Thinking about Management

This book is an invitation to engage in an exploration of some of the more puzzling aspects of the processes that have come to be called 'management'. It aims to provide a comprehensive but focused collection of readings to support and encourage wider consideration of alternative ways of thinking about management, and its effectiveness, in contemporary organisations. Aimed particularly at the advanced student of management, key features of this text include:

- a selection of contributions that derive from historically grounded and politically aware considerations, examining alternative approaches to understanding management, drawing on a wider source of perspectives than those that currently dominate management literature;
- an exploration of the uncertainties and apparent contradictions encountered in management action, grounded in the reflective practices of the contributors, employing examples and experiences from a wide range of organisations;
- improved access to ideas that are fundamental to understanding the complexities of management and will extend students' own ways of thinking about management;
- an informed contextual approach to the study of management, grouping together themes and ideas that aim to shed light upon the contested arenas of management action.

By emphasising the development of improved critical abilities in management practice, *Thinking about Management* will be an invaluable text for all management studies and MBA students.

David Golding is Senior Research Fellow at the Hull University Business School. He has over twenty years of experience of managing in industry and has spent fifteen years teaching and researching management. He has published widely in both management and sociology journals and contributed to a number of books on management.

David Currie is Senior Lecturer in the Department of Organisational Analysis and Human Resource Management, University of Lincolnshire and Humberside. He has fourteen years' experience of management in local government and ten years' experience of teaching and researching in management.

Thinking about Management

A reflective practice approach

**Edited by David Golding
and David Currie**

London and New York

First published 2000
by Routledge
11 New Fetter Lane, London EC4P 4EE

Simultaneously published in the USA and Canada
by Routledge
29 West 35th Street, New York, NY 10001

Routledge is an imprint of the Taylor & Francis Group

Typeset in Baskerville by Taylor & Francis Books Ltd
Printed and bound in Great Britain by TJ International Ltd, Padstow, Cornwall

British Library Cataloguing in Publication Data
A catalogue record for this book is available from the British Library

Library of Congress Cataloging in Publication Data
Thinking about management : a reflective practice approach / edited by
    David Golding and David Currie.
        Includes bibliographical references and index.
        1. Management. I. Golding, David, 1940– . II. Currie, David,
    1957– .
    HD31.T4875   2000
    658–dc21   99–37897

ISBN 0-415-20275-2 (hbk)
ISBN 0-415-20276-0 (pbk)

Contents

Notes on contributors   *vii*

Preface   *ix*

1 **The nature of management**   1

   DAVID GOLDING

2 **Encountering management**   17

   VINCENZO DISPENZA

3 **Treading treacle at parties and parapets: excursions into
   managerial ideology**   34

   JOE NASON

4 **The enactment of political tensions in management: a historical
   perspective**   51

   JUDITH GOLDING

5 **Reconstructing the study of management**   65

   ROBERT PROTHEROUGH

6 **Teaching management through reflective practice**   81

   JANET McGIVERN AND JANE THOMPSON

7 **Circles of uncertainty in management learning**   98

   JUDITH GOLDING

8 **Promises, promotion and pristine porcelain: rhetorics and
   essences in management action**   111

   FRED DOBSON

9 Nothing starts from nowhere   **125**

DAVID CURRIE

Reflective   **145**

DAVID GOLDING AND DAVID CURRIE

Name index   *147*
Subject index   *150*

Contributors

Vincenzo Dispenza initially worked in the construction industry in a family-owned business. He subsequently worked as a translator, interpreter and a teacher. He has lectured at the Hull Business School, University of Lincolnshire and Humberside, for ten years. He has taught management decision making and research methods in Africa, the Middle East and the Far East. He has published in the area of management development and his current research interests include the evaluation of management consultancy projects.

Fred Dobson spent over a decade lecturing in the field of Organisational Behaviour in Hull Business School, University of Lincolnshire and Humberside, following twenty years' experience in the running of SMEs. He is currently employed as an Academic Manager in the External Business Unit of the university, where he is responsible for initiating, launching and managing a series of training, consultancy and external business programmes.

Judith Golding is Senior Lecturer in the Hull University Business School. She has experience of working in a variety of organisations, including a period as personnel manager with a large Canadian food manufacturing company, and personal assistant to the group managing director of a large multinational media corporation. She has twenty years' experience of teaching and research in management and has published in a variety of journals in management and organisation studies.

Janet McGivern is Senior Lecturer in the Department of Organisational Analysis and HRM, University of Lincolnshire and Humberside. Her research interests include organisational analysis, individual learning, and the therapeutic use of group processes in management self-development. Janet has been writing with Jane Thompson for six years, exploring and designing innovative teaching and learning strategies for management education. Janet is a member of the editorial board for the *Journal of Gender Studies*.

Joe Nason is Senior Lecturer in the Hull Business School, University of Lincolnshire and Humberside. Prior to becoming a lecturer, he worked for over twenty-three years in a number of organisations within both the for-profit and not-for-profit sectors. His research interests are research methods, management development, and individual learning.

Robert Protherough has been at various times coal miner, journalist, teacher, editor, academic and consultant. At Hull University he was Senior Lecturer in the School of Education, but also worked in the schools of English and of Management. He has a particular interest in the management of the arts in education and in the training of professionals. He is the author of a dozen books, and has lectured and directed courses in North America, Australia, Africa and the Caribbean.

Jane Thompson is Senior Lecturer at the University of Lincolnshire and Humberside. She has written many publications in the area of teaching and learning, and gender and education. She is co-author (with Christopher Rowe) of *People and Chips, the Human Implications of Information Technology*, 3rd edn (1996). She is an area editor for the *Journal of Gender Studies*.

Preface

'If you ask me, management is simple enough to understand, but difficult to do.'

'Well, if that's the case, then it should be possible to train anyone to do it.'

'And so it would be, if only we knew what it was.'

This book arose out of a desire to address the kind of paradox that seems to underlie the above conversation. Management is often cast as being akin to the task of a juggler – i.e. quite difficult to do, but little doubt about what needs to be done. This may work very well at the level of performance, but if a juggler is asked to explain why they need to keep all the balls in the air, the response is likely to be 'to prevent them falling to the ground'.

While this may be a reasonable enough response for a juggler to make, such a self-fulfilling response may be less acceptable when we come to consider the contexts and responsibilities of management. The metaphor falls down, however, not because it is inappropriate but because it is incomplete, suggesting that we may need to look a little further than at what first meets the eye. For one thing, we may need to examine what lies behind the immediacy of some of the things that we have come to know as familiar management actions. In this book, we shall embark upon that process of questioning the nature and origins of some of the basic things that managers do.

Through successive examinations of familiar, everyday activities, we shall come to question the very nature of management. We will do this not from a detached or esoteric stance but for the very practical reason of engaging readers in reflections upon their own struggles to achieve that most elusive of organisational outcomes – survival! To be successful in this, we felt that such a book ought to be accessible to readers from a variety of different backgrounds, the only common starting point being a desire to extend their own understanding of management – in short, to anyone with the curiosity to wonder why such questions are not at the heart of all management education.

We decided that the best way to make such a book accessible would be to base it upon the experiences of actual managers, particularly if this could be made to reflect the kind of work undertaken in a wide variety of both types and sizes of organisation. On the other hand, we also felt that hard-nosed managerial experience should be only a starting point. The ability to generate learning from experience should be equally important, and we therefore chose managers whom we knew had been particularly effective in using their experiences in the teaching of management.

Accordingly, all the contributors to this book have been (or still are) practising managers. All of them have come to question in some way what they were (and are) doing, and all of them have used this questioning as a fundamental component in the contributions that they have made to the advancement of management teaching.

A common feature of the kind of questioning that has taken place during the careers of the contributors to this book has been a concern to explore the 'why' questions about management (as distinct from the 'how to do' questions). In particular, the contributors have been keen to explore questions such as 'why are we doing this?' In other words, 'how has it become possible (and acceptable) for me to be asked to do this in the first place – i.e. how has this situation arisen historically?'

Through the questioning of their experiences in this way, each of the contributors to this book has become committed to extending the ways in which management is understood. Each has been encouraged to share with readers something of how their own thinking has affected their work, and how they came to harness their experiences and reflections when they became involved in the teaching of management.

In focusing upon the experiences of the authors in thinking about what they were doing, one of the strands developed in the book concerns the idea of reflective practice. The analysis of this kind of process is designed to encourage broader thinking about management, by encouraging the dismantling of boundaries and promoting wider journeys of exploration than is sometimes the case. The book attempts to do this both in terms of methods of approach (e.g. by reflecting upon experience) and in terms of content (e.g. by focusing upon historical origins and alternative conceptual frameworks).

In the course of the book, readers will be introduced to a variety of theoretical traditions and disciplines, both those normally associated with management studies (e.g. social-science-based disciplines) and those that, until more recently, have been rather less associated with management studies (e.g. humanities-based disciplines). Through the development of successive contributions and alternative analyses, the book aims to encourage more debate about whether the subject of management can be considered a discrete discipline or whether management might be better seen as a multi-disciplinary subject.

The casting of the book as a critical text raises questions as to what a critical enterprise might entail. Clearly, we are not pursuing anything akin to the kind of traditions that prefer to see the idea of being critical as in some way a negative trait. On the contrary, in this book being critical is rather more concerned with the idea of being prepared to examine and question alternative ways of understanding particular significances – especially those alternative ways that may not have previously been considered, for whatever reasons.

In developing a critical stance towards management, the book has been structured to encourage an addressing of gradually more complex ideas. However, it is not necessary to read the book sequentially. Indeed, the authors have tried to suggest that learning should be flexible and just as likely to proceed in a cyclical manner as to unfold through a linear progression. Each chapter has been written from a different, although related, perspective and can therefore be approached without any prior reading being necessary. Equally, the editors have not sought to massage out any differences of opinion that may exist in the individual essays, taking the view that engaging with disparate positions ought to be the very stuff of management, but which is all too often concealed or avoided. In this book, juxtaposed perspectives have been left to stand side by side, as have repeated storylines. We regard such differences and agreements as legitimate and have not sought to 'pull it all together' in an attempt to produce a new meta-narrative of management.

The editorial process has been one of encouraging contributors to pursue the things that *they* have felt to be important in developing wider, more critical and more creative thinking about management. The book does not seek to be a comprehensive review of any of the various literatures on management, and neither does it aim to provide answers to questions about management. Indeed, in some cases it may not even provide very clear questions. What it does seek to do, however, is to be a resource and an inspiration, and to provide further legitimation for those students of management who wish to examine in more detail the functionally located texts that abound in management studies.

The book is aimed at two main groups of readers: first, those students of management on formal courses such as the various master's (e.g. MBA) and diploma (e.g. UK DMS, certificate and diploma) courses in general management, together with those following specialist master's courses and some of the more advanced final-year specialist students in management; second, the book aims to attract and encourage those practising managers who wish to extend their explorations of the concepts and boundaries of management.

The book is divided into nine chapters, beginning with an introductory chapter by David Golding that sets out the approach to be adopted in the book and outlines some of the origins of the idea of studying the subject of management through reflective practice.

In Chapter 2, Vince Dispenza sets out a framework for conceiving the ideas developed in this book in relation to the plethora of approaches that are encountered in the literature.

Joe Nason then begins the substantive exploration of management through reflective practice in Chapter 3. Examining some puzzling occurrences from an organisation in which he worked for several years, he suggests that subtexts and subverted agendas are most revealing in understanding organisational activities.

In Chapter 4, Judith Golding emphasises the importance of historical groundings for any comprehensive and secure understanding of management and suggests that managers forget the inherited aspects of organisational positions at their peril.

Robert Protherough argues, in Chapter 5, for an alternative to the kind of social-science-dominated approaches to understanding management. Echoing something of the old argument of art *versus* science debate in management, Robert suggests that a subject like management may have rather more in common with the humanities than with the social sciences.

In Chapter 6, Janet McGivern and Jane Thompson explore some of the alternative ways of teaching management and, drawing upon their own experiences in this, set several relevant resonances in motion.

In Chapter 7, Judith Golding explores the way in which attempts are made to reduce uncertainty in organisations and suggests that rather than trying to define uncertainty out of existence, a more fruitful alternative might be to attempt to harness uncertainty as a learning vehicle.

Fred Dobson examines some personal experiences and puzzlements in Chapter 8 and sets out how he came to understand the significance of what happened to him when he ran his own company, drawing upon and elucidating some unusual theoretical resources.

In the final chapter, David Currie explores some more creative ways of gaining access to the ideas that lie behind conceiving organisations as dynamic arenas in which members are interminably engaged in the social construction of reality.

In a book on reflective practice, so many people have contributed to the thinking behind the text that they are too numerous to acknowledge individually. Suffice it to say that if you knew any of us, you have probably influenced us, whether you were aware that you were doing so or not – although you are in no way held responsible for what has ensued! However, special thanks are due to John McCauley for a critical reading of an earlier draft of the book, Stuart Hay for continually challenging us to rethink our own thinking about management, and to Michelle Gallagher for help, support and encouragement in completing the task we had set ourselves.

David Golding
David Currie

1   The nature of management

David Golding

Introduction

The purpose of this chapter is to provide an introduction to both the content and the learning approaches to be adopted in this book. The chapter aims to introduce readers to a particular approach that is designed to encourage a more extensive consideration of issues that are at the heart of the practice of management.

Beginning with an analysis of some of the difficulties involved in trying to define management, the chapter goes on to suggest that a cyclical approach towards understanding the nature of management may be more appropriate than any approach that attempts to produce definitive statements about management. In the course of this analysis, the chapter will examine in particular four areas of concern which are held to be fundamental to the study of management:

- the importance of position in management relations (e.g. as might be reflected in a typical organisation chart);
- the management of meaning (e.g. the perspectives that might be reflected in particular management communications according to whose interests are being served);
- the emphasis placed upon management as a practical activity (in which the question of why anyone would want to conceive management as an impractical activity will be addressed); and
- reflective practice (in which an approach to the study of some of the essential paradoxes and contradictions of management will be developed).

The chapter will conclude with a discussion of the importance of tradition and historical perspective, in preparation for an exploration of some of the disparate ways in which attempts have been made to understand management in the literature, which will be the subject of Chapter 2. This in turn will form an introduction to the following chapters, each of which has been designed to approach management from a different perspective, deriving from the experiences and specific reflective practices of the respective authors.

Defining management

It might be expected that a book about management would begin with a definition of management, or at least with an attempt to provide readers with a statement locating the particular concerns that are to be the main focus of the book. In books concerned with the functions of management, this is often achieved by providing a list of topics which are to form the content of the book, coupled with an outline of the logic behind the order in which those topics are to be addressed.

Books about management which do not begin in this way fall into two main categories. There are those concerned with the application of skills and techniques in management, which may regard the provision of such a definition or locating statement as unnecessary, because the meaning of management is held to be self-evident. And there are those that take a critical stance towards management, which may regard the provision of such a definition as a rather more complicated matter than might at first appear, requiring some preparatory work to be undertaken before embarking upon the task. In the latter case, such preparatory work may on occasions become so extensive that it ends up being a topic for the whole book.

This opening has probably already conveyed something about the category into which the writers would place this particular book. In even suggesting that there might be some difficulties in defining management, it is evident that the writers regard the introduction to a subject such as management as far from straightforward, and that problems are likely to be encountered by anyone trying to come up with a workable definition of management.

It is our intention to pause at various stages throughout this book in order to consider the kind of questions being raised in a little more depth. We shall attempt to do this through the use of examples, mainly from our own experiences but also through the use of material selected for its relevance to the issues under discussion. We shall also invite readers to reflect upon their own experiences, whether as managers, employees, customers, end-users, etc., whether that is in a full-time, part-time, permanent or temporary engagement or from whatever kinds of organisational experience they may have had, and indeed wondered about. Our main intention in these pauses is to encourage wider reflection upon experiences as a means of expanding horizons beyond the normal range of acceptable explanations, and expected responses.

I want to start that process right away with an illustration from a few years ago, when I worked in the personnel department of the UK headquarters of a highly profitable American company. The company was a clear market leader in its field, with tentacles around the world. One evening, long after 'normal finishing time', I was sitting at my desk trying to sort out a sensible running order for my following day's work, which I knew was going to be somewhat hectic, when I sensed that someone was standing behind me.

I turned to see that it was the personnel director, who, without any preliminaries, said, 'Do you know what people call me David? People call me the axe-man.' (As it happened, I did indeed know this – he was the person who always did the firing, and not inconsiderable it was too). 'Do you think that's fair?' he went on, fortunately not waiting for an answer. 'After all, I'm only doing my job.'

On the face of it, this particular personnel director seemed to have a very straightforward way of defining his job – i.e. in terms of a circular argument comprising 'that which he had to do'. He was clearly quite comfortable with the label of 'axe-man' that had been applied to him, and he used it both to describe what he did to others and to avoid any significant consideration of how he reached decisions about what it was 'that he had to do'. (Only later did I learn that the personnel director's way of deciding what to do was simply to rely upon the managing director telling him what to do!).

Can you think of any examples from your own experience of significant labels being attached to managers as a means of conveying something about how they make sense of what they do, or perhaps more importantly, how their job is defined by others? Can you think of any examples of management in which a quite senior manager has been anxious to portray an active stance to their job (e.g., 'I fire people'), which on closer examination turns out to rely upon someone in higher authority telling them what to do?

It is unlikely to be just writers about management who see themselves as falling into different categories with respect to the task of defining management. People new to the study of management, too, invariably come to the subject with very different backgrounds and experiences, involving a variety of prior orientations and preconceptions. These differences frequently have more than passing significance not just for learning outcomes but also in the opening up of (and in the foreclosing of) agendas of what might be achieved through actual learning processes. Indeed, one manifestation of the difference between those who regard the defining of management as a simple matter and those who view the process as being fraught with difficulties can be illustrated by an example of an exchange between two students of management in a recent part-time MBA seminar. After a long discussion about a work-based problem, one student exclaimed with obvious frustration:

> This is getting us nowhere – look, all that really happened was that somebody stepped out of line. It was my job to do something about it – make sure that it didn't happen again.

A fellow student responded to this by saying:

> Aren't you the one who was telling us earlier that it's your job to encourage people to be creative in what they do? How do you tell the difference between being creative and stepping out of line?

To which the reply came:

> If you can't tell the difference you're not a manager!

Therein lies one of the difficulties of defining management. Two people disagreed, yet they disagreed not merely about the case under discussion but about something rather more extensive, involving matters at the heart of the problem of coming up with a workable definition of management. There seems to be little prospect in these circumstances of proceeding as though the differences are of little practical consequence.

On the contrary, the emotional content of the exchange seems to suggest that immense importance is placed upon resolving what some might want to see as a simple example of a practical management problem. Yet is it all so simple? Or could it be that the example contains a clue to the often curious nature of disputes about management? The people concerned seem unable to communicate with each other in terms that have any clear basis for establishing much of a degree of shared understanding. There seems to be a will to resolve the problem quickly and move on to the next, but this is accompanied by an apparent lack of any means of reaching an agreement.

It is as though a previously assumed common language between the parties involved has broken down. And if that is so, then what chance is there for reaching agreement upon anything? Will everything have to be negotiated? And renegotiated? And if not absolutely everything, then how far can we go before any communication begins to fracture, as our language reveals a lack of shared understanding?

Walter Cronkite, the famous US television newscaster, used to sign off each evening at the end of his newscast with the words 'That's the way it is tonight.' What did he mean by that? Did he mean that he (or more likely, they) had presented the news in the only way possible? Presumably not, yet the choice of words might give the impression that there had been no problems of meaning, interpretation or perspective that had led to particular versions of events being presented, rather than any alternative.

Of course, those who work in television news pride themselves on the maintenance of balance in their reports. But how is the word 'balance' used in such contexts? Invariably, it is used to defend news production teams from the criticism that they have presented only particular versions of events. Yet how could they have done otherwise? Of course they have presented particular versions of events: that is the nature of storytelling, whether in a children's nursery rhyme or in a television news broadcast.

However, the matter of balance is not taken lightly by those who work in television news, and it is certainly not considered a pedantic matter about the use of words. The espoused need to maintain balance governs almost everything they do, and yet the nature of that balance is seldom defined beyond the general aim of providing equal treatment for differing political perspectives, economic groupings, racial origins, etc. By repeating this aim often enough, it becomes possible to claim that a consensus exists and that by and large, balance is being maintained. The use of Cronkite-type phrases is thus made to seem perfectly normal, when clearly such a situation is not only unrepresentative but is also unattainable.

Can you think of any examples from your experience where language has been used in such a way as to suggest that there might be a consensus, but where upon examination it becomes evident that there is considerable doubt as to whether any agreement could ever exist? Can you think of any examples where questions about the use of words such as 'balance', 'normal', 'average', etc. have been subverted by defining them as pedantic.

In addition to divergences of opinion as to whether management can easily be defined, a further problem arises in that we are all too often faced with situations where the seemingly obvious becomes very elusive when we try to express what it is that we regard as being so obvious. Indeed, those kinds of situations are frequently encountered in management, and it will be one of the tasks of this book to attempt to unravel some of the reasons why that should be so.

Thinking about management

One function of this chapter is to begin the analysis of such contradictions, and in so doing introduce readers to an approach to the study of management that can be adopted both by those who are new to the subject and by those who have been grappling with such issues for many years. This approach has been devised to enable, if not to encourage, readers to undertake the study of management in a cyclical manner, as distinct from a linear approach, which might rely upon specific starting and ending points. A cyclical approach is relevant to disputes about management, because it encompasses the principle of periodic re-examination of previous assumptions.

In a subject such as management (which may seem simple enough on the surface but which turns out to be rather more complex than at first appeared) this is a particularly effective way of opening up areas which previously may have been neglected. This is why in addition to being aimed at students on formal courses in management, whether undergraduate, diploma or master's courses, the approach is also designed to commend itself to practitioners of management who are interested in developing their own abilities by thinking more extensively, and indeed in different ways, about management.

At the heart of this book's cyclical approach to the study of management is the notion of reflective practice. Essentially, this will be conceived as a process of thinking about action, in which alternative ways of framing particular actions may be considered. We shall not be concerned with generating technical analyses of the anatomies of thought but rather we shall concentrate on the ways in which the processes of reflection and consideration manifest themselves in our everyday lives. We shall thus be rather more concerned with the social effects of reflection (how, for example, inherent tensions between acquiescence and commitment to action are resolved in the individual) than we shall with any presumed structures and processes involved in the act of thinking.

Air traffic controllers have to make very quick decisions. These decisions have to assume that there will be a high degree of reliability in the quality of information they use, and the decisions also have to be communicated quickly and accurately to those awaiting instructions. The consequences of this not being the case are immense, and yet is this really a sensible example from which to make generalisations about the nature of management?

Individual managers may from time to time be engaged in activities requiring high degrees of accuracy and/or speed of decision, but this may not be a very representative basis from which to attempt a general statement about management. Furthermore, there may be at least a possibility that any attempt to produce a description of management based upon high-profile (even 'glamorous') functional examples is going to be misleading. The habit of using examples involving severe consequences (such as medical situations requiring complex transplants or delicate brain operations) may not be the best way to begin to understand management. Equally, some of the more mundane examples requiring rapid responses (such as the everyday occurrences in driving along a motorway) may be inappropriate starting points for attempting general conclusions about the processes involved in management.

That these kinds of situations are frequently used as starting points for understanding management is evidenced by the plethora of strong action-based conceptions of what 'doing management' constitutes. Indeed, the idea of a 'person of action' is one of the strongest images of management that pervades most industrial cultures. Perversely, this has led to the idea of the very process of thinking being equated with indecision.

As an example, I once worked for a manager who always responded to requests from his superiors to explain his actions with a quasi-military frontal attack. He would frequently say that attack was the best form of defence, and would invariably be seen going off to justify his actions with a cry of 'always ride towards the sound of the guns' (see Golding 1979).

Perhaps the main trouble with the idea of equating 'good management' with decisiveness is that sooner or later its proponents are likely to be brought up against the resistance of others to their so-called decisiveness. The temptation to immediately categorise such resistance in negative terms is obvious enough, but unfortunately this can soon lead to a situation in which any activity which does not count as being decisive is therefore defined as being indecisive – including the action of thinking about what needs to be done!

Can you think of a situation in which you acted out of a need to be seen to be doing something rather from a consideration of what needed to be done? And, conversely, can you think of a situation when you acted out of inertia rather than from what you instinctively knew ought to be done?

The kinds of tension generated in the apparent divergence between thought and action is an issue at the heart of the notion of reflective practice, and the practical problems that this presents will therefore be approached through analyses of the processes that are involved whenever we stop to think about what we are doing. In providing this focus, we shall need to bear in mind the way in which energy and time are important elements in the resolution of conflicts between taking time for consideration and the need for quick action. Indeed, we shall suggest that analysis of these very processes may lead us to a fruitful examination of some of the implications of alternative ways of framing particular actions. Thus we shall seek to derive a means by which learning can occur – i.e., through the process of reflection, which in turn may lead to internally derived change. An example of the potential effects of such reflection occurred on a recent residential course which formed part of a DMS/MBA programme:

The trouble is … in my job I don't have time to stop and think about what I'm doing at the time. I leave that until later … which often never comes, because in the evenings (if there is much of any evening left by the time I get home) I'm always too tired to do the things I promised myself I would do at the time. And so I just go on from day to day – not exactly making the same mistakes (I'd soon be fired if I did that) – but continuing to justify what I do in the same old ways. I think management ought to be redefined as dis-management … and then perhaps taking time to see what we do in a different light, might develop some credibility … or do I mean … I don't know … legitimacy … well yes that would make quite a change … especially with regard to what is seen as acceptable behaviour in my situation!

In line with such sentiments, this book will treat thinking as a dynamic process and will attempt to introduce readers to the importance of focused reflection as a source of change, especially as a means of creating change in the individual, although the book may have little to offer in the way of releasing time for doing that!

At various stages of the book, readers will be introduced to the kinds of problems encountered in attempts to understand management, and as suggested this chapter has already begun that process by highlighting the existence of difficulties inherent in attempts to define the very notion of management. The chapter now continues with a rather closer examination of four areas of concern which seem to raise questions that are at the heart of these difficulties. These four areas are:

1   The importance of position in management relations
2   The management of meaning
3   Management as a practical activity
4   Reflective practice

Discussion of the kinds of problems presented in these areas will form a basis for an introduction to some of the ways in which issues raised will be picked up and examined in greater detail in the following chapters of the book.

The importance of position in management relations

The circumspect nature of the opening of this book suggests that the authors consider their task to be a difficult one. For one thing, they seem to have decided that putting forward a preliminary definition of management could be counterproductive. At the same time, in appearing to be withholding something, the writers may give readers the impression that they are exercising some kind of power deriving from their privileged position. Most of the writers of this book would accept this to be the case and would concur that, indeed, this may have something to do with (if not being an enactment of) power relations between certain groups and individuals. Furthermore, since the focus of some of the chapters of this book will be upon the way in which power relations are often maintained by actions designed to conceal the exercise of power in those relations, the writers ought to address such matters with respect to their responsibilities to readers – if not to make an undertaking, at least to attempt to avoid engaging in that kind of concealment.

Indeed, since attempts to conceal the exercise of power are often achieved by underplaying the different interests of the parties involved, the writers of this book take it as incumbent upon themselves to at least try to make something of their own journeys towards understanding management a little more explicit – e.g. through the provision of illustrative material from their own experiences. They propose, for example, to try to make their own underlying assumptions and positions (so far as they are aware of them) a little more accessible to readers than might be customary in books of this nature – that process has already begun!

Each one of the writers of this book has worked as a practising manager in one form of organisation or another. As a result of those experiences, in their different ways, all have come to regard the process of reflecting upon their actions as an important component in their own learning and development. One of the aims of the book, therefore, is to attempt to share some of those reflections and thereby encourage readers to engage in their own reflections in order that they may become more aware of the wide range of factors that impact upon their actions.

In suggesting that some importance be given to position (and especially to hierarchical position), we have immediately stepped into a large hole of conceptual difficulty. A critical stance towards the three preceding paragraphs might point out that we have proceeded as though the notions of position and power, not to mention assumptions about hierarchy and the attending conceptual problems in the whole area of organisational structure, are unproblematic. Nothing could be further from the case. The writers of this book regard terms such as 'power' and 'position' as extremely problematic. Critical stances towards the three paragraphs are therefore entirely legitimate.

Such critical stances are also an important element in the nature of communication. As has already been suggested, wherever we are located in any organisation, we do not proceed with preordained shared understanding (although neither do we start with 'a blank sheet of paper'). Indeed, the study of communication ought to proceed with the paradox of meaning firmly in mind. We may not be able to satisfy our desire for agreement for shared understanding universally (even on the meaning of single words such as 'management'), but that does not prevent us proceeding. On the contrary, we all too often proceed on the assumption that our definitions of terms and situations are in essence shared by others, even though this is far from the case. So how is this possible?

An example of a comment at the end of an industrial relations seminar on a recent MBA programme will suffice to illustrate this:

> Well I'll tell you this for nothing. I'm a good deal more confused now than I was at the beginning of this course. I thought that I knew what industrial relations was. It's my job for goodness sake. Now I'm not so sure, in fact I've begun to wonder whether I shall ever be able to say what industrial relations is, and the strange thing is that I don't feel particularly uncomfortable about that!

This member of the seminar group was perhaps articulating one of the great paradoxes of exploring supposedly common-sense terms. We soon encounter the possibility that things are not as simple as they seem, and that reaching agreement upon definitions is fraught with difficulty, if not unattainable. Yet we define what we do (in practice) by the nature of the assumptions we make all the time. The member concerned in the above example, an industrial relations manager in a well-known manufacturing company, was expressing wonder at how it is not only possible to proceed with everyday definitions in the light of the impossibility of reaching agreement on those definitions but that it is actually necessary to do so.

The illnesses and damaging after-effects that military personnel sustain following active service have become of increasing concern in modern warfare. As a result of the experiences of those serving in recent Middle East conflicts, the notion of Gulf War syndrome has emerged. The idea that there is such a syndrome seems to have divided even the medical profession. There are doctors and consultants who take Gulf War syndrome very seriously, and there are those who argue that no such syndrome exists.

However, in the latter group the argument is with the categorisation, not with the symptoms. There is no real attempt to deny the seriousness of the presenting symptoms exhibited by victims. Rather the argument seems to be that there can be no single overriding description of the causes of such symptoms which could justify a general category of Gulf War syndrome. In other words, a scepticism is being shown towards the attribution of a single cause.

In fact, the attribution of single causes is a common feature of so-called advanced societies, so much so that it might be referred to as a single-cause neurosis. Perhaps there is nothing surprising in this. It may be that one of the overriding needs in a complex society is to develop as many all-embracing definitions as possible in order to simplify the complexities faced by members of that society. The importance of health and fitness in life mean that the medical world has a prime need for such simplifications – provided that they are sustainable. If they are not sustainable (and which medical definition, treatment and means of diagnosis has not fundamentally changed in the last twenty years), then such simplifications quickly become counterproductive.

Other examples of contentious general medical categories that are currently subject to extensive debate include irritable bowel syndrome and chronic fatigue syndrome. In each case, it may be that the only lasting benefit of such categories turns out to have been in drawing attention to the possibility that something was going seriously wrong. Beyond that, the application of general categories may actually inhibit progress because it may discourage the act of thinking the unthinkable. The main purpose of simplification is to save the effort involved in always having to start from first principles, yet prior categorisation may discourage exploration of the very routes along which lie the best chances of identifying a more specific treatment of the particular variations in symptoms being exhibited.

Can you think of any examples of particular situations in management being defined in terms of questionable general categories? And can you think of any examples of problems not being taken seriously because they have been defined in terms of general categories, the existence of which are subject to repeated doubts.

The approach in this book will be to confront some of the paradoxes of management (along with a whole variety of other ambiguities and contradictions), where on the one hand we may not be able to define something, but on the other hand, we are in effect defining it by the nature of what we do! In this way, perhaps the problem becomes not so much one of an inability to proceed until we have defined what we are going to do, as one of accepting that we will rarely be able to reach universal agreement about what we are going to do. As indicated, this does not mean that we cannot proceed, but nor does it mean that we should press on regardless of such problems. What it might mean is that we should treat the job of conceiving what we do as problematic, and therefore as something to be visited and revisited as a matter of routine.

The management of meaning

Since the process of providing an introduction to the book has already begun, despite the reticence exhibited, it might be useful to question a little further what kind of a process is involved when we seek to provide an introduction to what we perceive is to follow. As has already been suggested, in some traditions it is customary for introductions to books about management to occupy but a few paragraphs, if any. Yet in this book, it has already become apparent that such an undertaking is rapidly becoming the topic of this whole chapter, with, as implied earlier, the prospect of it becoming the subject of the whole book!

Have the writers taken leave of their senses? Or could it be that they regard the provision of an overview as a possible inhibiting factor in attempts to develop more exploratory approaches towards management? Could it be, in other words, that they consider such provision as counter to the aim of encouraging more reflective practice in others? Are they really attempting to make their own positions more transparent (in order to avoid too much of the kinds of concealment found in power relations), or are they simply avoiding their responsibilities towards their readers?

In other words, could it be that the writers view the provision of an overview as essentially one of managing meaning? And are they, therefore, trying to draw the attention of readers to the fact that, in reading an overview provided by other writers, they themselves are entering into a relationship with those writers in which meaning is being managed.

The notion of the management of meaning was first developed in a management context in an influential analysis by two important management thinkers, Dan Gowler and Karen Legge, who brought a refreshing anthropological perspective to the study of management (Gowler and Legge 1984). They suggested that from their own and others' observations it did seem that managers spent an awful lot of their working day talking, and that since much of that talk was designed to influence outcomes, an examination of how shared meanings were established would be fruitful. Their argument was that anyone undertaking such an examination would soon have to account for the differing degrees of influence (upon for example definitions of situations) according to presumed hierarchical positions. Before proceeding further with an analysis of the implications of such factors for the present discussion, perhaps a few examples of situations involving 'the management of meaning' would be appropriate.

When US writer Gore Vidal was asked whether he ever regretted not becoming a more active and institutionally involved politician (with the clear implication that he would have been a real contender for the White House) he replied that the tensions between being a writer and being a politician would perhaps have precluded that. Asked to expand on this distinction, he declared his view that whereas writers must always tell the truth (he exempted journalists from this requirement!) politicians must never give the game away.

The suggestion seems to have been that perhaps politicians are a good example of those doing jobs wherein it might be said that a large part of their existence is involved in the management of meaning. An example of this has perhaps been revealed in the UK BSE inquiry, which is charged with an investigation of the factors that led to the rise of BSE (commonly referred to as 'mad cow disease') in a large number of UK cattle herds during the 1980s. The inquiry has recently documented how the 1992 proposal to set up an independent animal feedstuffs advisory committee to monitor the cattle-rearing industry was resisted. Wintour (1998) reported in the British newspaper *The Observer* that Nicholas Soames, then the UK Agriculture Minister, wrote in an internal departmental minute that 'the group would overlap with other committees and add to the pressure for regulation when we are trying to go the other way'.

What was this 'other way' referred to? Why, deregulation of course – already decided upon as an important platform of the then UK government's policy, even it seems when faced with evidence of a considerable crisis. But that is at the heart of managing meaning: it is not the particulars that matter but the general direction which has to be maintained, or at least take on the appearance of being maintained. The current obsession in Western political circles with 'spin doctors' is a manifestation of this. This is someone who has put a particular slant on events in order to show themselves (and/or their own political party) in a more favourable light. This is particularly in evidence in the treatment of political matters in the British press, which has become so captivated with the process of 'spin' that they are in danger of losing sight of the 'task' in favour of describing the 'process'.

The present UK government is similarly in danger of losing sight of its targets, having become so concerned with managing meaning. The phrase 'staying on message' has become so much a part of the political lexicon that the medium has almost become more important than the message. In order to 'stay on message', the most outrageous of contradictions may be exhibited, but inconsistencies in pronouncements come to matter less than, as Gore Vidal might have put it, the crime of saying something that might disclose anything.

Politicians and others in public life are often adept at using contradictions to their own advantage. Perhaps a good example of the absurdity that this sometimes entails was parodied in the Gnome column of the British satirical magazine *Private Eye*: 'The idea that I would blackmail the Prime Minister to further my business interests is as outrageous as it is correct' (Strobes 1998).

Could it be that managers too develop an ability to turn contradictions to their advantage? Can you think of any examples of particular contradictions being ignored or denied in order to sustain a particular decision that had previously been taken? And can you think of any occasions upon which you have deliberately withheld information in order to obtain a preferred outcome – i.e. an outcome that gave you a greater advantage than would have any of the alternatives that may have been possible.

It is evident that the processes by which meaning is managed are important features in any communication, and it is therefore not surprising that they should be considered an especially relevant subject for analysis in a book about management. And since management may be seen as an expression (or representation) of particular power relations, it is not entirely inappropriate for the writers of a book such as this to exhibit a little reticence towards appearing too sure of themselves! On the other hand, it is all too easy to give the impression of having lapsed into evasiveness. This was rather potently brought home to the writer of this chapter in a conversation with a colleague from another university department:

'What is your book about?'

'Management.'

'Oh, that sounds interesting. What is your starting point?'

'Er, I'm not sure that I know how to convey that yet.'

'You haven't got far with it then?'

'Oh yes, it's more or less written.'

'I don't understand how it can be written if you don't know what your starting point is.'

'Oh I know what my starting point is (well one of them) but I don't yet know how to communicate that, not least because everyone starts from a different position. You see, we are trying to persuade people about to become managers, and those who already are practising managers, that it's a good idea to reflect upon what they will do (and have done) as a means of learning about why they will do (or did) certain things – and in so doing discover something about the assumptions they operate under – you know, the things they take (and have taken) for granted, as a means of encouraging them to look at alternatives.'

'That sounds more like a conclusion to me.'

'Well, that's the problem really. Writing books about management (and particularly those proposing a model of reflective practice) is not like writing a whodunit, where you have to conceal the ending in order that readers shall not be dissuaded from reading the whole book (notwithstanding that some readers will indeed subvert the 'rules of the game' by reading the ending first). In fact it's more likely to be the other way around. When you are not concerned with definitive answers, and each person has a different starting point, then it's more a question of not subverting the beginning, in order that different endings can be allowed – nay encouraged … and of course that is always likely to be in tension with any desire that you may have not to conceal your own position.'

In fact, the difficulty of knowing where to start is often an indication of the enormousness of the task, and clearly this book is no exception. We normally deal with such difficulties by avoiding them, ignoring them, or more likely stomping all over them as though they were not there. Rarely do we attempt to encompass them, and use them to our advantage. The writers of this book have chosen to do just that, by making explicit the nature of the difficulties as perceived, and in the process, attempting to convert them from obstacles into ways of proceeding.

Management as a practical activity

As an example of the processes involved in the management of meaning, consider the way in which managers use the term 'practical'. Managers are frequently heard to say that management is a practical activity? The contributors to this book (at least the writer of this first chapter) seek no argument with that. Of course management is a practical activity – in this book, that is taken to be self-evident. Indeed, as already indicated, the book is written by people who have extensive practical experience of management. But being practical, as distinct from what? As distinct from being theoretical? That would clearly place the notion of being theoretical as in some way the opposite of being practical. But is the relationship between theory and practice quite so straightforward? Maybe not, although what else could be the analytical opposite of being practical? Being impractical perhaps? Well, there would be a certain irony in that, because being theoretical is often regarded by managers as being impractical (e.g. 'if you sit there thinking about it, you'll never get anything done'). And yet, surely, thinking about what would be the most practical thing to do is a very practical thing to do!

Leaving aside for a moment the question of how such matters might be resolved, the significant factor with respect to issues of managing meaning (of which the relations between writers and readers of books about management are a part) is that a debate about the meaning of 'being practical' has been entered into. But a debate with whom? Perhaps 'debate' is not quite the right term. Perhaps an invitation to engage in a debate would be more appropriate. Such invitations are at the heart of processes of relations between writers and readers, involving the idea of invitations (accepted or declined, or indeed redefined). Yet this particular example of a debate, or invitation to engage in debate (or invitation to think about engaging in debate), has concerned only one small issue – that of 'being practical'. Suppose that this kind of analysis were to be applied to other aspects of the whole structure of complex relations involved in the processes of management.

But before considering this, also suppose that someone – writer or reader – had the means by which they could ensure that their particular definitions of terms such as 'being practical' became the preferred ones. To consider the implications of that could be a fruitful first step towards understanding what is involved in the processes of managing meaning. For while in our own small spheres we all have the facility to decide for ourselves what 'being practical' means, it is when we come to share our perspectives that we run into trouble. It is here, in the process of deciding upon an agreed definition (in this case, of 'being practical') that the importance of power relations becomes manifest, and in the course of which the management of meaning itself becomes a practical problem.

Reflective practice

We now come to the heart of why the job of defining management has been delayed. For one thing, even at a simple level, it raises the question of whose definition should we have begun with? That of the writer of this chapter? Or that of the writer of the second chapter? Or one of the other writers? Or would the expectation be that writers of a book such as this should have taken time to reach an agreement between themselves on the matter? And if so, how would we know that agreement had been reached? Whose word would we take for that? And given that definitions about terms like 'management' are likely to change over time, which definitions would be more relevant – those that the writers had at the time of reaching agreement (assuming that agreement had been reached) or those that they have today? Not to mention the matter of how long the process of reaching such an agreement might have taken. Or whether it would even have been possible (not to mention necessary).

On the other hand, perhaps we should have begun with some reader's definition(s). Yet if what has gone before is to believed, they too are likely to be fairly disparate (to say nothing of the difficulties in gaining access to them!). And yet in a curious way, might that not be the only starting point that any of us has?

Each of the chapters of this book may be seen as one response to this kind of problem, representing as they do alternative ways of approaching the task of thinking about management. Each chapter will comprise a different way of studying and engaging with the structures and processes of management as seen and experienced by the authors. This in itself is an invitation to engage in disentangling some of the processes involved in the management of meaning, and readers are encouraged to develop their own ideas further in their own reflections, drawing upon the kinds of cyclical process involved in the interplay between reading and note taking, reading and debating in groups, debating and rereading, rereading and re-entering debate, etc. – in short, the very stuff of learning to think about management.

The highly respected American sociologist C. Wright Mills (1959: 216–17) argued that the setting up of a file or journal was a good way to proceed in guiding the process of reflection.

In such a file as I am going to describe, there is joined personal experience and professional activities, studies under way and studies planned. In this file, you, as an intellectual crafts(person), will try to get together what you are doing intellectually, and what you are experiencing as a person. Here you will not be afraid to use your experience and relate it directly to various work in progress. By serving as a check on repetitious work, your file also enables you to conserve your energy. It also encourages you to capture 'fringe thoughts': various ideas which may be by-products of everyday life, snatches of conversation overheard on the street, or, for that matter, dreams. Once noted, these may lead to more systematic thinking, as well as lend intellectual relevance to more directed experience.

I have lost count of the number of times I have chided myself for not following this advice to the letter. How many ideas written on the backs of envelopes have I misplaced, now lost for ever, and all for lack of a 'file' or way of storing them, not to mention an effective means of later retrieving them? How many fruitful

avenues have I not pursued for lack of a memory with which to recall their significance (or indeed apparent lack of significance at the time, and yet a feeling that
they might be important if only …)?

One further point may be useful as a marker for the kind of assumption that readers
may encounter in this book, namely the importance that the writers in this volume attach
to the impact of history upon what we do. This may seem a little strange, if not initially
somewhat regressive, especially since so many books about management are concerned
with the future, and in particular with the importance of detailed planning as a prerequisite
for successful management. On the other hand, the concerns of practising managers are
often more focused upon the present – e.g. 'Now why did he/she do that?' So why this
focus upon the past?

We have no wish to move the focus of anyone away from planning, or from trying to
understand what may be happening right in front of them, but we do want to suggest that
an appreciation of the past may be crucial to an understanding of the present and to any
effective planning for the future. Indeed, the very processes of reflection require that the
past be taken into account. The writers of this book will therefore attempt to ground their
own reflections in appropriate historical perspectives in order to highlight the importance
of developing an appreciation of how we got to where we are today!

Moreover, is it not the case that in focusing upon the processes by which meaning is
managed, the writers and readers of this book cannot escape the effects of those self-same
processes as they are socially exchanged, drawing upon pre-existing levels of awareness of
the norms and rules of writing and reading? Thus the use of the book is subject to the way
in which the development of understanding is, or comes to be, a shared activity, whether
that applies to managers or to writers and readers of books about management.

As indicated, the book aims to harness this difficulty and convert it into a topic for
examination. Hence, one of the dimensions with which this book is concerned is the question of the extent to which we become essentially engaged in those same processes of
managing meaning. Any reader who has read so far is already engaged in that process.
Furthermore, since one of the themes of this book is to suggest that processes concerned in
the management of meaning are endemic to the whole field of management, a central
focus will be upon gaining awareness of the impact of historical precedents and traditions
by way of successive analyses of the kinds of management of meaning that have been
taking place under our very noses.

Concluding note – encountering management

This chapter has examined some of the problems facing those intent upon extending their
understanding of both the concept and the cluster of activities that have come to be known
as 'management'. It has been suggested that an approach that encourages periodic reflection upon the ways in which managers make sense of their experiences might be a more
fruitful way of exploring management than any approach that attempts to reach definitive
or generalised conclusions about the nature of management.

In the light of the foregoing, it might be useful to consider how someone new to the
study of management might begin to relate their own journey of exploration to the variety
of approaches that they will find in the literature. Indeed, given the diversity that they are

likely to encounter, it is clear that they will need a means of dealing with at least some of the apparent contradictions. In order to facilitate entry points into what lies ahead, the following chapter will attempt to provide such a means of locating particular explorations of management within what can sometimes seem an extensive, disparate and daunting literature.

References

Golding, D. (1979) 'Symbolism, sovereignty and domination in an industrial hierarchical organisation', *The Sociological Review* 27 (1): 169–77.

Gowler, D. and Legge, K. (1984) 'The meaning of management and the management of meaning: a view from social anthropology'. In M.J. Earle (ed.) *Perspectives on Management*, Oxford: Oxford University Press.

'Strobes, E.' (1998) 'Gnome', *Private Eye* 947, p.5.

Wintour, P. (1998) 'Closed minds let mad cows survive', *The Observer*, 29 March, p.12.

Wright Mills, C. (1959) *The Sociological Imagination*, New York: Oxford University Press.

Further reading

Other useful approaches to a critical perspective on management, drawing upon a variety of experiences and research materials, include the following:

Alvesson, M. and Willmott, H. (1996) *Making Sense of Management*, London: Sage.

Anthony, P.D. (1986) *The Foundation of Management*, London: Tavistock.

Linstead, S., Grafton Small, R. and Jeffcutt, P. (1996) *Understanding Management*, London: Sage.

Reed, M. (1989) *The Sociology of Management*, London: Harvester Wheatsheaf.

Watson, T.J. (1994) *In Search of Management*, London: Routledge.

2   Encountering management

Vincenzo Dispenza

Introduction

This chapter addresses issues about the development and representation of management theory and its relationship to management practice. A more accurate chapter title could therefore be 'Encountering management theories and perspectives'. Writers often confuse the theory of management work with management work itself and end up talking *about* managers rather than *to* managers. In the process, they make many assumptions about what managers do. As you read through the chapter, I would encourage you to think about how the issues raised relate to you as a manager in your own organisation. I would also ask you to remember that the ideas set out here are the personal reflections of the author. Another author might choose to categorise the development of management theory in a different way.

The broad aims of this chapter are as follows:

*   to provide you with a brief historical and theoretical context in which to locate your own assumptions about management;
*   to challenge the idea that management (as presented in much management and organisation literature) is an objective phenomenon;
*   to encourage you to recognise the validity of your own management experience in the face of an overwhelming body of management theory that attempts to present management as an objective and unbiased activity.

The chapter is divided into the following sections:

The canon of management   Addresses the notion that management and organisational theory has infiltrated society to such an extent that some taken-for-granted assumptions about management are rarely challenged. A recognisable body of theory has been used to promote organisational principles and management virtues over the years. The same writers' ideas are recycled in the literature, for consumption by current and future managers on courses such as Master of Business Administration (MBA).

Management in a historical context   Argues that management literature has largely presented the phenomenon of management in an ahistorical way. This has resulted in a substantial body of literature that emphasises the practical nature of management, thereby avoiding the need to locate management in a broader social or political context.

Management as a technical-rational pursuit   Management has traditionally been represented in a technical-rational way in the literature. That is, studies of management activity have tended to ignore the subjective dimensions of a manager's actions. The focus has traditionally been on managers as neutral organisational technicians who make decisions according to objective criteria, and in an unbiased way.

Management as a philosophical problem   Encourages the reader to question the nature of management, and to adopt a more reflective approach to their own experience.

Critical management   Recent authors have come to acknowledge management as a socially creative process. As the traditional roles of management have been called into question, new conceptualisations of management (based on a more empirical approach) have emerged. This section explores this development.

Management as a political necessity   Briefly draws upon the distinction between different views on conflict as a framework for locating assumptions about management action in organisations.

Management as cultural manipulation   Different theoretical perspectives on the meaning of culture (integration, fragmentation, ambiguity) are presented. The manager's role in promoting dominant organisational values is evaluated.

All the areas addressed under each heading deserve a more in-depth treatment than I am able to give here. By its very nature this chapter is an overview, a somewhat brief encounter. It is hoped that you will go away and read some of the authors mentioned in more detail.

The canon of management

Irrespective of whether you have studied management in the past, you are likely to have come across such names as Henri Fayol and Frederick Winslow Taylor. Authors such as these represent the canon of management and organisation theory. I use the term 'canon' in the sense of a sacred body of work that constitutes and represents the core beliefs of a recognisable area of social life. Just as a priest would study the Testaments at some stage or other, managers are more than likely to come into contact with the 'Old Testament' works of Henri Fayol and Frederick Taylor and the 'New Testament' works of writers such as Henry Mintzberg and Peter Drucker. The older works are generally accessed in introductory textbooks (Mullins 1998; Buchanan and Huczynski 1997) and the salient points synthesised and reproduced for consumption by the next generation of students.

Modern management theory developed with the advent of industrialisation and mass production. There was a corresponding awareness of the need for efficient management of organisations. Henri Fayol's thoughts on the management and organisation of work were first published in English in 1916. His 'fourteen principles' and his identification of key managerial activities have since entered the folklore of management. Fayol's thoughts have been particularly influential in the way we have come to conceptualise modern management. So too have Frederick Taylor's ideas on 'scientific management'. Taylor's contribution was to attempt to instil reason and logic into what he saw as inefficient practices and introduce a more scientific approach to the management of contemporary organisations. In highlighting key management activities, Fayol laid the foundation for what has become an identifiable area of work called 'management' and a corresponding body of literature called 'management theory'. The activities identified by Fayol included planning, organising, forecasting, commanding, organising and coordinating. When I ask my students what is meant by 'managing', these activities feature prominently in the lists of functions they identify. Undergraduates, in particular, find it easy to identify these activities, although their answers are not always based on experiences of managing or of being managed in organisations.

By being handed down to subsequent generations of students and managers, the notion of managerial activity, as described in a lot of management texts, has acquired a mythic status. This body of literature has been passed on to future managers as one would pass on a 'Highway Code' to a learner driver. Such a code may prove a useful theoretical guide to survival on the roads but is no substitute for experience. There are significant perils awaiting those who believe that the code must be right because experienced drivers (practising managers) develop their own idiosyncrasies and tactics for survival. Sticking to the code may prove hazardous for those who place too much credence on the myth of management activity as represented in the traditional management literature.

The rational, functional approaches to managing first identified by Fayol and others have influenced contemporary approaches to management. This is sometimes referred to as the *functionalist paradigm* (Burrell and Morgan 1979). Functionalist literature reflects a scientific, or pseudo-scientific, approach to management. It treats social science as if it were natural science; that is, it assumes that there are answers to management and organisational problems – the trick is to find them. A great deal of popular literature has emerged that treats management in a prescriptive way. This literature has sometimes been called 'guru theory' because of the tone adopted, which is often solution-based and evangelical rather than problem-based and critical. It has also been called 'Heathrow organisation theory', after the London airport. It is so called because this type of book is often to be found in airport bookshops and is often not very taxing, although many of the books purport to change the reader's life! The functionalist approach is well illustrated in decision-making theory by the emphasis on normative decision-making models. These models tend to assume that managers have perfect judgement and knowledge, and make decisions in an unbiased way (see, for example, Cooke and Slack 1991).

The canon represents a predominantly western-centred view (United States and Europe) of management, yet its influence is widespread. The following example illustrates two points: first, management theory has become an important export as education has become a global business; second, the way in which individuals conceptualise their work and their lives within the context of their own culture and experiences often bears little or no relationship to the classical management theory that they have been taught.

Goldfish or gurus?

I was chatting to a colleague from Malaysia who was in the process of completing an MSc in human resources management at a British university. In our discussion, it was evident that she was aware of classical management theory as well as being up to date on her chosen area of research. The conversation turned to the topic of her husband's business, which was highly successful. It became apparent as we spoke that my colleague attributed the success not to an awareness and application of management knowledge and skill, nor to economic or environmental factors, but to the fact that her husband had acquired some tropical fish, which had bred successfully. As they had flourished, so too had the business. From a predominantly Western, rational approach to management it would be easy to dismiss this causal relationship as irrational. However, it serves as a useful reminder that prescriptive management theory, although prevalent throughout the world via the growth of MBAs in particular, denies, for instance, the fact that there may be a spiritual dimension to existence.

Nonetheless, the set of guiding principles provided by the early writers has largely been adhered to by subsequent generations of organisation and management theorists. Classical ideas have been developed, updated and often criticised, but paradoxically any criticism has enhanced their profile, as a glance at many contemporary textbooks of organisation theory will testify.

Management in a historical context

In the same way that the British physicist Isaac Newton developed a label for, and an understanding of, the concept of gravity (rather than inventing gravity itself), management has long existed in different guises. Perhaps the language of dominance, for example 'slavery', 'serfdom and 'feudalism', has developed into the more commonly recognisable managerial terminology of today, for example 'teamwork', 'empowerment' and 'networking'.

Very rarely do management theorists venture into the prehistory of management. On occasion, however, writers draw upon influential thinkers of the past to address contemporary management concerns, for example Machiavelli (Jay 1970) and Rousseau (Storey 1983). One of the outcomes of this unwillingness to venture into the prehistory of management is that management becomes regarded as an ahistorical phenomenon. This facilitates the mythification of management. Its roots are rarely questioned or explored, and as a consequence it acquires a mythic status.

The role of myth in establishing 'blissful clarity'

According to French philosopher and social commentator, Roland Barthes (1973: 143):

> in passing from history to nature, myth acts economically; it abolishes the complexity of human acts, it gives them the simplicity of essences, it does away with all the dialectics, with any going beyond what is immediately

visible, it organises a world which is without contradictions because it is without depth, a world wide open and wallowing in the evident, it establishes a blissful clarity; things appear to mean something by themselves.

An example of this can be found in Henry Mintzberg's influential article 'The Manager's Job: Folklore and Fact'. Mintzberg sets out to challenge Henri Fayol's classical formula of management as planning, organising, controlling and coordinating. He uses a small sample of senior managers in order to reach his conclusions. Mintzberg's stated intention is to encourage the reader to challenge Fayol's ideas and point them to a more useful description of managing. Although he draws upon the work of a classical writer, he adopts an essentially ahistorical perspective. Rather than questioning the basis of managerial authority, the author concludes by describing a new set of management roles that can be treated as a revision of Fayol's original list. Mintzberg's work, although methodologically reliant on a limited sample size, has been extremely influential in management theory. This can be explained in different ways. It could be that the work has resonated with the experience of managers and/or writers on management. It could also mean that individuals seem to need the security of a universal theory, a universal truth. As Barthes suggests, such blissful clarity is a myth.

Management as a technical-rational pursuit

The classical preoccupation with management as a technical-rational pursuit is reflected in the apparent obsession with the structure of organisations. More recent writers (Burns and Stalker 1961; Mintzberg and Quinn 1988) have carried on the tradition of concentrating on *forms* of structure and establishing design principles. Emphasis is placed on the need to design organisations so that they perform to their optimum capability or, at the very least, in an efficient manner. This focus on the forms of organisational structure has tended to divert attention from important issues about the *nature* of structure. For example, German sociologist Max Weber's notion of bureaucracy promotes organisational virtues such as reliance on formal rules and regulations; reliance on formal roles and role relationships rather than less formal interactions; job specialisation, routinisation and clear task definition; and reliance on formal authority rather than personal power.

Subsequent generations of organisational theorists have built upon the tenets of the concept of structure and, in choosing to refine it, have diverted attention from the moral and ethical dimensions of organisations as mechanisms of control. The underlying assumptions regarding the validity of organisations as rational phenomena have largely been perpetuated and reinforced rather than examined and explored.

By categorising emergent new practices in terms of established theory, writers imply a progressive chronological link that perpetuates the classical principles of organisation design. Burns and Stalker (1961), for example, develop the traditional concept of bureaucracy by differentiating between mechanistic and organic structures.

Mintzberg (Mintzberg and Quinn 1988) refines the concept of bureaucracy by distinguishing between machine bureaucracy and professional bureaucracy.

In classical management theory, the most commonly stated aims of organisational structure are to coordinate potentially disparate and often contradictory aims and behaviours; to achieve effective and efficient economic and social performance; and to create a framework of social relationships flexible enough to meet the needs of the environment while maintaining internal clarity of purpose and direction. These aims reflect a traditional focus on the rational-economic forms of structure.

However, a more radical perspective might view organisations as the arenas of class conflict, in which different social stakeholder groups struggle to assert their rights, thus stressing the exploitative nature of structure. So some of the aims of structure may be to get more effort out of people for less money, to ensure that managers' right to manage is perpetuated, and to control potentially deviant behaviour.

Organisations inevitably reflect the societies of which they are a part. Through early socialisation processes such as schooling, we are asked to accept hierarchy as a legitimate and natural phenomenon. In effect, people expect to associate with others in a hierarchical way. Managers are expected to manage, and when they are not seen to be managing according to widely recognised criteria their competence may be called into question. The managerial activities identified by Fayol and others soon become redefined as managerial duties.

As stated earlier, managing has predominantly been presented by authors as a rational activity. Classical management theory has therefore concentrated largely on the functions of managing in and around organisations rather than on questioning the underlying values. This promotes a view of managers as organisational technicians. Organisation theory has grown in parallel with management theory and, in a similar way, the structuring of organisations has been represented as an essentially politically neutral (or value-free) function designed to facilitate communication and the achievement of organisational goals.

Management, as an academic discipline, is a relatively recent phenomenon, as the rapid growth of business schools in the United States and the United Kingdom has shown. It is an eclectic phenomenon drawing upon a number of established academic disciplines, such as psychology, sociology and anthropology. One of the difficulties in determining what constitutes management theory results from the fact that it reflects what is, in practice, not so easily definable. The word 'manager' has some meaning, but without a specific context the meaning attached is general in the extreme.

Under the influence of classical theorists, the main function of management has generally been regarded as the efficient and effective control and coordination of resources in organisations. With the advent of the human relations school came a growing recognition that people are a key organisational resource to be managed. Management theory therefore appropriated softer disciplines such as psychology, sociology, social psychology and anthropology to help to make sense of the complexity of human nature and human interaction. A large body of theory has developed to address the inherent problems of managing people.

While there has been a growth in literature which reflects a more eclectic and imaginative approach to the study of management, it is less clear whether this has filtered into the everyday reality of how organisations actually operate. A glance at popular introductory management texts suggests that more innovative and critical theorists are becoming accepted as orthodox, notably Gareth Morgan and Gibson Burrell. Yet everyone is a product of their own time, and their works, too, are firmly rooted in prior evidence of a classical training. Gareth Morgan's *Images of Organization* and Gibson Burrell's *Pandemonium* are innovative developments of their joint seminal work *Sociological Paradigms and Organisational Control*. Incidentally, the use of metaphor to understand management and organisational life has become an important feature of critical theory, largely due to Morgan's influence.

My own experience of talking to managers suggests that innovative theory is filtering into organisational life, but management in organisations is still mainly conceptualised in terms of discrete functions – for example, production, sales, marketing, finance. Management education reflects this. Typically, MBA courses consist of a series of separate units, which follow Management Charter Initiative (MCI) guidelines and reflect a functional conceptualisation of organisation. One such function is human resources management (HRM). HRM has gained a higher profile in organisations in recent years. A great many textbooks treat the subject of HRM in a largely functional and descriptive way (for example, Beardwell and Holden 1994). As with other organisational components, HRM has developed its own specific vocabulary and set of activities, such as recruitment and selection, employee resourcing, or employee relations. Again, these components reflect a transferable structure supported by professional body status – in the case of HRM, the Institute of Personnel and Development (IPD). Occasionally, there are more critical approaches (Legge 1995). In the main, however, HRM as an academic discipline and an organisational reality is dealt with in a functional way. Students are required to learn the curriculum and acquire the skills needed to become competent practitioners.

Perfect recruitment and selection: a warning

The following extract from a song serves as a reminder that functional specialism does not always result in perfect knowledge and favourable outcomes.

> Lay my head on the surgeon's table.
> Take my fingerprints if you are able.
> Pick my brain, pick my pockets.
> Steal my eyeballs and come back for the sockets.
> Run every kind of test from A to Z.
> And you'll still know nothing 'bout me.
>
> Run my name through your computer.
> Mention me in passing to your college tutor.
> Check my records, check my facts.
> Check if I paid my income tax.
> Pore over everything in my C.V.
> But you'll still know nothing 'bout me.

'Nothing 'Bout Me (Epilogue)'
words and music by Sting ©1993.

Reproduced by permission of EMI Music Publishing
Ltd/Magnetic Publishing Ltd, London WC2H 0EA.

Management as a philosophical problem

As an MBA student I was posed the question 'Is a philosophy of management possible?' At the time, I found the juxtaposition of philosophy and management spellbinding, mainly because I regarded them as incompatible. I used the work of the German philosopher Ludwig Wittgenstein to try to make sense of the question. Wittgenstein (Magee 1987) argues that in order to determine the meaning of a word we should not turn to a dictionary but to the particular context in which that word is being used. In the context of this chapter I refer to philosophy as a process rather than a product. To philosophise is to ask the fundamental questions and to continually evaluate and improve practice through intellectual enquiry and debate. Interestingly, when philosophy is employed in the context of 'management-speak' it becomes a product rather than a process. We therefore talk about a management philosophy in the sense of an ideology or a set of values.

Cooper (1990) argues that philosophy should be used to challenge the ways in which our reality is constructed and manipulated through the construction of language. Management language is continually changing. What used to be called 'sacking' is now euphemistically called 'outplacement'. But is the outcome the same? Or are we dressing up the same unpalatable acts in a more palatable language? 'Outplacement' certainly sounds a less contentious and more objective process than 'sacking'. But has this resulted in it becoming a more scientific pursuit?

Is management a science?

> Wittgenstein thought that if you want to understand a type of discourse, such as religious discourse or any other type of discourse, look at the role that it actually plays in people's lives. For him, intellectual life was to try to treat all intellectual endeavours as if they were attempting to be like a science. He thought that science had its place like anything else, but that it was a mistake to treat subjects which were plainly not forms of science and technology as if they were second-rate attempts to achieve science and technology.
>
> (Searle in Magee 1987: 335)

This raises important issues regarding Taylor's legacy of management as a science. Can you think of examples from your own experience that indicate that managers' actions are sometimes presented in a more scientific way than is actually the case?

The use of 'management speak' may be intended to represent managers as objective, and to represent management as a science. It may also have to do with justifying it as an academic discipline and validating it as a profession. Most of the managers I have come to know while teaching on the MBA are more concerned with exploring the 'softer' side of managing: that is, the uncertainties and ambiguities that come about as a result of having to deal with people. The phrase 'if it weren't for the people problems, this job would be easy' reflects the notion that management cannot purely be rationalised as a scientific phenomenon. In attempts to deal with the 'people problems', a variety of ideas have been borrowed from the social sciences and presented to managers in a prescriptive manner. So, for instance, the apparent obsession with motivation and the ubiquitous 'Maslow's hierarchy of needs' may be seen as yet another pseudo-scientific managerial attempt to understand what makes employees tick. The fact that Maslow has been taken out of his original humanist context and made use of in a utilitarian way makes no odds. It seems that much of the traditional functional literature is based on an assumption that everything (including personal motivation) is manageable. This is an illusion perpetuated by authors who seek to provide managers with a flawed sense of certainty, and whose real agenda may be to meet managers' wants rather than their needs.

The tendency of classical theorists to provide universal solutions has persisted to the present day, and contemporary management theorists concentrate on developing prescriptive solutions to organisational and management problems (for example, the McKinsey 7-S Framework, Total Quality Management, Business Process Re-engineering). This is the kind of thing that Wittgenstein warned us about. Management is in danger of being crystallised and described in absolute terms. In reducing management to a set of universal guiding principles, the complexity and contradictions inherent in the day-to-day problems of practice are denied. As a result, managers may come to compare their experiences of management unfavourably with the simplified version presented to them in introductory texts. At best, they may see little relevance in textbook theory; at worst, they may see their own attempts at managing as flawed in comparison with what they are led to believe should happen.

Examples of 'management speak'

new speak	*didn't that used to be ... ?*
communication strategy	talking to people
associate	employee
outplacement	sacking people
rationalisation	sacking people
downsizing	sacking people
empowerment	delegation
networking	politicking

Critical management

By drawing upon a variety of theoretical sources, more recent organisational theorists have begun to distinguish between subjective interpretation and objective acceptance of organisational phenomena. Writers have begun to address, for example, the extent to which structure is the product of human consciousness rather than having an objective meaning outside of individual consciousness. For instance, by drawing upon the work of Berger and Luckmann (1966), the notion that reality is largely the product of human interaction has been acknowledged. This has led to explorations of how structure is maintained and perpetuated through everyday interactions, and organisational members are viewed as actors who create a world that they experience as objective. Structures subsequently take on a life of their own and influence the way in which individuals act. Morgan (1997) refers to this as the 'enactment view'. This could be described as a dialectical relationship. In other words, members of an organisation (managers in particular) create, enact and perpetuate organisational structure through their activities and interventions. The structure, in turn, influences individuals by determining their behaviour. Structure acquires 'agency' and becomes a driver of peoples' thoughts and actions.

Think of the last time you heard someone refer to organisational processes and practices in an objective way. For example, 'it's the way it's done … it always has been', or 'the structure is always changing here … it never seems to last more than two years'. Do you think that the processes or practices you recalled were a result of anyone's decisions? Why do you think we might refer to real people's decisions in such an objective and impersonal way?

According to Berger and Luckmann (1966), people are capable of inventing a world that they then experience as something other than a product of their own making. The authors go on to suggest that (1) society is a human invention and (2) an objective reality, and therefore (3) people are social products. They warn that any analysis of the social world that fails to acknowledge any of these three tenets will be distorted. The relationship between humans and the world they create is a dialectical one, so, for example, the product (management) 'acts back' upon the producer (manager, student of management, general public). The image of management as perpetuated in classical management literature, and the image of what constitutes good management, may lead an individual to self-censor their decision to become a manager. So the facts that most managers are male and that management is often described in terms of traditional male-oriented attributes may lead women to self-censor themselves out of a possible career in management because they may regard it as an unsuitable area of work. Similarly, those females who choose a management career may find themselves playing according to patriarchal rules. Whether this process of self-censoring and 'playing the male game' is conscious or not is a moot point.

Playing the male game?

I recently attended a presentation by four female students, who had set themselves the aim of exploring the similarities and differences between the ways in which male and female managers made decisions. They touched upon the concept of patriarchal organisation and the extent to which females become chameleons in a male-oriented world of management. As a result of the content of their presentation I became aware that two of the group were wearing what might be considered 'traditional male attire' (trouser suits). I later told them that I found this interesting, given the nature of their topic. However, they replied that their choice of clothes was entirely due to the cold weather, and they found it difficult to entertain the idea that it might be due to some subconscious process of trying to comply with a male stereotype. Given the context of their presentation, I was viewing it as a possible example of the 'acting back' process and of the enactment view mentioned earlier. Our actions are not entirely consciously determined, and the institutions we create and perpetuate through our own actions take on a creative function of their own.

Every social interaction involves communication at either an explicit or implicit level. The implicit level of meaning is created and perpetuated by the use of signs, myth and language that promote managers as rational and purposive. This obscures the moral, social and political dimensions of management. Signs play an important part in our learning from a very early age. Inanimate objects become an influential (conscious or subconscious) driver for our actions. A philosophical examination of these inanimate objects is important in the context of management, as symbols take on a powerful role in signifying meaning to the extent that they acquire the 'agency' of structure. For example, the suit and tie, the leather chair, the slightly larger office space, all act as symbols. All 'mean' something in the context of working in organisations. Recognising the agency of such factors can be an empowering experience.

The practical power of symbolism

A rapidly growing and extremely successful organisation was experiencing some difficulties with its sales force. All the sales representatives were young males, and although the sales manager believed that much of the recent success was due to the high level of competition between these young men, he had a problem. The level of accidents involving company cars, which all happened to be a popular make of German sports car, was unacceptable. In fact, there was an average of two incidents a month, usually but not always minor, but invariably leading to vehicles being out of action. The manager decided that the solution to the problem lay in the cause, which he believed to be bravado and carelessness. Consequently, the company purchased a rather less powerful and less fashionable, second-hand vehicle, which became known as the 'joke car'. All the sales representatives were informed that anyone involved in an accident which led to their own vehicle needing attention would be required to drive the 'joke car' instead. The number of incidents decreased significantly.

The enactment view is particularly relevant when addressing the changing role of managers in the structuring process. In recent years, the emphasis has shifted from organisational structure to corporate culture, and managers have been encouraged to view themselves more as social rather than technical organisational agents. The emphasis has moved away from direct to indirect control.

With the advent of globalisation, more turbulent economic environments and rapid technological advances, classical management theory has been increasingly viewed as anachronistic due to its reductionist approach. The universal principles promoted by the early theorists have been challenged by writers adopting a more critical approach to the study of management and organisations. This term, 'critical', underscores the perception of classical management as the dominant force in the literature. Critical approaches are based on an assumption that managing is a complex, demanding and often problematic process and, therefore, should not be presented in a simplistic way. To do so would be to ignore the 'real life' problems of managing. The contradictions and complexities of managing should be embraced in an attempt to develop the skills and knowledge required to be a more thoughtful and effective manager.

Anthony (1986) distinguishes between what he calls the 'official' theory of management and the 'real' theory of management. He describes official theory as a rational process that emphasises objectivity rather than subjectivity, as a purposive activity that emphasises direction and achievement, primarily directed at making a profit and getting things done in the name of the organisation. He identifies real theory as social and political behaviour in organisations. He arrives at this position by arguing that real theory focuses on what he suggests happens in 'real life' (empirically), for example:

> the inability of superordinates to learn from their subordinates about what was going on, the self protective feigning of ignorance, the side-stepping of official procedures to gain personal advantage, the deliberate use of change and confusion … the construction and maintenance of ambiguous rules, and the claims and obligations of friendship.
>
> (*ibid.*: 178)

In terms of real theory, management is far from a rational activity, instead emphasising politics and a 'what's in it for me?' attitude. It is purposive, but only in the sense of achieving personal goals, and it is primarily directed at maintaining personal power and not necessarily maximising organisational profits. A common thread in the growing tradition of critical management studies is the tendency to be critical of official theory.

Critical management theorists are often categorised under the broader label of 'postmodernism'. Postmodernism questions the basic rational assumptions on which preceding theories have been founded. Just like classical theorists, postmodern organisational writers have borrowed concepts and vocabulary from other disciplines and areas of study. Postmodernism has long been recognised as a phenomenon in the world of architecture, literature and the visual arts, where painters and writers have challenged accepted definitions of what constitutes art. In a similar way, postmodern organisational analysts have challenged traditionally held views of what constitutes the purpose and practice of organisations. In doing so, they have turned their attentions to less traditional topics such as emotions in organisations (Fineman 1993) and sexuality in organisations (Hearn and Parkin 1987).

Management as a political necessity

Industrial sociologist Alan Fox (1966) first developed what has generally become known as the traditional view of organisational conflict. The unitarist view, with its emphasis on harmony and integration, regards managers as organisational peacekeepers. Conflict is seen as an unnecessary evil, to be minimised and certainly not tolerated or seen as legitimate. Any conflict that does emerge is therefore seen largely as a failure to manage organisational processes adequately. Problems can be explained in terms of difficulties of communication. For example, the emphasis may be placed on process details (managers not communicating well enough or often enough) rather than political issues (the incompatible needs of different stakeholders). In contrast to the unitarist perspective, Fox (1966) identified the pluralist perspective. Pluralism, with its acknowledgement of the needs of different stakeholders, recognises the inevitability of organisational conflict. Managers are seen as playing a part in managing the tensions between different stakeholder groups.

Both perspectives acknowledge the pivotal role of managers in maintaining employee relations in the work context. Although they may disagree on the purpose of management in the process of managing organisational conflict, managers' right to manage is not queried. However, a more radical perspective on conflict points to the exploitative nature of management in organisations. Organisational conflict is regarded as a structural phenomenon resulting from competing social forces, which clash on a daily basis. Managers manage on behalf of the owners of the means of production (shareholders and owners of capital) and therefore exploit those who provide the labour (workers). This perspective imbues the notion of managing with a much more macro-political quality. Nevertheless, the reductionist nature of all three arguments (unitarist, pluralist, radical) means that many managers, who see themselves as 'just making a living', may regard the debate as irrelevant to their existence. However, I wonder whether the issues raised by these theories are experienced by managers at a visceral level. Managers experience at first hand the pressures of being placed in contradictory and often untenable positions between those they manage and those who manage them. Intellectual detachment is often a luxury.

Bacharach and Lawler (in Fincham and Rhodes 1988) point to a divergence of views presented in relation to managers as political agents within organisations. The authors reject the 'happy family' (unitarist) view of organisations presented in a great deal of management theory and the 'class conflict' (radical) view projected by others. Instead, they take over what they regard as the middle ground, that is, a view of organisations as 'politically negotiated orders'. The authors try to avoid making a judgement on the use of politics in organisations, preferring to see it in terms of an organisational fact of life, where members of an organisation compete for the same resources.

Dunford (1992) suggests that the subject of power has traditionally been treated as secondary in studies of organisational behaviour, and power has been viewed in pejorative terms in the context of the dominant view of organisations as machine-like structures. This contrasts with the view expressed by authors such as Bacharach and Lawler. This divergence reflects the different perspectives on power and politics that are found in many academic texts, in which the existence and use of power and politics are assumed to be either legitimate or illegitimate.

This notion of legitimacy and illegitimacy can be examined further by looking at different perspectives concerning the management of technological change and, in particular, by addressing the issues inherent in the technological determinism versus strategic choice debate. Technological determinists argue that the choices made regarding the selection and implementation of new technology is determined by the function of technology and its environmental requirements. Those who favour the strategic-choice perspective, on the other hand, argue that structure is the choice of power holders in the organisation, who often use the determinist argument as a rationale to implement their own ideas (hence, its political connotations). To illustrate this, I shall look at the example of a relatively recent organisational phenomenon – call centres.

How can I help you?

A call centre is a centralised call management facility designed specifically to deal with large numbers of telephone enquiries from customers. Operators are usually located in huge open-plan offices and are given a predetermined script to learn and adhere to. They are monitored by a supervisor, who uses surveillance technology to listen in selectively on conversations between operators and customers. Supervisors may draw operators' attention to any lapses in the set script and to what may be considered unnecessary conversation with customers. Each call has a target optimum time limit, and operators are trained in techniques such as 'closing down' a conversation.

From a determinist perspective, it could be argued that this way of working is a consequence of environmental pressures to reduce costs. This is achieved through economies of scale, by centralising call management and by job specialisation. As more organisations offer this kind of efficient, extended, specialised service, the customer will come to expect it. Organisations that do not use technology to offer the same level and type of service will be left behind. In contrast, from a strategic-choice perspective, the decision to structure work in this way has less to do with technological developments and competition than with the motives of managers to monitor and control operators in order to achieve a cost-effective service. The rationale that customers demand this kind of service could be challenged. The fact that many customers try to engage operators at a human level would be used as evidence to suggest that operators are being unnecessarily dehumanised and mechanised in the name of technological determinism.

Management as cultural manipulation

Increasingly, managers are being required to 'walk the walk and talk the talk', that is, to see their role as part of the process of promoting cultural values as well as 'getting the job done'.

According to Morgan (1997):

> management has always been to some extent an ideological practice, promoting appropriate attitudes, values, and norms as means of motivating and controlling employees. What is new in many recent developments is the not-so-subtle way in which ideological manipulation and control is being advocated as an essential managerial strategy … used to create an Orwellian world of corporate newspeak, where the culture controls rather than expresses human character.

This might be seen as a rather bleak view of managing culture, but it has long been implied that managing corporate culture is an important instrument in winning over 'hearts and minds' (Deal and Kennedy 1982; Peters and Waterman 1982). It is hardly surprising, therefore, that managing culture as a means of gaining competitive advantage has been regarded by some as a sinister development in the evolution of management theory.

In what is considered to be a postmodern approach to the subject of organisational culture, Frost *et al.* (1991) categorise the vast array of theories according to three distinct perspectives: (1) integration, (2) differentiation, and (3) ambiguity/fragmentation.

The integration perspective presents and promotes the idea that culture is unified and unifying. Organisational culture is talked about in terms of integrating and bringing together all members of the organisation. Writers adopting this perspective focus on discussing the importance of shared values and common goals and beliefs. There are obvious parallels here with the unitary perspective of organisational conflict.

The differentiation perspective addresses issues of diversity. Emphasis is placed on the existence of subcultures as opposed to an overriding, cohesive culture. The presence of subcultures is recognised as an inevitable result of the differentiated nature of organisations and society. Individuals and groups will have their own particular needs, wants, beliefs and values, whether organisational or personal. This will lead to the creation of subcultures. The potential for conflict is therefore acknowledged. There are parallels here with the pluralist view of conflict in organisations.

The ambiguity/fragmentation perspective offers a completely distinct view of culture. The notion of clearly intelligible patterns of behaviour and shared meanings is challenged. Meanings are seen as much more fluid and transient than the other two perspectives would have us believe. Organisations are arenas in which social actors are continuously negotiating and renegotiating meaning, so the extent to which culture can be clearly identified and managed is much more problematic.

Dunford (1992) suggests that the integration perspective is particularly appealing to managers as it provides a tidier and more holistic view of culture. As a result, it gives managers the necessary illusion that culture may be managed easily. The fact that it may not be the most appropriate frame of reference by which to make sense of the complexities and contradictions involved in managing organisations is irrelevant. Its main purpose is to provide managers with a neater model for making sense of how things should be.

Research into management practice often highlights the fact that a great deal of managers' time is spent fire-fighting, that is, dealing with pressing problems in a reactive and hurried way. Not surprisingly, rather than develop the diagnostic capability to deal with their own unique circumstances, managers may choose to simplify the problems they face by turning their attention to approaches that offer an easy solution or by denying that there is a problem at all. As managers have traditionally been portrayed as politically neutral organisational agents, attention has been diverted from the view that managers play a crucial role in creating organisational reality. However, management writers have increasingly come to regard political activity as a valid area for research.

Conclusion

One of Joseph Stalin's early actions when he took over the leadership of the Soviet Union was to systematically replace the senior engineers who had worked under the old tsarist regime. The aim was to substitute them with soviet engineers, who, while as technically gifted as their predecessors, would not openly question the wider socio-political context of their work. What relevance has this for contemporary management and, in particular, for practising managers? Management does not exist in a cultural or historical vacuum; it is a socio-political phenomenon, the ramifications of which are more than purely economic. Successive governments have recognised the value in appealing to the 'business community'. At one level, managers are recognised as important stakeholders in society; at another level, management is often depicted as a politically neutral process. However, there is a danger in accepting any representation of management as politically neutral. Managers play a significant role in the societies in which most of us live and work. Like the tsarist engineers, managers should widen their vision from the practical to the political and from the pragmatic to the philosophical, because actions that are described as being pragmatic may hide a political motive.

Management takes place in a context of exchanges of labour for some kind of reward. Managers play a key role in this exchange process by trying to get 'more for less', that is, increasing profit, reducing costs and adding value. This process and all its associated actions has become so normal as to appear natural. Just as the soviet engineers had no experience of working in an alternative system and were therefore more likely to accept their role as purely technical and therefore apolitical, managers may view their role as practical and apolitical.

Postscript

I have argued that the same authors seem to appear in management and organisation textbooks, and that paradoxically any criticism gives greater legitimacy to classical management ideas. A glance at the reference section to this chapter might suggest that I have 'fallen into the same trap' and have helped to reproduce the canon. It seems that nothing starts from nowhere.

References

Anthony, P.D. (1986) *The Foundation of Management*, London: Tavistock.

Barthes , R. (1973) *Mythologies*, St Albans: Paladin.

Beardwell, I. and Holden, L. (1994) *Human Resource Management. A Contemporary Perspective*, London: Pitman.

Berger, P.L. and Luckmann, T. (1966) *The Social Construction of Reality*, Harmondsworth: Penguin.

Buchanan, D. and Huczynski, A. (1997) *Organizational Behaviour. An Introductory Text* (third edition), Hemel Hempstead: Prentice Hall.

Burns, T. and Stalker, G.M. (1961) *The Management of Innovation*, London: Tavistock.

Burrell, G. (1997) *Pandemonium*, London: Sage.

Burrell, G. and Morgan, G. (1979) *Sociological Paradigms and Organisational Analysis*, London: Heinemann.

Cooke, S. and Slack, N. (1991) *Making Management Decisions* (second edition), Hemel Hempstead: Prentice Hall.

Cooper, D.E. (1990) *Existentialism*, Oxford: Basil Blackwell.

Deal, T.E. and Kennedy, A.A. (1982) *Corporate Cultures: The Rites and Rituals of Corporate Life*, Reading, Mass.: Addison-Wesley.

Dunford, R. (1992) *Organisational Behaviour. An Organisational Analysis Perspective*, Englewood Cliffs, New Jersey: Addison Wesley Business Series.

Fayol, H. (1949) *General and Industrial Management*, London: Pitman.

Fincham, R. and Rhodes, P. (1988) *The Individual, Work and Organization*, London: Weidenfeld & Nicholson.

Fineman, S. (ed.) (1993) *Emotions in Organizations*, London: Sage.

Fox, A. (1966) 'Industrial Sociology and Industrial Relations', Royal Commission on Trade Unions and Employers' Associations, Research Papers 3, London: HMSO.

Frost, P.J, Moore, L.F., Louis, M.R., Lundberg, C.C. and Martin, J. (eds) (1991) *Reframing Organizational Culture*, London: Sage.

Hearn, J. and Parkin, W. (1987) *'Sex' at 'Work'. The Power and Paradox of Organisation Sexuality*, Brighton: Wheatsheaf Books.

Heidegger, M. (1968) *What is Called Thinking?*, New York: Harper & Row.

Jay, A. (1970) *Management and Machiavelli*, Harmondsworth: Penguin.

Legge, K. (1995) *Human Resource Management: Rhetorics and Realities*, London: Macmillan.

Magee, B. (1987) *The Great Philosophers*, London: BBC Books.

Mintzberg, H. (1975) 'The manager's job: folklore and fact', *Harvard Business Review*, July–August: 49–61.

Mintzberg, H. and Quinn, J. (1988) *The Strategy Process: Concepts, Contexts and Cases* (third edition), London: Prentice Hall.

Morgan, G. (1993) *Imaginization*, London: Sage.

Morgan, G. (1997) *Images of Organization* (second edition), London: Sage.

Mullins, L.J. (1998) *Management and Organisational Behaviour* (fifth edition), London: FT/Pitman.

Peters, T.J. and Waterman, D.H. (1982) *In Search of Excellence*, London: Harper & Row.

Storey, J. (1983) *Managerial Prerogative and the Question of Control*, London: Kegan Paul.

Taylor, F.W. (1911) *Principles of Scientific Management*, New York: Harper.

Turner , B.A. (ed.) (1990) *Organizational Symbolism*, Berlin: de Gruyter.

3 Treading treacle at parties and parapets

Excursions into managerial ideology

Joe Nason

Introduction

This chapter is concerned with illuminating the taken-for-granted assumptions that underpin the ideologically driven nature of management activities. Many would argue that the 'quintessential role' of management is control (Storey 1983: 96). By drawing upon a breadth of organisational theory and personal experiences, the position being adopted here suggests that, although the fundamental daily experience of management in action may not be consciously perceived as control, 'doing' management in an organisational context invariably manifests itself as such. This is in part due to the ideological preconditioning of those involved. Although it may not be in their own interests, managers are seen as the key players in symbolically perpetuating, transmitting and reinforcing this situation, thus ensuring that the prevailing dominant ideology is sustained. In Western societies, this mainly reflects capital and capitalist rationality.

Context

If one of the aims of this book is to support and encourage wider consideration of alternative ways of thinking about management, this chapter seeks to contribute to that aim by taking a critical stance towards the very social phenomenon typified (Schutz 1962) by what we call management. To achieve this, the chapter will draw upon a diverse number of disciplines in an attempt to 'reveal society for what it is, to unmask its essence and mode of operation' (Burrell and Morgan 1979: 284). This broad, eclectic approach is common in work of this nature, which tends to be labelled as critical management or organisational studies (Alvesson and Willmott 1992: 9; 1996: 20). One of the purposes of the broad approach is to provide a framework from which dominant societal values, or as they are often termed 'ideological beliefs', can be questioned (*ibid.*: 10). These beliefs arise, in large part, from a process that is often termed 'socialisation' or 'ideological preconditioning'. Through this process, we are exposed to a system of ideas (both implicit and explicit), as a result of which we learn the ways to behave and think considered normal or appropriate for that society. Once internalised, these dominant cultural values or ideological beliefs tend to be accepted as natural. Thus we rarely question them. Hence the need to question and illuminate the taken-for-granted assumptions upon which these beliefs are built and maintained (Friere 1972). Through this process of questioning, this chapter seeks to encourage more enlightened and informed forms of practice (Alvesson and Willmott 1992: 10), particularly with regard to the practice of management. By drawing upon personal experience and combining this with a focus upon the theory and practice of management, underpinned by philosophical intervention, my intention is to provide you, the reader, with a catalyst to critically examine the taken-for-granted world of management. This approach is intended to make you reflect upon your own experiences, thus encouraging you to develop your own skills as 'reflective practitioners' (Argyris and Schon 1978).

Managerial experience: treading treacle

Tony Watson, professor of organisational and managerial behaviour at Nottingham Business School, makes explicit through his research into managerial activity (1994) that managers are aware of the pressures and contradictions that permeate their daily existence in organisations. They frequently feel and exude feelings of frustration and stress arising from the very systems they are supposed to control. Another common source of their frustration, he suggests, is their inability to gain the full cooperation and commitment of their peers, their staff and even more senior colleagues. He reached this conclusion after working for a year alongside managers at ZTC Ryland as a participant observer, studying the nature of management. At the time of his research, ZTC Ryland employed around 3,000 people in developing, manufacturing and selling telecommunications products. In his own words, his research presented a superb opportunity to look at a fairly mainstream British company (*ibid.*: 4).

My personal experience of managing in a number of organisations, both large and small, coincides with what Watson observed. Whether it was in my early days as a relatively junior manager or in my latter as quite a senior one, I often felt frustrated trying to do my job. At times, the pressures and contradictions made it feel as though I was walking through treacle to get the job done. More often than not, 'the system' was to blame, the system being the internal operating procedures and norms of organisational life that held the organisation together. The system was not only a convenient scapegoat at times but was also the foundation from which I tried to make sense of the pressures and contradictions of the job – a job which I was well trained for and considered by many to be very good at. During these times, I experienced the pressure, frustration and contradictions but had little or no exposure to any ideas for making sense of the situation, other than blaming 'the system'. I had been socialised into thinking in a particular way with little or no encouragement to expand upon or break out of this.

Several years on, through an understanding and application of critical approaches to studying management and organisations, I now make sense of my managerial experiences in a different way – a way that is not offered as an absolute truth but rather as an alternative explanation. This kind of alternative perspective has furnished me with a different understanding of why, despite working so hard and achieving results, I often felt frustrated and powerless. The remainder of this chapter takes one such experience and proceeds by an emergent theoretical analysis to provide insights into how developing the capability to generate alternative perspectives may be seen as the essence of reflective practice. Where appropriate, other experiences will be included in the analysis to enrich the approach.

Parties and parapets: sharing an experience

Setting the scene

The scene is the sports and social club of the Enigma International service centre in Hometown (names disguised to respect confidentiality). Enigma International is a large

British multinational company. At the time of this story, the UK operating division of the company was split into twelve geographical areas, covering England, Scotland and Wales. Each of these areas was served by a number of strategically situated service centres. The nature of the business required personnel to be spread throughout the country. Each service centre virtually mirrored the others. Procedures and operating policies tended to be standardised, as you would expect in a large, bureaucratic organisation.

At this time I was employed by Enigma as a senior industrial and commercial sales engineer. My role entailed marketing their core product and supporting this activity through marketing and managing two other augmented ones. In financial terms, this equated to a business portfolio worth in excess of £25 million per annum. Within the Enigma structure, my position was the highest of the middle management grades. The next rung up the ladder was classified as a senior management position. My base was the Hometown service centre. Over 100 people were employed there. As with any organisation, some people worked harder than others, but on the whole the majority of staff worked hard and were conscientious.

On the occasion in question, a party was being held at the company's sports and social club in recognition of the official closure of the service centre. I am still not sure what I was doing there. I do know that when I arrived, I was certainly not in the mood to party.

The service centre was being closed in the name of efficiency and rationalisation. Yet it was one of the most profitable in the country. However, it was the furthest away from the territorial headquarters. The closure had been phased over a period of time. During this period, a lot of uncertainty and anxiety was experienced by staff. The centre was being merged with one that already existed in a city 40 miles away. Staff there were also suffering from uncertainty and anxiety. As part of the rationalisation process, people from both centres were applying for their own jobs.

The operating structure had been changed; however, in practical terms there were still more people than jobs available. To make matters worse for the lower grades of staff, jobs were ring-fenced and cascaded down. What this meant was that if you did not get your own job, you were automatically offered the one beneath it.

It is difficult adequately to describe how the staff felt. The phased closure had taken over a year from announcement to reality. During this time, I had witnessed people openly demonstrating high levels of stress, fear, anger and frustration. It was not unknown for people to start crying in the office. Indeed, there had even been a fatality in the other service centre. An employee died from a heart attack at work. Of course, it would be impossible to attribute this unfortunate event to the pending closure/merger. However, one cannot help but wonder how much the stress of the process affected this individual.

As part of the closure/merger strategy, there were a large number of 'awareness' meetings and team briefings. According to senior management, these were intended to keep people informed of what was going on in an attempt to reduce their anxiety. However, whatever was said, there always appeared to be an underlying message, namely that we should all still be committed to the company. It was not really Enigma's fault that this was happening. The hardship had to be endured because of the pressure of market forces. The future survival of Enigma depended upon the changes. As such, it was in our own interests to cooperate. We should all be working hard to ensure that the transition was as smooth as possible. Despite the tensions and frustrations, this message seemed natural and proper. We all complied, even the people who were being made redundant. We kept our heads down and worked very hard. No doubt, the fear of us also losing our jobs had something to do with this.

As the of day closure approached, the number of staff in the office diminished rapidly. Some staff had taken redundancy. Others were travelling daily to the other service centre 40 miles away or had relocated themselves and their families. I cannot over-stress how emotionally disturbing this experience was for those involved. It was undoubtedly one of the worst periods of my life. To see colleagues and friends suffer the consequences of this prolonged closure was not pleasant. I can feel the anger re-emerging, even now, as I write.

On a personal level, my job was safe. The title of my role had changed; the content, salary and working conditions remained the same. My only problem was that my new operating base was 40 miles away. After being offered my own job, my immediate response was one of relief. However, anger soon followed. This was fuelled by the way we had been treated, in conjunction with a need to know why all this had been deemed necessary. Even if the closure/merger was required, surely senior management could have handled it in a more humane way? After all, the people being most effected were the ones who had worked for years to make Enigma successful. They were the employees who the senior management had historically relied upon for loyalty and commitment: the ones who had given it. These were the people who not only helped to build Enigma but were also known personally to local management. In an attempt to resolve my personal feelings of tension, I asked to see 'Bill', the most senior manager in the area, who had the responsibility for the merger of the two service centres. Bill readily agreed to the appointment. I had always found him to be a decent person. He, like us, was just a pawn in a living game of chess. Or at least that was how I saw it.

Although the scene is being set in the sports and social club, to help to contextualise the story it is important that you are aware of preceding events. Hence the need for this background information. The meeting with Bill was of particular importance. When we met, he seemed tired and had aged visibly. I felt that the process must be affecting him badly. We exchanged pleasantries and soon progressed to the formal purpose and intention of the meeting. Bill rigorously defended the company position and operating policy. He reiterated that the changes had been necessary and that these were in our own interests. He also pointed out that my future career looked very healthy. His expectation was that my progression to senior management would happen before very long. However, he suggested that my attitude would have to change slightly for this to happen. It had been noticed that I had a tendency to question operating policies and senior management directives rather than just follow them. This fuelled my anger. Yes, I did tend to question, but only when a policy caused operational problems. The decision to close the service centre had caused considerable operating difficulties. Senior management did not seem to accept responsibility for any of these difficulties, so I had challenged this on numerous occasions.

My response emphasised that questioning could be a positive attribute in that it concerned itself with improving the work situation. This was not accepted. Questioning was seen as negative because it challenged the decisions of more senior management. This, it was stressed, was being pointed out to me for my own good. It emerged that the only reason that I had not been promoted previously was my habit of questioning operating policy. Anything except conforming was seen as negative. My competence was not in question, but some facets of my behaviour and commitment most certainly were. Bill concluded the meeting by reminding me that the way to progress was to curb my tendency to question. If I could do that, promotion would be likely to follow quickly. My response was to thank him. We shook hands and parted. Upon leaving his office, my thoughts and feelings were very mixed.

Part of me felt anger. My questioning was seen as negative and problematic. What was I supposed to do – be walked upon without squealing? Yet my behaviour was blocking promotion opportunities. The potential for higher salary and position fed my ego. Perhaps the compensation for conforming made it worth while. These were very contradictory positions, and I did not know what to do.

As it transpired, over the next few weeks my level of questioning intensified. Perhaps it had become habit, or part of my scripted behaviour. It seemed as if I could not stop myself challenging the senior management team on the inadequacies of the new operating policy. Furthermore, I was not going to allow myself to become an organisational scapegoat for inappropriate systems and procedures. I worked hard to overcome the daily operating problems that arose from the closure/merger. However, whenever I met any of the senior management team, I continued to point out the inadequacies of the new set-up to them. I usually followed up such encounters by outlining specific circumstances, identifying operating problems arising from the new operating system and so on, in a memo to senior management. Before long, the senior management team seemed to walk the other way when they saw me coming. When we did meet, their body language and general approach suggested that they found my behaviour uncomfortable.

Let's party

So there I was, having just arrived at the sports and social club. The party was already in full swing. A first-rate buffet had been laid on, and everyone's first few drinks were 'on the house'. The place seemed alive, the babble of voices almost overshadowing the music that blasted out from the disco. People seemed happy. Looking around the room, you could not help but notice that they seemed almost relieved. The closure had finally come. Now it was time to move on with the new ways of working. This party could be seen as an important rite of passage, a symbolic act of closure.

My sombre mood changed. Perhaps a combination of alcohol, the good food and my saturation in a party atmosphere made me feel better. Whatever it was, something affected me. I began to feel a lot better about the whole experience. I remember talking to friends and colleagues, even saying that I now felt bad about the way I had openly challenged and questioned the actions of senior management. I remember thinking that perhaps an apology was in order. My job was a good one and it had been recognised that my promotion prospects were good if my attitude changed. The immediate dilemma was: to what extent had that been jeopardised by my recent behaviour? It was time to build some bridges. Little did I know that the opportunity would soon arise.

Three senior managers were at the party, 'Bill', 'Tony' and 'Mike'. They had spent most of the evening standing together in a tight triad but had just begun to circulate. Perhaps they felt that it was now safe to do so. The reorganisation had angered a lot of people who were gathered in the room. Standing at the bar waiting to be served, I noticed Bill walking up behind me. His hand touched my shoulder and he said something like 'I'll get this Joe'. He ordered himself a refill and paid for the drinks. We stood talking. He said that he was pleased to see me at the party. We talked for a while, during which we exchanged pleasantries and discussed the future of Enigma. My attitude was positive in that I started talking about the opportunities that lay ahead and expressed certainty that any operational difficulties could soon be overcome, labelling these as nothing more than teething problems. His demeanour suggested that he was delighted with what had been said. We separated on very good terms. As he was walking away, he stopped and re-approached me. Taking me to one side, out of earshot of anyone else, he reminded me that 'if I stopped putting my head above the parapet I could really progress'. These were his exact words. My response was to thank him for his concern and patience. We shook hands and I asssured him that I recognised that my future lay with the continued success of Enigma. I felt good. It was time for me to mingle.

Within about ten minutes, Tony and I were talking. The conversation was very similar to the one with Bill. As the talk was drawing to a natural close, Tony said something that momentarily stopped me in my tracks. He said, 'Joe, I want to see you get on, so do yourself a favour and stop putting your head above the parapet!'

In my experience, although the phrase 'putting your head above the parapet' is not uncommon, to have it directed towards you twice within the space of ten minutes, by two different people, is unusual. My mind raced. Was this coincidence, or had I been the subject of some private discussion? I felt a little uneasy but did my best not to show it; Tony and I parted on overtly good terms. It was time for another drink. Standing at the bar, soaking up the atmosphere, I remember telling myself not to be so paranoid. Even if they had been talking about me, so what? Their advice was good for my career. Drink in hand, I continued to mingle.

Would you believe that within a few minutes, Mike was standing in front of me chatting politely. Once again, the conversation was very similar. However, this time I felt that I had been sought out. Reflecting as we spoke, I recalled that both Bill and Tony had approached me. I did not let my inner feelings show, and Mike and I developed a reasonable rapport. We started to laugh over something trivial. As the laughter subsided, Mike said, 'Joe, you're a good guy. You could go a long way in Enigma if only you would stop putting your head above the parapet'. He moved on to mingle elsewhere soon after uttering these words.

Left on my own again, my unease grew rapidly. My immediate thought was that the phrase 'putting your head above the parapet' three times in such a short time was more than coincidence. Was it possible that all three 'chats' were part of a conspiracy to persuade me to take more ownership of the new operating systems? Then again, were they simply coincidental? However, what did seem obvious was that whatever was going on at the party, my future interests were tied inextricably to the continued success of Enigma. That caused some personal concern and tension. I did not know why, but such was the extent of my unease that I decided to leave the party shortly after the third conversation.

My main concern now was to try to make sense of the experience. Conforming may have been good for my career, but I was not sure that it was good for me as a person.

Have you ever experienced similar tensions? Can you relate to my story? Perhaps you have found yourself compromising your own values for those espoused by those more senior than you in the company. Have you ever had to attend a 'social function' because you were expected to attend, rather than because you wanted to? Have you ever 'bitten your tongue' and kept quiet when you really wanted to speak out at work but were concerned about the consequences of doing so? Have you ever put your head above the parapet? If so, what happened? How did it feel? Why did you do it?

Making sense of experience: a theoretical analysis

> practice is never theory free, for it is always guided by an image of what one is trying to do. The real issue is whether or not we are aware of the theory guiding our actions.
>
> (Morgan 1986: 336)

It is clear that any experience can be interpreted, and made sense of, in different ways. It is equally clear that the broader our knowledge base, the more eclectic our reading, the greater the exposure to ideas that allow the generation of alternative insights into how we make sense of our experiences. What follows is an emergent analysis, which provides the potential to locate the party and parapet story in a broader social context. The analysis is underpinned by writers on more general aspects of the human condition, as well as those who have engaged in a critical examination of management. Where appropriate, other experiences are included to enrich the debate.

One of the central themes of critical theory in relation to management studies is that of ideology. It was explained in the introduction to this chapter that the piece concerns the ideologically driven nature of managerial activity. The analysis will proceed by locating ideology within a critical framework, with due attention paid to the possibility that some of the terminology used in the analysis may be unfamiliar to some students of management.

Operationalising ideology and hegemony

Ideology

As a result of the party, two things were clear to me. First, that coercive attempts were being made to control my behaviour, as I kept being told to keep 'my head down'. The second, that I was not being told why this was necessary. Intuitively, this felt strange. My later reading of ideology and hegemony has allowed me to reflect upon and make sense of this feeling. The *need* to be told may well be ideologically derived, whereas not being told why could emanate from our hegemonic conditioning.

Karl Mannheim (1960: 245), a sociologist who has written extensively on the concept of ideology, reminds us that 'the same word or concept, in most cases means very different things when used by differently situated persons.' Hence the need for me to operationalise, or make explicit, how concepts such as 'ideology' and 'hegemony' are to be employed in the specific context of my analysis. Terry Eagleton, a professor of English literature with a particular interest in ideology, succinctly outlines the problem of specific definition (1994: 14–15). He suggests that 'it is hardly an exaggeration to claim that there are almost as many theorists of ideology as there are theories for it' (*ibid*.: 14). Recognising the validity of what Eagleton is suggesting means that to attempt to 'define' ideology would be a contradictory exercise. To do so would be to over-simplify a complex phenomenon. Hence, rather than defining, my intention is to operationalise by explaining how the concept tends to be employed in work of this nature.

Jorge Larrain, a sociologist who has written a seminal piece of work on this subject, suggests that from the critical perspective ideology can be seen to have a negative rather than positive connotation (Larrain 1979). However, it should be recognised that he uses the notions of 'positive' and 'negative' not as value statements but as conditions of self-awareness. Positive relates to the conscious world, i.e. beliefs, whereas negative relates to the unconscious lack of awareness of where those beliefs, and the implicit assumptions that underpin them, come from. Thus in the more traditional positive sense, ideology tends to refer to the world views or cultural values of a group that have been internalised through the process of socialisation. The values underpinning such collective world views are often implicit rather than explicit, and they tend to be unspoken, based upon taken-for-granted assumptions about the way that things are in the social world. The cognitive validity (i.e. the degree of understanding and relevance) of these implicit assumptions is seen as a separate issue, whereas from the more critical perspective ideology refers to the relationship between these implicit assumptions and the way in which the ideas they are based upon shape our core cultural values. Hence in a critical analysis the cognitive validity of these ideas is immediately called into question.

It is often argued from the critical perspective that ideology becomes concerned with creating a distorted or false consciousness through which those who control ideas shape how people think and make sense of their lives. Those who control ideas are those with the greatest societal power base. Powerful groups, from this perspective, influence the ideas of those below them through the dissemination of ideology, to persuade the majority that their subordinate position is normal and natural, and that they have the right to command power and respect (*ibid*. 47–8). Ideology thus comes to be seen as a social product, emerging from historical contradictions in society. In particular, in the context of critical management studies, those contradictions deriving from the social relations that develop as a result of the division of labour in the workplace become of major interest. Ideology becomes a deceptive device that obscures the underlying nature of these relations, hiding not only deception but also subordination and exploitation.

One example taken from the parties and parapets story would be the way in which the managers did not disclose that they had spoken about me together. Yet it was obvious that they had. Such behaviour is deceptive and may concern itself with perpetuating the existing social relations of production within Enigma. My experience suggests that when confronted (as you have been here) with such a possibility or interpretation it often tends to be rejected immediately. So to emphasise this point further, another experience will be drawn upon, this time to highlight the potential for subordination and exploitation.

Exploitation – a matter of choice?

In my work at the university, a large proportion of my time is spent working with practising managers on a part-time MBA programme. One evening, we were exploring issues such as deception and the potential for domination and exploitation through the underlying nature of the social relations of production. The class members rejected this. They did not see themselves as being dominated or exploited through some obscure deceptive ideological device. I think they thought that I was talking nonsense. In an attempt to make them more aware of the potential of what was being suggested, I asked them to locate themselves within the labour process. To achieve this, I started by asking how many hours a week they worked. This tended to be between 50 and 65 hours. As they began to explore this experience, the students started talking about the problems associated with working these hours. Issues of personal stress and tiredness, in conjunction with the impact on their families and home life, became the focus of debate. The ever-increasing demands on their time was seen as a major source of tension. At an appropriate point, I intervened, asking how many hours they are contracted to work and if overtime payments were available. The general response was that they had contracts that state a notional time of about 38 hours, but due to their staff positions overtime payment was not an option. Yet, week in, week out, they are expected to work many hours over what they are contracted for. As this obvious truism became clearer to the students, the potential for their own domination and exploitation became clearer. The students then really opened up, talking about their own fears and powerlessness at work. Remember, these were practising managers. Many even spoke about not being the first to leave open-plan offices at night for fear of being seen as not committed enough.

One of the most extreme examples cited was by a production manager of a large engineering works. This factory worked a 24-hour shift system. On the last Saturday of every month, the production director would call a breakfast meeting at 6.30am to discuss the month's production. The attendance of all production managers and supervisors was mandatory. As the Friday night shift did not end until 5am, the practical ramifications of this were that in order to have accurate figures for the meeting managers were having to go in at 4am to prepare their data. This was after having worked a full week. They feared for their jobs if they did not attend the meeting, so they complied. This is an extreme case, but it highlights clearly the deceptive exploitative practices that were referred to earlier. Can you think of any similar experiences?

Perhaps a shorter way to exemplify the general point that I am attempting to make here is to ask you to think about the old saying 'a fair day's work for a fair day's pay'. Now ask yourself, who really decides what is fair? Is it you, or those who employ you?

Hegemony

The concept of 'hegemony' was originally developed by the neo-Marxist Antonio Gramsci (1971; Apple 1979: 4; Bocock 1986: 11).

Antonio Gramsci

Gramsci, an Italian Marxist and political theorist whose concept of 'hegemony' has been very influential in modern sociology, was born into a poor family in Sardinia in 1891. In 1911, he won a scholarship to the University of Turin, where he read linguistics. He did not finish his degree, leaving university to become a journalist and adviser to the Turin factory councils movement of 1919–20. He was one of the earliest advocates of involving factory workers in key decision making. In 1926, he was jailed for his anti-fascist beliefs. At his trial, the government prosecutor demanded that the judge 'stop this brain working for twenty years'. Gramsci spent the last ten years of his life in fascist prisons and clinics, but this did not silence him. Rather it inspired him to write his major theoretical treatise, *Prison Notebooks*. In this text, among other subjects, he explores in depth the concept of 'hegemony'. For Gramsci, ideological struggles are really struggles for hegemonic control, which shape and influence the hearts and minds of working-class people such that they think in ways that benefit and advantage existing dominant societal holders of power rather than themselves.

Gramsci (1971: 207) described the state as

> the entire complex of practical and theoretical activities with which the ruling class not only justifies and maintains its dominance, but manages to maintain the active consent of those over whom it rules.

If the ruling class manages to maintain control by gaining the consent and approval of a society such that the political, moral and cultural values of the ruling class appear natural, then in Gramsci's terms hegemony has been achieved.

> At base hegemony is all about ideology. But it is ideology writ large: the idea of an all encompassing dominant ideology whose scope extends through all social, cultural and economic spheres of society … Hegemony is the concept that a Marxist would use to describe a world view whose effect is to congeal the dominance of one economic class over another into cultural permanence.
>
> (Bocock 1986: 11)

It is acknowledged that to some the notion of a ruling class may be problematic. In the context of this work, ruling classes may be likened to John Child's (1977) notion of 'dominant coalitions', the members of which are the management elite in the organisational hierarchy.

Managerial prerogative

Have you ever really wondered what gives managers the right to manage? Or put another way, what gives them the right to control the actions of other people? This right to manage is often termed the 'managerial prerogative'. At work, we may be asked to do something that we do not want to do. We may moan, complain or even take some form of sanction, but invariably we do what is asked of us – even when it causes personal stress or anxiety. Why do we allow this to happen? Critical theorists would argue that the reason we do so has more to do with our socialisation or ideological preconditioning than with anything else. They suggest that the social reality that we create obscures the nature of the social relations between workers and managers in the labour process. This is achieved to the extent that it seems natural for someone 'more senior' to control our actions in the workplace.

This process of obscuring, it can be argued, is almost a kindness. Indeed, Larrain (1979) suggests that it is almost a practical necessity in that it distracts the majority of us from realising our position of potential oppression and exploitation in the labour process. This is achieved ideologically by creating societal illusions and mystifications (*ibid.*: 185). In the context of work, one such illusion could be the managerial prerogative itself, i.e. the right to manage.

Our hegemonic conditioning ensures that our consciousness becomes saturated, such that the world we live in becomes our common-sense world, the only world that we can perceive as viable (Apple 1979: 4). Political and moral alternatives to such a world tend to be seen as untenable, even incomprehensible. Such a position, it would appear, was demonstrated by the senior managers referred to earlier in my story. All of them felt that their advice to me was in my own interests, despite the personal tensions and anxieties that I experienced. Perhaps it was more in their interests than mine. My behaviour made me difficult to control.

Although hegemony may be similar to ideology, they are not the same thing. Hegemony is a broader concept: it may include various ideological beliefs, but is not reducible to one single belief. For example, ideologies like the ones espoused by the leaders of the main British political parties, William Hague's Conservatives or Prime Minister Tony Blair's New Labour tend to be imposed. Hegemony, on the other hand, presupposes consent, or at least the engineering of consent. A change of government may result in a change of ideology (the means); however, it would not threaten the dominant hegemony (the ends). At a basic level, they may be distinguished by describing ideology as 'a system of ideas', whereas hegemony is 'a lived, habitual social practice which probably encompasses the unconscious' (Eagleton 1991: 112).

Practical reflection

Have you ever noticed much change in the workplace following a change of government? One government may have the stated ideology of pursuing managerialism; the other may take a more socialist stance in that its stated aim is to give the workers more say. This has tended to be the situation in Britain between the Conservative and Labour governments for as long as I can remember. My experience of mainland Europe suggests that a similar picture exists there. My experience also suggests that, whichever government is in power, workers will find themselves in very similar circumstances. They tend to work hard for their employers and have little or no say in their remuneration packages (although they may think they have). From the critical perspective, the workplace is subject to the same forces of domination and exploitation in the pursuit of profit maximisation, or cost minimisation, regardless of the ideological beliefs espoused by the ruling party. This arises because the ideologies operate within a hegemonic framework, which has not been challenged or changed. It is as a result of our hegemonic conditioning, according to Gramsci, that exploitation and domination in the labour process tends to appear natural, inevitable and therefore acceptable. This results in the underlying ideological beliefs of capitalism rarely being questioned.

As Nichols and Armstrong (1976), two organisational researchers interested in the labour process, have observed, the real triumph of capitalist hegemony is that, for the most part, those workers do not affirm or deny its values. For them, capitalism is just part of an unalterable order of things (not necessarily a proper one). It is a world they did not choose, cannot make and cannot alter. For this reason, capitalism (like God) is not the sort of thing you should think about too much (*ibid.*: 59).

By distinguishing them in this way, hegemony can be seen to be similar to Marx's notion of ideology. This also rejected the idea of an independent form of free consciousness as 'what men think is necessarily referred to and conditioned by the historical reality of society' (Larrain 1979: 39). Having now operationalised ideology and hegemony, we can further explore how this relates to organisation members' experiences of managerial control.

Developing skills as a reflective practitioner

One of the aims of this book is to facilitate the process whereby readers develop the capability to reflect upon current practice with a view to generating alternative ways of thinking about management. In other words, to help them to reflect upon their own experiences so that they may generate alternative ideas and insights into current practice. If someone has the ability to do this, they are often called a 'reflective practitioner'.

It may sound as though this is an easy enough task; however, my experience suggests that the process can be very difficult to perform. Various people offer differing explanations of why this should be the case. For me, the work of Gramsci offers a very plausible explanation.

He suggests that, contrary to popular belief, the development of the capability for critical thought, analysis and general awareness does not automatically emerge from experience. Rather, the ability for critical thought develops out of the emergence of a powerful counter-hegemonic force that is capable of disseminating alternative perspectives, which highlight how a lot of our 'common sense' and instinctual values are culturally learned. Without this counter-hegemonic experience, you are unable (partially) to escape the ideas and false consciousness of a particular society. If you can 'break free' and begin to reflect upon your experiences in different ways, then this generates the capability for more enlightened forms of practice. I would argue that you are then on your way to becoming a reflective practitioner.

However, ask yourself how you usually react when you come across something that threatens your comfort zone (your 'common sense' and 'instinctual values'). Do you embrace the experience, or do you tend to shy away from the uncertainty it creates? My experience suggests that most of us can feel threatened by such experiences rather than embracing them as opportunities. Certainly, when I feel threatened I tend to stay in my comfort zones. To become reflective practitioners, we must learn to live at times with the uncertainty that arises from embracing the unknown and accepting opinions that at first appear unpalatable. Writing a chapter for this book, for example, has provided me with a host of solicited (and some unsolicited) critical comments, and it is very difficult to remain engaged in a reflective process as opposed to becoming defensive, angry, confused and so on.

The reality of managing: reflections on personal experience

When an actor takes on an established social role, usually he finds that a particular front has already been established for it. Whether his acquisition of the role was primarily motivated by the desire to perform the given task or by the desire to maintain the corresponding front, the actor will find he must do both.

(Goffman 1959: 37)

By playing roles, the individual participates in a social world. By internalising these roles, the same world becomes subjectively real to him.

(Berger and Luckmann 1966: 91)

Some years ago, while still working in industry (and researching for my PhD on a part-time basis) I asked my immediate manager, Mike, what the job of a manager was really all about. His reply reflected what is often termed the 'functional' or 'classical' model in that he regurgitated Fayol's words that a manager 'plans, organises, coordinates and controls'. We spent a few minutes discussing this approach. I then asked him what he had done the previous day.

On hearing the question, he paused for a few moments, laughed and said, 'Not a great deal of what I just said a manager's job was all about.' We then laughed together and he commented that he had never really reflected before on what his job entailed. He just seemed to know what he had to do and got on with it. He was, in his own words, a very practical man. However, he thought my question was a super way of exposing the 'real' nature of managerial work. I told him that it was not my idea and that I had borrowed the approach from Mintzberg (1973: 1). He laughed again and told me that my honesty would get me nowhere.

Several years later, in my role as a management developer I have adopted the same approach many times. If you ask a manager what their job entails, they say one thing; if you then ask them what they did the previous day you generate a different answer. This simple exercise usually stimulates a lively discussion about the practical nature of management. If you have never done this exercise before, why not try it for yourself?

Parties and parapets revisited

> It is not difficult to deprive the great majority of independent thought, but the minority who will retain an inclination to criticise must be silenced.
>
> (Hayek 1944: 118)

The basis of my interpretation centres on reflection about why putting my head above the parapet was seen as so threatening by the senior management – although it is highly unlikely that even now, after the passage of several years, they would actually admit that they found my behaviour threatening. However, the energy and time that they devoted to convincing me to conform rather than question suggests to me that they were in a defensive position. I suspect that their real concerns grew from my questioning of company policy and procedures. In other words, their fear emanated from my questioning of the validity of a system that had played a major role in structuring their reality. My questioning threatened the implicit belief system, the unspoken, taken-for-granted assumptions upon which that reality was socially constructed. In other words, I was threatening their dominant ideological values derived from capitalist rationality. This was never articulated. Rather, it was reformulated in the guise of giving me 'good career advice'. What could not be allowed in Enigma was someone approaching a very senior level who had the ability and motivation to analyse the company critically or rigorously. The quiet words at the party, advising me to conform, were concerned with management control at a hegemonic level. I had to embrace and consent to my own conformity if I wished to gain entry to the highest levels of management. In my experience, such conformity is required in most organisations. The most effective form of managerial control is indoctrinating others into your belief system. If successful, you will not have to waste your time and energy getting others to do what you want – they will do it anyway, as it will now appear to them to be the natural thing to do. The ideologically derived nature of management control ensures that this is likely to happen more often than not. It also tends to ensure that those involved in the labour process (both operational managers and wage labour) are unaware of why it happens. They are just left feeling the tensions and contradictions of organisational life, treading treacle to try to get the job done. Such is the power of our hegemonic conditioning.

As for myself, back in Enigma, it could be argued that I was lucky to have kept my job given my ability to question the dominant ideology in the company. I saw my individuality and creativity as a strength. Indeed, much of the company rhetoric proclaimed the value of just such attributes. However, from the critical perspective offered in this chapter, organisations can be seen as structures of control. Far from being desirable, individuality and creativity have great potential to undermine the ideological foundations of managed organisations.

Wilsher (1993: 36), commenting on research from Cranfield and Manchester, noted that:

> It is often the more imaginative, self confident and go getting individuals – the ones who argue at committee meetings – who tend to find the black bin bag waiting on their desks, while the non-boat rocking colleagues with a strongly developed aptitude for office politics are the ones who successfully survive.

The experience of the closure of the service centre had a profound impact upon me. It could be argued that the process itself was a counter-hegemonic experience, as my previous perceptions of the organisation and its senior management were shattered. Watching the effects of site closure, including redundancy, and staff relocation on those subjected to the process was not a pleasant experience. It certainly made me question the morality of management and brought to life the real political nature of the managerial process. What was worse than watching the effects of the site closure was experiencing it for myself.

Conclusion

Alistair Mant, an influential management researcher, suggests that 'the term management should be used to describe three related phenomena: an activity, an occupational group and the values or ideology of that group' (1976, quoted in Johnson and Gill 1993: vii).

This chapter, through focusing on the applied lens of a critical paradigm, has located and explained the way in which I now make sense of what happened to me at the party. By drawing from a number of sources, I have attempted through reflective practice to illustrate that although the daily experience of management in practice may not consciously appear as control, 'doing' management invariably manifests itself as such. Control is seen as the ideologically derived, quintessential aspect of management that underpins and highlights the interrelated nature of Mant's three phenomena. It is worth repeating: the quintessential role of management is control.

An ending or a beginning?

It is worth repeating – the quintessential role of management is control. Perhaps if I say it often enough I can indoctrinate you into believing it! But I need to remind myself that it is just one perspective. Of course, it is *my* perspective and as such is one I value. But I would rather leave you with the space to make your mind up, come to your own conclusions, develop your own perspective. So, in drawing my party to an end, let me invite you to party on.

Bibliography

Alvesson, M. and Willmott, H. (eds) (1992) *Critical Management Studies*, London: Sage.

Alvesson, M. and Willmott, H. (1996) *Making Sense of Management*, London: Sage.

Anthony, P.D. (1977) *The Ideology of Management*, London: Tavistock.

Anthony, P.D. (1986) *The Foundation of Management*, London: Tavistock.

Anthony, P.D. (1994) 'The alienation of the academy', guest lecture, University of Humberside, Hull (September).

Apple, M. (1979) *Ideology and Curriculum*, London: Routledge & Kegan Paul.

Argyris, C. and Schon, I. (1978) *Organisation Learning: A Theory of Action Perspective*, Englewood Cliffs, New Jersey: Addison Wesley.

Berger, P.L. and Luckmann, T. (1966) *The Social Construction of Reality*, Harmondsworth: Penguin.

Beynon, H. (1973) *Working for Ford*, Harmondsworth: Penguin.

Bocock, R. (1986) *Hegemony*, London: Tavistock.

Burrell, G. (1988) 'Modernism, post modernism and organisational analysis 2: the contribution of Michael Foucault', *Organisational Studies*: 221–35.

Burrell, G. and Morgan, G. (1979) *Sociological Paradigms and Organisational Analysis*, London: Heinemann.

Child, J. (1977) *Organization*, London: Harper & Row.

Clegg, S. (ed.) (1989) *Organisational Theory and Class Analysis*, New York: de Gruyter.

Clegg, S. (1993) *Modern Organisations*, London: Sage.

Dalton, M. (1959) *Men who Manage*, New York: Wiley.

Eagleton, T. (1991) *Ideology*, London: Vess.

Eagleton, T. (ed.) (1994) *Ideology*, London: Longman.

Earle, M.J. (ed.) (1985) *Perspectives on Management*, London: Oxford University Press.

Edwards, P. (1986) *Conflict at Work*, Oxford: Basil Blackwell.

Fox. A. (1985) *Man Mismanagement*, London: Hutchinson.

Friere, P. (1972) *Pedagogy of the Oppressed*, Harmondsworth: Penguin.

Gill, J. and Johnson, P. (1991) *Research Methods for Managers*, London: Paul Chapman.

Goffman, E. (1959) *The Presentation of Self in Everyday Life*, London: Penguin.

Golding, D. (1979) 'Some symbolic manifestations of power in industrial organisations', unpublished PhD thesis, Sheffield Hallam University.

Gramsci, A. (1971) *Prison Notebooks*, London: Lawrence & Wishart.

Hayek, F. (1944) *The Road to Serfdom*, London: Routledge.

Johnson, P. and Gill, J. (1993) *Management Control and Organisational Behaviour*, London: Paul Chapman.

Larrain, J. (1979) *The Concept of Ideology*, London: Hutchinson.

Lukes, S. (1974) *Power, A Radical View*, London: Macmillan.

Mangham, I. (1988) *Effecting Organisational Change*, London: Basil Blackwell.

Mannheim, K. (1960) *Ideology and Utopia*, London: Routledge.

Marcuse, H. (1972) *One Dimensional Man*, London: Abacus.

Marx, K. (1962) *Das Kapital*, Vol. 1, London: Penguin.

Marx, K. (1979) *Wage Labour and Capital*, London: Central Books.

Marx, K. and Engels, F. (1976) *Collected Works*, London: Lawrence & Wishart.

Matteson, M. and Ivancevich, S. (1989) *Management and Organisational Behaviour Classics*, Illinois: BPI Irwin.

Mintzberg, H. (1973) *The Nature of Managerial Work*, New York, Harper & Row.

Mintzberg, H. (1989) *Mintzberg on Management*, London: Macmillan.

Morgan, G. (1986) *Images of Organisations*, London: Sage.

Nason, F.J. (1999) *Management Education – Ideology in Action* (forthcoming).

Nason, F.J. and Golding, D. (1998) 'Approaching observation'. In G. Simon and C. Cassell (eds) *Quantitative Methods and Analysis in Organisational Research*, London: Sage.

Nichols, T. (1969) *Ownership Control and Ideology*, London: Allen & Unwin.

Nichols, T. and Armstrong, P. (1976) *Workers Divided*, London: Fontana.

Pettigrew, A. (1973) *The Politics of Organisational Decision Making*, London: Tavistock.

Reed, M. (1989) *The Sociology of Management*, Hemel Hempstead: Harvester Wheatsheaf.

Reed, M. and Anthony, P. (1992) 'Professionalising management and managing professionalisation: British management in the 1980s', *Journal of Management Studies*, September: 591–613.

Salaman, G. (1979) *Work Organisations: Resistance and Control*, London: Longman.

Sayles, L.R. (1964) *Leadership – What Effective Managers Really Do and How they Do It*, Maidenhead: McGraw-Hill.

Schutz, A. (1962) *Collected Papers Vol. 1: The Problem of Social Reality*, The Hague: Martinus Nijhoff.

Slack, N., Chambers, S., Harland, C., Harrison, A. and Johnston, R. (1995) *Operations Management*, London: Pitman.

Storey, J. (1983) *Managerial Prerogative and the Question of Control*, London: Routledge & Kegan Paul.

Taylor, F.W. (1911) *Principles of Scientific Management*, New York: Harper.

Thompson, J.B. (1984) *Studies in the Theory of Ideology*, Cambridge: Polity Press.

Watson, A. (1994) *In Search of Management*, London: Routledge.

Wilkinson, A. and Willmott, H. (1995) *Making Quality Critical*, London: Routledge.

Willmott, H.C. (1987) 'Studying managerial work: a critique and a proposal', *Journal of Management Studies*, May: 249–70.

Wilsher P. (1993) 'The mixed up manager', *Management Today*, October.

Wright, O.W., Hachen, D., Costello, C. and Sprague, J. (1982) 'The American class structure', *American Sociological Review* 47.

Further reading

Alvesson and Willmott (1996) provides an excellent overview, exploring how critical theory has evolved, its relevance to modern management and why it should be considered important by practising managers. Anthony (1986) exposes the need for managerial activity to be subjected to moral and philosophical as well as economic investigation. Eagleton (1994) provides a collection of readings that bring together in one text many of the differing perspectives on the complex nature of ideology. Lukes (1974) explores how our socialisation processes may be used as a hegemonic device to shape our beliefs in a way that works against our own interests. Storey (1983) examines the position of management in attempting to control the labour process.

4 The enactment of political tensions in management

A historical perspective

Judith Golding

Introduction

This chapter explores a particular way of examining the historical origins of those activities, beliefs and ideologies that in the modern world have come to be known as 'management'. In the course of this analysis, the chapter focuses on the foundations of a specific form of inequality in organisations.

Inequality has many dimensions, and members of organisations perceive and experience the effects of inequalities in various ways (not just in terms of the more high-profile elements of gender, race and disability but also in terms of age, size, regional origin, accent and many other sources of apparently 'innocent' discrimination). In analysing these experiences, this chapter seeks to illuminate the origins of one special feature of organisations that makes such discrimination, in all its forms, possible. It examines in some detail the foundation of inequality, which is contained within the nature of hierarchical organisations – i.e. some people have positions that are said to be (and are enforced as such when deemed necessary) 'above' others in terms of a command structure, no matter how relaxed or tight that structure might be.

The chapter goes on to examine this foundation of inequality in a context of deference (i.e. the deferring of one person to another in terms of perceived responsibilities, according to their positions on a hierarchical scale). The chapter will trace the historical foundations of deferential relationships from ancient master/slave relations, via the particular manifestations of deference laid down in the formative years of joint stock companies, through to the large and complex organisations that we know today.

Using examples of the absurdities of deference taken from a large multinational organisation in which the author worked, the idea of regaining a lost historical grounding of the origins of inequality in organisational relations, from which the notion of management has emerged, will be examined.

Organisation and hierarchy

Any serious examination of the kinds of hierarchical relationship that exist in organisations (i.e. as represented on a typical 'organisation chart') will reveal a serious discrepancy between the treatment of hierarchy in much of the mainstream management literature and the actual accounts given by those engaged in such relationships. It is as though management is deemed to have occurred through the execution of a series of technical functions not requiring the co-operation and commitment of any of the individuals involved.

There have been attempts to redefine the nature and consequences of hierarchical relationships in the critical literature (e.g. Alvesson and Willmott 1992; 1996), but this seems to have been largely ignored by those following a path that emphasises the discovery of those aspects of management that can be held up as good examples to copy (e.g. those following the path of Peters and Waterman 1982). Indeed, the contributions of those recommending such a path might suggest that the history of management reflects a linear pattern of successive improvements in the conditions in which organisational work is carried out. Nothing could be further from the case, and yet in the absence of any treatment of inequalities deriving from hierarchical relationships, one can only assume that such factors are felt to be inconsequential. Perhaps it is not surprising therefore, that there has been such a neglect of the accounts of those experiencing the effects of such inequalities.

The whole history of industrialisation has been one of increasing efficiency, resulting in successive benefits being passed on to workers, for example through a progressive reduction in the number of hours worked per week. Or has it? Judging by experiences in the last decade of the twentieth century, perhaps a reduction in the number of hours that are paid for would be a more accurate reflection of the conditions. More and more workers are complaining of overwork and reporting that they are expected to work many more hours than they are paid for, with the health problems associated with overwork becoming of increasing concern (see Sparks *et al.* 1997).

Indeed, drawing attention to the way in which a tightening of operating procedures is often cast as an improvement in working conditions might be a more appropriate way of capturing the essence of those recurring features in the history of organisations. The kinds of metaphor used to reflect increasing efficiency in organisations (e.g. slimming down, trimming excess, returning to basics, focusing on essentials, becoming lean and mean) remind me of the old story of the Yorkshireman trying to economise on the feeding of his dog, wherein it is said that he had just got the animal used to living on 'nowt' when it died!

As an example of this kind of doublespeak, the US film industry has become so focused upon the consequences of failure at the box office that streams of film writers are being employed to make successive revisions to scripts – to such an extent that it is becoming impossible to determine who should be credited with authorship. In fact, a panel from the Writers' Guild is often employed to give a ruling on an equitable apportioning of effort (not to mention pay), the irony being that this is cast as a reflection of the general improvement in fairness of working conditions in the industry.

Can you think of any examples of managers being unable to account for precise responsibility in this way? And can you think of any occasion upon which a reduction in the consumption of resources has been reframed as an improvement in working conditions?

The neglect of the experiences of vast numbers of employees has been unfortunate, since even a cursory examination of the experiences of those engaged in hierarchical relationships will show that the factors that comprise perceived inequalities have not fundamentally changed. This is not to suggest that conditions both within and without organisations have not changed at all. Of course conditions have changed, in some cases drastically. Sadly, however, the extent of those changes has sometimes been over-emphasised, not least because of the associated attempts to portray organisations as politically neutral places, operating in historical vacuums. An illustration involving part of an overheard conversation between two returning final-year undergraduate students of management in a university in the north of England will underline the extent of the neglect.

> I was looking through the book list, and I couldn't find anything relating to … 'running an outlet' … you know like say [the burger bar] I worked in last summer. Everything seemed to be related to what they might be doing at head office … which very few of us will ever get to see.

> Well yes, but you should worry. I was showing one of the books on the list … I agree that it was the only one I could find in the library … but anyway, I was showing it to my dad, and all he could say was, 'Oh yes, and how do any of these companies ever get to fire anyone then?' And you know why that interested him …?

The seriousness of neglecting the kind of impact that hierarchical relations have upon the lives of those working in organisations (in this case involving an issue of how it is possible for one person to terminate the employment of another) is amply demonstrated by the way in which the father of one of the students expressed frustration at the abstracted and general nature of the book that he was shown from the book list of a course in management. Indeed, management textbooks (especially those of the Peters and Waterman kind) rarely give space to the kind of thing that seemed to have interested the father of the second speaker, and even those in the functional areas charged with attending to matters such as the termination of someone's employment (i.e. human resource management and personnel management) often restrict themselves to questions of how to handle situations of redundancy, rather than to questions concerning how it is possible for such things to be accomplished. The idea of hierarchy being central to this accomplishment is not a favourite topic in the functional management literature.

Moreover, this lack of attention to the hierarchical factors that enable redundancies to be accomplished is reflected in other areas too. The introductions of new technology is a good example. New technology is often treated as though its introduction is inevitable – the element of 'the new' becoming a self-fulfilling prophecy because if you do not keep up to date, you will not survive. Now who could argue with that? No one really, but in the meantime, questions about who decides, why, and what the consequences might be are at the very least blurred, if not entirely side-stepped.

It is a considerable irony that the failure of those charged with the task of teaching and writing about management (especially those following prescriptive traditions) to address matters of most concern to those experiencing the cold, hard edges of organisational life is nowhere more apparent than in the treatment of new technology as though it were a politically neutral issue. Restricting the analysis for the time being to information technology, the word 'new' raises significant questions about the use of language. How many times can something be new? Whose (hierarchical) interests are being served by calling it new? Perhaps everything can be said to be new the first time an unfamiliar application is introduced, but this has occurred so often, in so many stages, at so many times during our own century that the notion itself is in danger of being exposed as a euphemism for someone's intention to make someone else redundant. Nevertheless, we seem destined to learn little from repeated examples. Thus mistakes of conception (is it new?), application (is it appropriate?) and effects (will it achieve what we want, without unintended consequences?) have occurred in many cases.

> It is sometimes sobering to look back upon particular experiences with a view to reassessing the position you adopted and the predictions you made at the time. I was reflecting recently upon a research project that I had undertaken about fifteen years ago and was shocked to realise the extent to which I had underestimated the impact of the introduction of a new word-processing system.
>
> This was at the headquarters of the National Coal Board in the UK, and most of my attention had been focused upon the potential impact on the jobs of the office staff concerned. I had been intent upon trying to assess the 'real' intentions of the managers who were responsible for introducing the new word-processing system, but looking back that was the least of the problems, because a mere fifteen years later, not only have all the office staff gone but so has the headquarters building, together with the entire National Coal Board and almost the whole of the coal-mining industry!
>
> I would have made an immediate resolution not to be drawn into a position of underestimating the potential for change in any situation, were it not that I have made that resolution before only to be caught out by my own failure to realise the extent to which unanticipated change can occur without there being any kind of limit that makes sense at the time.
>
> Perhaps a more considered reflection upon historical precedent would have helped me here – in the sense that very few organisations survive in the longer term, despite the emphasis upon activities that might lead one to assume that the opposite was the case.

On the other hand, there are occasions upon which the introduction of 'new' technology is more overtly cast in a light in which supposed changes in organisational structure are said to be necessary. In the case of information technology, the improved access to information that developments will bring is said to necessitate (and indeed to lead to) flatter structures, because reporting systems will become more streamlined with improvements in information flow (for example, information obtained from electricity and gas meter readings can be fed straight into a 'billing' programme, without the need for a layer of supervisors to collate and assemble the information from the work of a group of meter readers).

The main problem with that kind of analysis is that despite the obvious advantages in situations such as the meter-reading example, the opposite has been the result in too many other cases. Thus to take one small example, increasing decentralisation of control over the quality of milk production was said to be an inevitable consequence of advances in information technology in the early 1980s. This patently did not occur (see Rowe 1986), the actual result being more central control over quality standards (as a result of improvements in quality of information) than it did in decentralisation of responsibility for achieving that quality. This kind of experience seems to have been neglected by the proponents of yet newer panaceas of organisational levelling processes (such that 'de-layering' has become a buzzword in the face of increased centralisation of control!).

In this chapter, I want to suggest that we have lost our way in terms of conceptualising our experiences, and that the experiences of people occupying different hierarchical positions in organisations derives largely from the historical development of command structures that have been in existence for much longer than most analysts would claim for the whole history of management studies. The neglect of such basic tensions in so much of the mainstream management literature may be one reason why we have lost our way. A relocation may provide one way of recapturing a more grounded understanding of the nature of management. For while changes may be for ever occurring in organisational relations, those changes are more often incremental (although wholesale changes of personnel may be involved) that are seldom as fundamental as analysts would sometimes have us believe (i.e. they seldom involve real changes in hierarchical structures).

In pursuing this somewhat unusual path, I want to illustrate some of the origins of the great divide, which seems destined to be perpetuated, between generalised theories of management and the experiences of employees in organisations. It is perhaps one of the paradoxes of management thought that while some of the more functionalist management writers (e.g. Kanter 1977) have highlighted the common dichotomy between publicly expressed values relating to the organisational life of a company and people's privately felt beliefs, the explanation of that dichotomy is so often insufficiently followed through. For the clash between individual human aspirations and what are characteristically reified as 'organisational goals' is still demonstrably evident in so many management texts. One reason for this is surely that proponents rarely ground their analyses in historical contexts.

Management writers have all too often pursued their analyses on the assumption that it is sufficient to look for elements of transitory change and to see those changes as having no particular significance and no historical antecedents. Garson (1972), for example, in a comparison between what is cast as a relaxed, democratic style of employee control and a rigid system, has emphasised the essentially 'cultural' nature of such dichotomies. The implication is that in different locations the kinds of tension that are found are not only diverse but also owe their existence to presumably quite distinct foundations.

In this chapter, I want to suggest that the kinds of tension found in unequal hierarchical relationships are not new. They are at the heart of what US commentator Edwards (1979) has called the contested terrain that forms the essence of organisational relations (i.e. the fact that people see things differently according to their different positions in the command structure). These differences are demonstrably part of our inheritance and may even be the unavoidable manifestations of our age-old struggles. Any analysis that forgets this is likely to founder in the desert of aspirations into which so many students of management are led, with little hope of making contact with any secure conceptual foundation.

Managers are often very critical of their situations. However, their critiques are often limited to a consideration of their own involvement in events about which they are not satisfied. They may sometimes ask questions as to why they are doing what they are doing, but such questions generally focus on the details of a particular complaint that they have. Rarely do managers ask themselves how it is possible for them to be asked (required?) to do what they are doing – i.e. on whose behalf are they being asked? Whose interests are being served (i.e. beyond those of their immediate superiors)?

Fundamental critiques of the reasons why we have managers are seldom entertained. Indeed, in my own job, I am sometimes told that asking such questions will only make managers more dissatisfied than they already are. It is even said sometimes, by those who work in universities, that it is not the job of management education to make managers more dissatisfied than they were before.

Could this kind of thinking have resulted in setting the sights of management education too low? Could it be that we have gone rather too far along the road of vocationalism (i.e. the kind of education that is designed for a specific purpose deriving from employment needs and prevailing labour market conditions)? Could it be that a return to education *away from* (e.g. away from control) as distinct from education *towards* (i.e. towards specific goals) might be of some benefit in a subject such as management studies, with its plethora of excessively functional agendas.

The concept of deference

In drawing upon the kind of account that people give when asked to describe their situations, this chapter will suggest that one way of understanding the kind of superior/subordinate relations found in a typical organisational command structures is to place them in a framework of deference.

Initially, it may seem a little strange to focus upon the idea of deference. After all, deferential relationships are nowadays thought of as part of a history that no longer applies to modern organisations operating in a more sophisticated world in which organisations with flatter structures have led to the establishment of more enlightened (if not more democratic) relationships. I want to suggest that this is far from the case, even if democracy and/or deference are treated as relative concepts (relative deprivation, in all its forms, being a favourite defence of the proponents of the 'Ah well, our organisations are not like that now' thesis). Indeed, I want to show that claims for flatter structures and more enlightened relations have a rather hollow ring to them when placed against the ways in which people categorise their relationships when asked to reflect upon their experiences.

The relationship between labour and capital is an important one in any organisation. The way in which employees are often treated as secondary to the achievement of adequate returns on capital sets the scene for a great deal of what happens in organisational relations. In Western cultures, the survival of an organisation is often held to depend upon keeping shareholders happy, and while this is obviously an important constituent in the history of organisations, the extent to which labour (in the form of actual employees) is held to be in service to capital (i.e. capable of producing the required returns on capital) is fundamental.

This element of 'service' might be an important starting point for an analysis of deference in organisational relations. In this analysis, I want to begin rather earlier than that, with an examination of the way in which the derivation of deferential relationships can be seen clearly in even older systems of patronage, which have had great strength historically, as particularly well evidenced in England in the seventeenth and eighteenth centuries.

Goffman (1956: 475) has identified the essentially symbolic nature of deference. He suggests that deference can be seen as a transaction in which one person renders superiority to another by deferring to their position, and that this may therefore reflect only a difference in position (i.e. stemming from their different roles). In other words, it may not relate to what they think about each other personally:

> By deference I shall refer to that component of activity which functions as a symbolic means by which appreciation is regularly conveyed to a recipient of this recipient, or of something of which this recipient is taken as a symbol, extension or agent ... Those who render deference to an individual may feel, of course, that that they are doing this merely because (he/she) is an instance of a category, or a representative of something, and that they are giving (him/her) (his/her) due not because of what they think of (him/her) 'personally' but in spite of it.

The symbolic feature referred to is not simply a feature of particular transactions. On the contrary, it is clear that a whole infrastructure of tradition exists associated with the derivation and maintenance of deference. As an example of how widespread this tradition is in some occupations, Newby (1977) concluded in his now well-established study of agricultural workers that deference was not attitudinal (i.e. not just a feature of the way in which particular farm workers deferred to farm owners) but was a fundamental element of social structure associated with the development of their particular roles.

The historical significance of deference in hierarchical relationships

The most obvious historical antecedent of deferential hierarchical relationships is in master and slave relations, which historically have formed the basis of many of the strands that we now come to define as 'organisation'.

Most periods of history have their own versions of master and slave relationships, and most people have a clear (if not distressing) image of the kind of cruel exploitation associated with eighteenth- and nineteenth-century examples (particularly those involving African victims in the Americas). However, it is also clearly possible to identify examples of slavery in ancient civilisations. The undoubtedly equal severity and starkness of these images has had the effect of creating a distancing – such that conceptions of such relations generally proceed as though their basic tenets belong to former times, with little relevance for our own times. The intellectual impact of these antecedent relations has thus been lost to whole areas of analysis, such as that bounded by organisation theory.

I want to attempt to resurrect some elements of those images for a moment, although rather than document further examples from the eighteenth and nineteenth centuries (such as the Africa/Americas experiences) or indeed from ancient times, I want to highlight aspects of deference deriving from master/slave relationships that do not have quite the same overt cruelty but which are nonetheless (and perhaps because of their relatively benign existence) more common than popular images would have us believe, although literally they may be rather more concerned with the 'master' side of the equation than with the 'slave'. In other words, I want to relate the notion of 'master' to 'manager', while not suggesting that employees are necessarily of the same order as 'slave' (i.e. I am not suggesting that employees are literally chained and unable to move; I am merely highlighting that they can normally only move to another 'master').

One the obvious examples is undoubtedly in the work of scribes, so common before the advent of the printing press. For hundreds of years, this role was what we would now call a personal assistant (employee) to the great officials of the state and Church (managers). It was a role normally attained through the patronage system and involved placing the needs of the master (manager) above those of the scribe (employee). Thus the needs of the master were always given a higher priority than those of the scribe, and the scribe was expected to leave the satisfaction of their own needs until the wishes of the master had been fulfilled. In relating this to complex modern organisations it is fairly easy to produce examples showing that the opposite is the case (indeed, Donald Roy (1955) extensively documented such opposing examples of employee actualisation in the 1950s). Clearly, then, employees do not follow the axiom as closely as their forebears would have had to do. However, I want to suggest that the general principle is still true, as can be seen in situations of crisis (e.g. how can a person who is being told that they are to be made redundant satisfy their own needs before those of the person giving them the news?).

One reaction of those considering the application of a master/slave relationship to modern organisations is to say that the notion of 'slave' is inappropriate, if only because employees are free to leave and move on. Just where they would move on to, and under what conditions they would manage to make alternative arrangements for earning a living, is seldom pursued, because there is a worrying similarity to be confronted.

Paul Foot, an influential journalist with a critical eye upon the way in which the BBC is being managed, recently wrote, in *The Guardian* newspaper:

> Every day, it seems, a first rate journalist is sacked by the BBC. Isabel Hilton was sacked the other day as a *World Tonight* presenter. She consistently failed to show even a trace of the two qualities most required of BBC interviewers nowadays – deference and ignorance. She had to go.
>
> Last week, Chris Dunkley was sacked from his long-standing job of presenting the reactions of BBC listeners. His problem was not just humour and style. Sometimes he even dared to suggest that BBC bosses can be wrong. He had to go.
>
> (Foot 1998: 16)

Could Mr Foot have had his tongue in cheek? I think not, especially when setting this against the comments of a former BBC governor, for according to *The Guardian*'s media correspondent, Janine Gibson (1999: 3), the crime writer

Baroness P.D. James had said that 'Creativity in sound and vision doesn't flourish in an atmosphere of despotism, coercion and fear.'

Baroness James was not the first to cast organisations in terms of climates of fear. Joseph Heller (1974: 19), in his novel *Something Happened*, did this too:

> In the office in which I work there are five people of whom I am afraid. Each of these five people is afraid of four people (excluding overlaps), for a total of twenty, and each of these twenty people is afraid of six people, making a total of one hundred and twenty people who are feared by at least one person. Each of these one hundred and twenty people is afraid of the other one hundred and nineteen, and all of these one hundred and forty-five people are afraid of the twelve men at the top who helped found and build the company, and who now own and direct it.

Can you think of an event in which people failed to disclose what they really thought before an important decision was made? And can you think of any occasions upon which the opposite was the case?

Many of our great writers and composers produced work under conditions of patronage. It was said to be a protective environment, but one suspects that their success was not unrelated to their ability to steer their talents to fit the desires of their masters (for example, J.S. Bach's organ and choral music may have been regarded as his prime contribution by his patrons in the church, but his solo violin and cello, and his orchestral music have historically become equally regarded and cherished).

A similar relationship between the sermons and the poetry of the English poet John Donne can be highlighted. Indeed, in the sixteenth century, Donne (now remembered as a great poet) was secretary to Lord Egerton, who held high offices of state under Elizabeth I. However, because Donne, born of bourgeois stock, ignored the socially accepted norms of the day by marrying a young aristocratic girl without consent, he lost this patronage. In spite of his obvious skills as an administrator and diplomatic emissary, this loss of patronage was permanent, to his eternal chagrin.

One can only wonder how his case would have been treated by an industrial tribunal, but the difficulty is that we normally respond to such thoughts by focusing upon the details of the case – marrying without consent (Ah well, that couldn't have happened nowadays could it? We are much more relaxed about these things). I want to suggest that such reactions confirm that we have become confused by our insistence upon focusing on the details rather than examining the principle. Whereas it is only the details that have changed, the principle still holds, in that redundancies do still occur as a result of disapproval of changes in marital relations. (Even as I write, the treatment of a former England rugby captain, whose testimonial has been cancelled – with clear consequences for his 'pension' – supposedly as a result of his leaving his present partner, confirms this. To say nothing of the recent difficulties encountered by the US president, which suggests that in the last resort even chief executives may have to account to their masters!)

One reason for this concentration upon detail to the neglect of principle derives from the fact that this element of 'service to a great patron' has continued rather more strongly than we would sometimes care to admit. It can clearly be seen to have continued into the beginnings of what has come to be called the industrial age. Indeed, the larger variety of roles connected with the growth of joint stock companies in the eighteenth and nineteenth centuries were often overtly cast as requiring an increasing workforce, each member of which would be required to enter into a specifically described subordinate relationship in the service of a master.

Moreover, the patronage system continued, in some instances into the present century. My own grandfather, for instance, in 1912, worked for (and even the language used carries the connotation of master and slave – i.e. 'worked for') a millionaire diamond merchant in London. The post was obtained by recommendation; and in this case the patronage extended to the family, such that when my grandfather died at the early age of 32, the patron made sure that his widow was given a job and helped with the expenses of educating the children.

The phrase 'it's not what you know but who you know' survives to this day, but in the early part of this century, another era marked by periods of high unemployment, much industrial and office work was poorly paid, and deference was seen to be an essential virtue of a good worker. (Could it be that current ritualisation of customer service through the use of standardised phrases such as 'thank you for calling, how may I help you?' has derived from such foundations?)

Concurrent with the development of structures of deference, however, went a reciprocal employer's obligation to treat workers reasonably and look after their interests. Thus the foundations of the paternalistic employer/employee relationship were laid. Conceptions of these relationships have tended to focus upon the reciprocity elements, which are evident enough, although the treatment of these relationships as equal is not quite so evident when subjected to closer examination.

One example of the inequality element is illustrated by my mother's experience, being told when she began work in 1928 to 'study the needs of the directors and you will do well'. How well did she do? It depends upon which success criteria are used, but she was glad to work unpaid overtime to please her employer and was delighted to be invited, with other staff, to the chairman's grand home in the country for an annual visit that included tea, cakes and tennis.

The kind of patronage system illustrated in such examples underlines the importance that they had in the development of whole structures of deferential relationships, as can be identified in the emergence of larger organisations in the nineteenth century. At the heart of the gradual increases in size of operation was the idea of the extension of an individual's work capacity, where huge collections of individuals came together with a view to (and in the service of) increasing an owner's production capabilities.

Patronage is often thought of as a rather outdated system of funding, but perhaps there are more examples of modern patronage than we care to admit. The funding of research might be a case in point, where indeed researchers are sometimes required to sign away their rights to publish their results unless they have prior approval of the funding body, even where this is a national government posing as a neutral provider of resources for the advancement of knowledge.

Perhaps sponsorship of sporting events is also a special case, in the form of a corporate patronage system. The power of the master (masquerading as sponsor) in such relationships is amply demonstrated by the climb-downs of most Western governments (masquerading as slaves to the multinationals?) from their initial insistence that the governing body of Formula One motor sport arrange for the removal of tobacco advertising from grand prix racing cars now, rather than arranging for it to be phased out over the next ten years.

Can you think of any occasion upon which the supposed neutrality of parties to an agreement has been compromised by the funding arrangements between them? Can you think of an example of anyone being required to withhold information by request of another person or body whose interests might not be best served by a disclosure?

Braverman (1974) has identified the functional basis of the emergence of particular role structures that enabled the extension of one individual's output as 'a pure expression of the Babbage principle'. This principle, deriving from the work of Charles Babbage (1832) in the nineteenth century, expresses the idea that as extensions of work capacity develop, it becomes wasteful for better-skilled and/or educated people (not to say better-paid people) to be employed in work that can be performed effectively by those who are less skilled/educated/paid, and that those with little or no special training are better suited to the performance of routine tasks, not only because they are cheaper to employ but also because they will perform routines more effectively (and more deferentially), being less distracted by other thoughts.

This extension of the manager's work capacity argument is at the heart of increasing specialisation, but how far has it led to decreasing deference in relations? Some examples might be useful at this stage – examples taken from my own experience of working in (very) hierarchical organisations.

Case studies in rituals of deference in organisations

Illustration I

The assistant managing director of a large multinational company in the media and entertainments industry was driven to work each day by his chauffeur, who had strict instructions to arrive at the office at 8.30 every morning. The office was an elegant and very large Georgian house in Mayfair in the heart of London. The office had large double front doors, which were opened only in anticipation of the arrival of the assistant managing director. As his car drew to a halt, the door porter stepped out, and the chauffeur handed him the assistant managing director's briefcase. As the assistant managing director walked from his car and across the marble floor of the entrance hall to the lift, the porter handed the case to a messenger boy. While the assistant managing director proceeded into the lift and rose to the second floor, the boy ran up the two flights of stairs and handed the case to him as he stepped out of the lift. When asked how he felt about this ritual, the assistant managing director said that he felt the staff in general thought it appropriate and those involved would be disappointed and feel ignored if the practice were to be stopped.

This example of deference in a multinational organisation (in the not too distant past!) conveys a picture of an assistant managing director accounting for his actions (justifying the demonstration of difference in hierarchical level) as fitting some kind of need that people have for rituals of deference. It is indeed sometimes suggested that workers like to have such rituals, but I would suggest not necessarily those designed to emphasise their inferiority in rank. Perhaps in any case this kind of claim pales in the face of the following example.

Illustration II

This same company had 'merged with' ('taken over' might have been a more appropriate description, in spite of carefully worded agreements concerning future activities) a considerable number of companies loosely connected with the entertainments industry. When a member of the directorate of one of these companies was asked to visit the same assistant managing director who featured in the previous illustration, another instructive ritual took place. The visitor was not specifically greeted at the door, or assisted at the lift! What the visitor was required to do, however, was to arrive early. Indeed, this was ensured by giving each visitor an appointment time fifteen minutes before the assistant managing director intended to see him (gender specificity intentional). The visitor was greeted on the second floor by one of the assistant managing director's secretaries and was escorted to a small private lounge. He was offered a hot, cold or alcoholic drink by the secretary and was then left to his own devices. Whatever the reason for the visit, this procedure was followed to the letter, whether the visit was for routine reporting purposes; whether the visitor was about to be informed of a promotion; or indeed whether he was about to be informed of his imminent departure from the company!

The purposes of this ritual, in the view of the assistant managing director's secretaries, who were themselves part of the ritual, was that it gave the visitor time to collect his thoughts, and that in any case the assistant managing director's time was so valuable that a possible wait for a tardy visitor, would be a needless expense. Experience had shown that visitors in general did seem considerably quieter (and in many cases more apprehensive, and no doubt more deferential) when it was time to be shown into the assistant managing director's office than they had upon arrival. Could it be that the ritual was designed to achieve this demonstration of superiority in rank, or is it just an example of routine organisational practice?

Perhaps the organisation from which the above examples were taken was unusual in the overtness of such rituals of deference, but that merely underlines the argument, because increasing covertness is hardly likely to reveal a serious rebuttal of the call to take more account of the importance of secure historical groundings in the structural elements that ought to be at the very heart of intellectual developments in a discipline such as management studies.

Concluding note

This chapter has examined the historical precedents of one particular aspect of organisational structure, involving the relations between superiors and subordinates. It has examined one of the main foundations of such relations and has suggested that they still form a major part of the way in which transactions, both social and monetary, are conducted in modern organisations.

The chapter has highlighted the way in which these relations are conducted in a manner that ultimately reflects a command structure (no matter how loosely) in which some people are held to be responsible for the actions of others, and correspondingly most people are required to report to another in some way.

In tracing the intellectual, and indeed inspirational, origins of superior/subordinate relations, the chapter has highlighted the part played by deference and by systems of patronage in the development of modern organisations.

Note

This chapter is based upon an original idea, previously published as 'Some problems in the concept of secretary' in *International Studies of Management and Organization* XVI (1), Spring 1986: 94–111. Due acknowledgement is made to the editors and proprietors of that journal for permission to draw upon the original materials in the development of the arguments presented in this chapter.

References

Alvesson, M. and Willmott, H. (eds) (1992) *Critical Management Studies*, London: Sage.

Alvesson, M. and Willmott, H. (1996) *Making Sense of Management*, London: Sage.

Babbage, C. (1832) *On the Economy of Machinery and Manufactures*, London.

Braverman, H. (1974) *Labour and Monopoly Capital – The Degradation of Work in the Twentieth Century*, New York: Monthly Review Press.

Edwards, R. (1979) *Contested Terrain – The Transformation of the Workplace in the Twentieth Century*, London: Heinemann.

Foot, P. (1998) 'It makes you sick', *The Guardian*, 15 December, p.16.

Garson, B. (1972) *All the Live-long Day*, New York: Doubleday.

Gibson, J. (1999) 'Birt's BBC denounced by ex-chairman Hussey', *The Guardian*, 4 March, p.3.

Goffman, E. (1956) 'The nature of deference and demeanor', *American Anthropologist* 58: 473–502.

Heller, J. (1974) *Something Happened*, London: Jonathan Cape.

Kanter, R.M. (1977) *Men and Women of the Corporation*, New York: Basic Books.

Newby, H. (1977) *The Deferential Worker: A Study of Farmworkers in East Anglia*, London: Allen Lane.

Peters, T.J. and Waterman, R.H. (1982) *In Search of Excellence*, New York: Harper & Row.

Rowe, C. (1986) *People and Chips*, London: Paradigm.

Roy, D. (1955) 'Making out: a worker's counter-system of control of work situation and relationships', *American Journal of Sociology* 60: 255–66.

Sparks, K., Cooper, C., Fried, Y. and Shiron, A. (1997) 'The effects of hours of work on health: A meta-analytic review', *Journal of Occupational and Organizational Psychology* 70 (4), December: 391–408.

Further reading

For a more extensive treatment of the nature and origins of superior/subordinate relations in organisations, see

Clegg, S. (1977) *Power, Rule and Domination*, London: Routledge & Kegan Paul.

Lukes, S. (1974) *Power: A Radical View*, London: Macmillan.

For an elucidation of the concept of deference in relationships, see

Goffman, E. (1956) 'The nature of deference and demeanor', *American Anthropologist* 58: 473–502.

For a comprehensive study of the relevance of deference in the relations of agricultural workers in the UK, see

Newby, H. (1977) *The Deferential Worker: A Study of Farmworkers in East Anglia*, London: Allen Lane.

5 Reconstructing the study of management

Robert Protherough

Introduction

This chapter argues that the urgent need for reconstructing management studies is, ironically, the direct result of the subject's popularity and rapid growth. The speed with which it has evolved has masked the lack of consensus about what should be studied and how. Partly because of ignorance about the subject's origins, it has been too easily assumed that embedded within it were universal truths and practices that would be equally applicable in all cultures. Management has long had a built-in 'colonising' tendency, absorbing other fields of knowledge or activity into itself. This, in addition to academic conservatism, has strengthened resistance to those changes (in curriculum and methodology) that are widely seen as necessary at present. In the last part of the chapter, proposals for restructuring are put forward that would involve widening the mainstream curriculum. Alternative ways of thinking and studying are offered, with examples that draw particularly on literary studies.

The rapid growth of management studies

In the United Kingdom, as in many other countries, there was no clear academic career path into management before the Second World War. It was not until the 1960s that postgraduate business schools were set up in London and Manchester, but there are now over 100, producing more than 8,000 masters of business administration each year (Caulkin 1998). By 1985, it was estimated that over 100 universities and colleges were providing business or management courses for 70,000 people (Barry 1989). During the Thatcher years, management education became 'an almost uniquely favoured field of academia' (Grey and Mitev 1995: 85), and at the time of writing (1998) more students at first-degree level are taking courses in business and management than in any other subject (Caulkin 1998, citing Association of Business Schools statistics). In the United States, it could be recorded in the 1980s that each year 'virtually one in every four of the nation's nearly one million new graduates takes a degree in business. Business enrolments dwarf those of all other fields of study' (Johnston 1986: 2).

Before reading further, consider what results this astonishing growth rate would have had on the curriculum of management studies and on applicants for posts in management. How far would you agree with my four points below? What other points would you wish to add?

- The apparently unchallengeable position of management silences criticism. Such extraordinary popularity seems to imply that little can be wrong with the existing courses, and that therefore there is no need to change.
- The corresponding rapid expansion of academic departments, lectureships and publications has meant that staff see their interests in maintaining rather than questioning the situation, and pressure has kept them so busy coping with numbers that they have had no time for more radical course design or revision.
- That growth has put more power in the hands of management academics, who exert increasing influence in their universities and indirectly help to shape the way in which the whole education process is viewed and planned.
- Management education has become monolithic and imperialistic, dominating the entry to careers in business. Because of the numbers of business graduates, it is much less likely than in the past that well-qualified graduates in other subjects will find themselves posts in management. As a result, management loses the potential widening of focus that they brought with them.

The constitution of management as an academic subject

The way in which management studies originated as an academic field has heavily conditioned its later development. Originally concerned with the training of horses (the Italian sense) or running a household (the French one) (Williams 1983) the term 'management' has vastly extended its meaning and hugely gained in status. However, there was never a stage at which coherent thinking and planning went into just what knowledge base the emerging discipline should have, what abilities it might inculcate in students and what methods were best designed to develop them. There seems to have been an unquestioned assumption that universal managerial theories and practices existed and could be straightforwardly conveyed to students in university courses. Cross-cultural studies question this. In Germany, there was scepticism about whether 'management' exists as a separate, definable entity; in Japan, there has been a heavy emphasis on in-company training; in France, management education was launched outside the universities; and so on. Significantly, whereas in the United States the study of management began in the most prestigious Ivy League universities, in Britain Oxford and Cambridge were the last to accept it.

What does 'management' comprise? When the Association of Teachers in Management in the United Kingdom framed a 'symposium' of papers on management studies in 1966, it drew on sixteen subjects, and the editor said frankly that this was on the 'cafeteria' principle, so that courses could 'try out anything which takes their fancy' (Pugh 1966: 2). What was to be taught was clearly seen as less significant than the urgent need for 'academic respectability' and 'professionalization'. 'High standards for entry, a long and arduous course, a respectable failure rate (i.e. respectably high), these are the requirements for respectability' (*ibid.*: 1). Twenty years later, an international volume concluded that 'there is little agreement on what subjects should constitute a management training or education course' and went on to list forty-three disciplines or skills currently being offered (Byrt 1989: 213–14).

What do you see as the necessary components for a course that leads to a qualification in management? The titles of first degrees on offer at British universities link business and management with such subjects as computer science, European studies, law, marketing, accounting, human resources, economics, finance, operations management and social administration. You can combine management with international politics, contract law, dance and drama or the European Union. According to which course you choose, you may or may not receive teaching in enterprise skills, research skills, software development, social issues or team building.

Look critically at the management curriculum of some institution known to you, consider what justification is offered for the items included and think about what is excluded.

The struggle for status implied in the 1966 symposium referred to above ('A degree in management – Huh! They'll be having one in paper hanging next!') has always greeted any proposal for a 'new' subject to be admitted to the university world. Each fresh entry involves threatening changes in the power structure, status, territory and values of the other curricular groups involved, a redrawing of the map of knowledge, an adjustment of boundaries. This was plainly the case in the evolution of management as a subject, in which a number of quite different and only loosely associated groups, with varying claims to 'academic respectability', came together to claim disciplinary status. Springing up in one location after another, the new 'subject', like others before it, defined itself in a piecemeal ('cafeteria') way. It did this largely in terms of related but better-established disciplines, taking on the traditional ways of thinking and acting found in economics and mathematics, law, sociology, social psychology and social anthropology. In the early stages, this meant drawing on specialists in those subjects for teaching and assessment, and later the importing and redefining of their materials and methods.

A common view is that the different sub-fields that combine to make up management education simply took over ('reappropriated' or 'colonised') the findings of these other disciplines, cannibalising their language forms. However, it could also be argued that those disciplines have continued to dominate by pulling the thinking in management education in the direction of their own specialisms and discourses to the exclusion of others. All academic 'disciplines' or 'communities of practice' embed their implicit cultures – beliefs and values – in characteristic language usages (in much the same way as do industrial or commercial organisations). These particular registers maintain their identity by defining what is to be included in and what excluded from their culture, what is and what is not valid to think and say. To use the right language acts as a membership card, giving you entry to the select group. In the case of management studies, the 'right' language has remained predominantly that of the social sciences, which helped to frame it.

While establishing itself in the academic world, the developing subject has also had to maintain close links with the managerial world for which it provides a preparation. There are special problems for 'applied' subjects (medicine, law, engineering, education, pharmacy, management), which are, by definition, concerned with practical ends as well as with theoretical knowledge and which exist simultaneously on at least two distinct knowledge maps. Compared with 'pure' subjects, it is frequently difficult to separate the academic field from the area of everyday professional practice in which it is rooted. Scholars of management have to operate within two different value systems: viewed with suspicion as 'theorists' by some of those in industry and commerce, and seen as marginal in universities that only consider standards of research and publication. Their success has to be judged in both academic and utilitarian terms.

The struggle for existence and academic respectability, in association with practical credibility, very briefly sketched here, can be held to have shaped the subject in a number of ways:

- There was a failure to create a coherent discipline with a defined area of expertise for two main reasons. First, the agenda was 'struggled over by contending interests and groups who lack any shared sense of strategic objectives' (Reed and Anthony 1992: 593). The different contributing subjects and professions, with only a tenuous connection between them, each tended to see themselves as central. Second, as courses have mushroomed in different universities, their actual content has varied according to existing expertise and power struggles rather than being decided by any agreed overall principles.
- The language forms in which conventional, mainstream management courses 'came to be' were drawn overwhelmingly from different branches of the social sciences, bringing with them the assumptions of their original disciplines and giving 'spurious credibility' to certain forms of managerial expertise (Alvesson and Willmott 1996: 43).
- There was and remains a confusion about what education and training should be like and about the appropriate methods to achieve these ends, particularly as management (unlike the other 'new' academic subjects) was not 'grounded' in an existing area of the school curriculum.
- The concern for professional acceptance and approval has resulted in an emphasis on listing those managerial competencies thought to be required in the industrial world, stressing the technical, scientific method and quantitative research.

Demands for change in management education

It is richly ironic that the study of management should be so popular at precisely the time when openings for managers seem to be decreasing through 'delayering', when career paths are unclear, and when both the role and the training are being increasingly questioned. The 'staggering' restructuring of managerial work in the last decade has resulted in a high and disproportionate thinning out of management posts in the great majority of firms (Ehrensahl 1995) and in discontent with the role (Scase and Goffee 1989), so that some senior executives are apparently rejecting even the title 'manager' (Burrell 1992: 68).

Arguing from quite different theoretical perspectives, a number of scholars in the field have united in their concern about the ineffectiveness of most of what passes for management education. Indeed, some would argue that the establishment of management as a separate field has been gravely misguided. Critics believe that 'there is something seriously amiss' (Grey and Mitev 1995: 73), that there is widespread 'disillusionment with traditional forms of management theory and practice' (Alvesson and Willmott 1992: 3), and that 'much of management education is irrelevant and some of the rest is naive' (Anthony 1986: 141). Viewed from the workplace, in one survey that asked about the best preparation for a managerial career, only 7 per cent of managers mentioned degrees in business studies (Thompson 1987: 70). More detailed criticisms are clearly related to the points made in the opening sections of this chapter. Authors point to 'the lack of a clear disciplinary focus' (Kallinikos 1996: 49) and to a knowledge base that 'is fragmented and disputed' (French and Grey 1996: 9). 'Remarkably little is known about the particular skills or competencies required by managers' with varied functions in different organisations (Barry 1989: 75), and consequently courses offer 'a misconceived theoretical explanation' of management's role and performance, making only a tenuous connection between the abstractions of study and actual work (Anthony 1986: 2).

In brutally summarised form, critics are complaining of the prevalence of instrumental machine metaphors for industrial organisations and a preoccupation with the scientific or the technical function of management seen in exaggerated concern for rational systems models that are inflexible and bureaucratic. They criticise over-easy assumptions that management theory is somehow morally and politically neutral, impartial and objective, that its practice is self-evidently valuable, and that greater efficiency or effectiveness is the chief or only goal.

For years, people have been saying, with apparent general agreement, that 'sustained excellence in management will require, above all, adaptability to change' (Business–Higher Education Forum 1985: 2), that 'managers will have to take uncertainty into their own world' (Beck and Cox 1980: 3), that 'innovation is vital' (Clegg and Palmer 1996: 218). Any look along the library's management shelves will show how frequently book titles contain the words 'change' and 'new', together with 'transition' or 'transformation', 'innovation', 'rebirth' or even 're-engineering'. But what does this general concern mean in practice? It is nearly 20 years since a major conference concluded that 'we know very little about how to bring about … changes in managerial attitudes' or roles (Beck and Cox 1980: 3). How do we prepare students for problems that as yet we do not recognise?

The challenge for management education is to become an effective agent for change in a faculty culture that is highly resistant to it. However, as yet there seems little evidence that courses give much consideration to the ways in which patterns of work are adapting as a result of global economic, cultural and political changes. Instead there is concentration on specific skills that will become obsolete before they can be put into practice (Reed and Anthony 1992: 600–1). Managers need an education radically different from the one traditionally offered, and 'the emphasis on specific techniques must be reduced, since these become rapidly dated', and replaced by human and analytical skills, 'learning to learn', flexibility, concern for values, awareness of other cultures and behaviours, and the capacity 'to see different perspectives, different conceptions of truth and right' (French and Grey 1996: 3; Mutch 1997; Thomas and Anthony 1996: 30–1).

To meet these criticisms and suggestions, the recurrent argument is for some widening of a narrow curriculum and methodology, in which at present the 'management' element overwhelms the 'education'. There is little to suggest that a sound general education damages later managerial performance, whereas 'there is mounting evidence which suggests that a specialised management education does nothing or does harm' (Thomas and Anthony 1996: 31). Significant change is brought about by people who have not been blinkered by traditional managerial assumptions. 'They are often not the experts or the specialists. Rather they are "boundary crossers" or "generalists" who move across fields or among sectors' (Kanter 1991: 55). Research in the United States has found that although liberal arts graduates are disadvantaged on entering industry compared with business graduates, later on they tend to do better. Useem (1986: 100) concludes that management courses 'that do not presently provide a full liberal learning experience should consider ways of doing so. Otherwise, they may be educating students for their first job but not their full career.'

There is nothing new in arguing that the management curriculum should be widened. In 1959, two major American studies (funded by the Carnegie Corporation and the Ford Foundation) recommended that half of the curriculum in business and management studies at undergraduate level should be in general education, promoting close ties with liberal arts disciplines, 'notably literature, psychology, history, political science, and mathematics-science' (Jones 1986: 128). However, it has not proved easy to design programmes that will achieve this and effectively bridge the divide between business and 'liberal' learning (*ibid*.: 124, 136). Business schools may acknowledge that the aesthetic ought somehow to be accommodated within the 'hard core' of management, but with little sense of how this might be achieved or willingness to take other subjects on their own terms. Some theorists argue that the situation has become so grave that conventional business education may have to be abandoned altogether.

> When he was asked where young people might be sent to be educated in new ways of thinking, in 'path-finding', Professor Leavitt at the London Business School said:
>
>> We might want to send them to places that appear very distant from our contemporary management scene. We could send them to live among artists and architects, or among philosophers and religionists, or among theoretical physicists; but *whatever we do, we should not send them to business schools*.
>
> (Leavitt 1983: 12, my emphasis)
>
> Do you agree with him, or do you think that he was exaggerating?
> If you feel that changes are needed in a curriculum that is nearer to training than to education, then just how do you believe that it might be brought about? How would you respond to Reed and Anthony (1992: 608), who rather desperately conclude that 'It may not matter too much what the subject matter is as long as we encourage our students and our managers to think and as long as we believe that what we are doing is valuable rather than profitable.'

The final section of this chapter proposes an apparently minor form of broadening that actually might have the potential to bring about a more radical reappraisal of the nature, aims and methods of management studies. It draws specific examples from my own initial discipline of literature, rather than generalising more widely, but without any suggestion that this is the only way of expanding or reconstructing the subject. The argument is not for the value of any one particular element of the humanities or arts in the education of managers. Others have written of the possible gains that could be derived from a study of visual arts, drama, fiction, history, ethics and so on. Unfortunately, changing a curriculum is like moving a cemetery – it may be clearly desirable but in practice it is difficult. It is particularly hard in the case of management because of the subject's built-in tendency to turn everything else into a pale version of itself.

The dominance of managerialism: resistance to change

Management education, as Anthony has pointed out, is a closed system primarily 'concerned with reinforcement', designed 'to protect status rather than to pursue effectiveness'. Even if serious criticisms are sustained and dissatisfaction is widespread, 'the consequence would be likely to be renewed efforts at reinforcement rather than any more radical change' (Anthony 1986: 138–9). The swift establishment of the subject has confirmed those colonising tendencies that almost automatically seek to appropriate other spheres by defining them in managerial terms, substituting managerial discourse for their own. Such linguistic 'privileging' presupposes the rightness of managerial forms of organisation, norms and values and excludes others (Hassard 1993: 18). Frequently, the result is to exclude the personal and the emotional. So 'volume-related production schedule adjustment' is a managerial way of describing the closure of a factory, and 'negative patient care outcome' means death. The wider field of education itself has increasingly been translated into market models of producers and consumers, controlled by administrators, regulated by a complex system of accountability and appraisal, and dominated by concepts of 'efficiency' (Ball 1990; Grey and Mitev 1995).

In a critique of educational management, theorist Mike Bottery (1988: 343) produced a 'Devil's Dictionary' of management terms used in the United Kingdom with his own definitions of their meanings. Here are some of them, lightly edited:

effective management	the head getting his or her own way in the quickest and most convenient manner
good practice	what the head/local educational authority/ Department for Education wants
inputs/outputs	pupils, children
management style	changing behaviour to get what you want
teaching units	teachers
teamwork	getting together a team who will work towards what the head wants
resource power	the bribes available to the head to get the staff to do what he wants them to

You might like to compile some entries for a similar Devil's Dictionary, drawing on management in some field known to you in your own country.

As in education, the worlds of travel, sport and amusement have been converted into 'the leisure industry'. There seems a clear connection between calling the arts a 'cultural industry' and the increasing tendency to view them in the light of management theory. From the 1980s onwards the traditional languages of the arts were increasingly supplanted by the vocabulary of economics or management as speakers for the arts strove to justify their work in unfamiliar language that would make sense to businessmen, accountants and politicians (Protherough 1999).

This colonising tendency exists strongly in management education. Even when it is felt that art forms might be used as part of the programme, it is all too easy to reduce them to familiar case studies to be employed within existing managerial techniques. For example, when it was proposed to 'use' Shakespeare's *Henry V* in a workshop for managers, the organisers said that the purpose was to demonstrate how the play reveals the 'leadership qualities' of Henry, described in the subheading as 'a perfect role model' for businessmen. Significantly, those attending were supplied with a video of Laurence Olivier's classic film, in which the heavily cut text emphasised Henry as hero on a white horse (rather than, say, Kenneth Branagh's 'Dirty Harry') (MacLeod 1996). The experience described would have been very different from grappling in a literature or drama class with the intense critical disagreements described in all modern editions over the play's ideological ambivalence and moral ambiguities. By avoiding questions about Henry's political motives, his responses to the common soldiers, his order to kill the French prisoners, and his attitude towards Katherine, complexity was ironed out to teach a managerial lesson.

A similar process can be seen at work in the presentation of fiction, traditionally offered as a straightforward, uncontentious source of information. So 'through literature dealing with organisation we can extend the range of our knowledge ... vicarious knowledge can substitute for personal experience' (Waldo 1968: 5). A recent volume has the unexceptionable opening words 'The purpose of this book is to show how good novels can educate better managers'. However, the actual approach demonstrates that the chosen works of fiction are not being offered openly for response, as they would be in a literature group, but as a kind of substitute for case studies, with their underlying assumptions, to make predetermined points: 'We hope to show that novels contain useful material for managers' (Czarniawska-Joerges and Guillet de Monthoux 1994: 14). Two assumptions are made, both of which demonstrate that fiction is not being seen on its own terms. The first is that novels teach simple, transferable lessons that the reader can 'use', that they 'can be direct models for our undertakings' and help us to 'learn about ... being a manager' (*ibid.*: 61, 116). The second is that novels 'simulate real life', mirror 'a real world' and offer 'accurate reporting of facts' (*ibid.*: 3–4). The language consistently stresses 'facts' and 'knowledge', which are said to be 'depicted', 'portrayed' or 'presented', with an over-neat concept of transferability. Such an approach ignores the extent to which fiction constructs the reality that it describes.

Without wishing to be unfair to a well-intentioned volume, it must be maintained that to read in this way is to misunderstand the nature of literature. Saying what a book is 'about' or 'shows' immediately closes down other valid lines of interpretation. Novels do not contain a single meaning and cannot be reduced to providing neat morals like proverbs. Texts speak simultaneously in different voices; they are shot through with contradictory attitudes, ideas and images. In other words, it is not legitimate (or even, probably, effective) to manipulate fiction in a way that diminishes its status as fiction. Literature has to be read as literature, not as something else, with awareness that a text can say one thing and do another, can be read differently by the same reader at different times and in different places. Instrumental uses of literature of the kind described above fail, not only because they treat literature as though it were something else but also because they are based on outmoded and inaccurate models of the reading process.

The point can be summed up succinctly: if material from an arts or humanities background is introduced into management studies with a clear view of what it is to 'show' or to 'do', then it is being misused. Literary texts should open up a range of responses, ethical problems should admit of no 'right' answers, and historical studies should illustrate that past events can be interpreted and valued in different ways. If that is the case, then what might the arts and humanities contribute to education in management and administration?

Humanities in management education: a case for literature

My argument is that the particular topic (literature, history, philosophy or theology) is less significant than the way in which it is incorporated into the programme, the perceptions of its function, and the manner in which it is taught and studied. The key questions are: what actual experiences might this provide for students? what significance does it attach to varying ways of knowing and learning? what kinds of teaching will best unlock its potential? how does it question current politically constructed curriculum models?

As suggested above, what matters is not 'using' literature or music or painting in a management way, looking to them for extractable meaning, but accepting them on their own terms as providing encounters of a different nature that will challenge viewers and readers 'to think not only about what is presented, but also about what one's own frameworks are' (Mangham 1987: xii). Five brief points can be made to sketch how this might happen and what values such studies could bring to management education.

1   Responding to a story (or a painting or a concert) is a matter of immediate experience rather than abstract conceptualising. Instead of seeing theory as some separate overarching structure to be understood and applied, the reading of literature is in itself to practise or engage with theory, to live it. A book diminishes or even eliminates the sense of division between the thinking mind and the objects of thought. Students who describe their reading of novels almost always do so in terms of a direct relationship between their own lives and the imagined life of the book, varying in where they place themselves on the continuum between involvement and detachment (Protherough 1983). That relationship is at once intellectual and emotional; poems and stories offer a practical field for critical thinking and for lessons in feeling. In addition, sharing one's response to a text with others involves tolerance of ambiguity, sensitivity, and awareness of different views. Because interpretations and judgements are never final, students are confronted in practice with what it means to live with the uncertainty and paradox that are found in management situations. To use the much-quoted terminology of the Marxist thinker Mikhail Bakhtin, working with literature replaces any quest for a 'monologue' (accepting a single voice presenting a particular experience or 'lesson') in favour of 'dialogue' (encounters with different voices, styles and interpretations) without any attempt to achieve some final authoritative judgement or interpretation (Bakhtin, 1981). It can thus help to develop those qualities that are nowadays so frequently mentioned as essential for managerial leadership: imagination, empathy, critical judgement.

A side-effect of such work is that it encourages students to understand the different rhetorical means through which reality is constructed. They can view more sceptically the claims of some scientists and economists that their texts are 'true' compared with the falsehoods of fiction. Literary and linguistic studies can help them to see that sociologists and economists are also 'tellers of stories and makers of poems' (Atkinson 1990: 10; McCloskey 1990: 5). It is naive to believe that 'scientific texts are transparent, a matter of "mere communication", simply "writing up" the "theoretical results" and "empirical findings"' (McCloskey 1990: 10–11). The traditional conventions of science writing distance what is reported by using the passive voice and by an unspoken or unwritten 'trust me' (or us), grounded in the author's membership of a restricted scientific community to which the implied reader also belongs (Harré 1990: 81–101). It can be fascinating and productive to examine Harvard-style case studies – sometimes presented as 'factual' or 'neutral' – with history or literature students.

2   Developing the skill of critical reading has major implications for teaching methods. It is revealing that in the mass of writing about management education there should be so little about managing the actual situations in which learning and teaching go on. When devising a new course in management, Thompson and McGivern (1996) found that drawing heavily on imaginative literature went hand in hand with learning how to learn from experience and with a shift away from lectures to workshops and seminars. The teacher role is reframed, away from resident expert with the answers and towards the consultant who confronts students with uncertainty (Raab 1997). Empirical work in management studies has begun to substantiate the view, familiar for some time in the teaching of literature (Protherough 1983; 1986), that response-based approaches to texts through free discussion are more productive than teacher-directed methods intended to 'help' students towards understanding. In a significant small-scale study, one researcher found that groups of management students given a set of tutor's questions to answer (in writing and later discussion) produced work that was 'inferior', 'banal and simplistic' and 'superficial' compared with those who discussed the text in small groups and then shared their reactions (Cohen 1998a). Although this work has to be treated guardedly, because of the familiar difficulties of assessing qualities of response, it gives support to views that 'teacher as facilitator' and avoidance of pre-planned conclusions may be more productive of insight than 'the "traditional" sense of the teacher imparting "facts" to passive students' (Cohen 1998a: 13).

Literature encourages lecturers to stop seeing teaching as their primary function and to take greater responsibility for student learning by encouraging reflection, making creative, imaginative jumps, seeing connections, applying reasoned criticism, formulating and communicating ideas and judgements, working together, hearing other views and reconsidering one's own. Working critically on texts can demonstrate how works created for one context take on different meanings in later presentations and revisions, as the following example shows.

In a recent programme centred on Shakespeare's *Romeo and Juliet*, students engaged in these shared activities:

- Establishing 'their' chosen form of text for a short passage from the play after examining it as printed in the two Quarto editions and in two modern versions – all different.
- Considering 'whose' the story is by examining the play's differences from its origins in Italian and French sources, leading to the long English poem on which Shakespeare chiefly drew.
- Discussing the play's 'afterlife', its continuing appeal transformed into other dramas, opera, ballet, musicals and paintings, seeing Shakespeare as just one part (although a very significant one) of a long chain of retellings.

- Comparing parts of the play as rehandled in film versions by Zeffirelli (a Renaissance setting) and Baz Luhrmann (transposed to a modern Verona Beach of guns and gas stations) to introduce questions of interpretation, emphasis and emotional impact.

Consider what abilities and skills are being developed in such a programme of work and how appropriate they are for students of management. You might also consider how far such approaches might be applied to the study of a management text known to you.

3   While literature has sometimes been misused in the search for neat, extractable lessons, it is undeniably true that it can provide materials for understanding management and industry if the methods of literary criticism are applied to appropriate texts (Cohen 1998b). 'Appropriate' here may be taken to mean literature that directly describes aspects of industrial life, like the familiar and possibly overused *Hard Times* of Charles Dickens, Mrs Gaskell's *North and South* and the more recent *Nice Work* of David Lodge. Such texts have to be probed and questioned in the manner described above, rather than treated as directly representational. There are many less familiar texts that can be used to promote interestingly conflicting responses.

As one example, Jonathan Coe's novel *The House of Sleep* (1997) contains a lively description of academic and medical specialists who are forced to attend a course of management training conducted by 'one of the country's most prestigious firms of management consultants' at an expensive hotel. The two trainers are young men who have 'majored in Organisational Change' and gained a diploma in 'Group Relations, Meeting Planning and Human Resource Development', respectively. These two greet their clients with the words: 'As qualified facilitators, our task during this session will be to engage you in a series of role-playing modules and creativity enhancement procedures … tested and approved by some of America's most successful corporations.' The group activities involve arranging matchsticks, making sculptures out of pipe cleaners, pasting original collages from colour advertisements ('Modify that Paradigm') and a game called 'alien babies', which involved buckets of water, ropes and jelly babies. In pairs, students can be asked:

- improvise an account of the course given to a friend, first by one of the trainers and then by one of the elderly participants;
- discuss whether this account makes you want to read the novel from which it is taken or whether it puts you off; or
- in your experience, how far should a satirical picture of this kind be (1) accurate, (2) fair?

Other texts, which on the surface have much less direct connection with management and industry, can still be 'appropriate' because they have proved (perhaps for this reason) stimulating in prompting questions about the individual in society, and the quest for meaning. An impressive range of poems, plays and novels has been used at the University of Lincolnshire and Humberside (Thompson and McGivern 1996: 27–8). Works that have been widely used in management courses include Franz Kafka's *The Trial*, Samuel Beckett's *Waiting for Godot* and Joseph Heller's *Catch-22*, which live out uncertainty and demand that readers formulate their own interpretations. To introduce students to concepts of deconstruction and intertextuality at a simple level, studies of stories originally written for children can be valuable, because they subject what is apparently simple and safe to critical challenge (Grey 1998). For example, groups can compare the complex range of different versions of *Little Red Riding Hood* in the oral tradition, in the classic handlings of Perrault and Grimm, in the modern revisions of Thurber, Roald Dahl and feminist workshops, or in Gillian Cross's award-winning *Wolf* (1992), which transposes the story to modern London, with new dangers for the heroine. Such close study and discussion of simple material raise profound questions of cultural change, appropriate roles, shifting relationships, and the problems of moral judgement.

4   A concern for literature signals that people, with their words, relationships and feelings, are being placed at the centre of understanding the business enterprise. Reading novels and plays inevitably involves assessing people's interactions, weighing values, making moral judgements. The shortcomings of impersonal and rationally detached views of management have been pressed particularly by feminist thinkers arguing for increasing 'feminisation' of management, but the arguments have made less impact within management education (Sinclair 1997). The methods of literary criticism can be applied not only to analysing such images as 'captains of industry' and 'entrepreneurs' but also to understanding ourselves and others at work as 'fictionally' constructed. More widely, we can also 'read' the lives of organisations themselves as texts, and the human interactions there as forms of language games. Organisations are not to be seen as machines but as complex and shifting human systems. The 'reality' of the industrial world can only be apprehended through the language or other symbol systems in which it is realised. 'Narrative is one of the many means by which cultures are formed and transmitted', through symbolism, metaphor, rituals and myth (Anthony 1994: 31–2). Newcomers to a community are inducted into the continually reshaped set of stories about key events, memorable characters, the differences between then and now. They begin to frame their own stories and to link them to those of others. Gradually, they are creating the organisation as it exists for them. 'A great deal of the reality of organisations … as it is perceived by their inhabitants, takes narrative form. What it is like to work for Ford, what Ford is, is narrative' (Anthony 1986: 189). An organisation can be 'read' as a conversation or as a dramatic performance (Broekstra 1998; Mangham 1978), and the 'reader' can operate like Sherlock Holmes, seeking 'the hidden meanings, consequences and motives behind acts, decisions and social behaviour' (de Vries and Miller 1987: 234).

In this way, social and industrial disputes can be seen as competing stories in 'a theatre of conflict', embodying different interpretations of events, a process of 'learning the plot' (Downing 1997). The situation changes when a new story is accepted as replacing or reframing an old one. For example, the contradictory stories of how and why people are regarded as worthy of promotion in the career game has been entertainingly deconstructed by Omar Aktouf (1996). The sort of rhetorical analysis described in the second point above demonstrates that the conventions and traditions through which organisations realise themselves, their myths, metaphors and symbols, can be studied from a variety of positions: psychoanalytical, anthropological, sociological, artistic (Andrews 1992; Hassard and Parker 1993). However, each of these approaches will prefer certain 'readings' to others; as in literature, there is no one 'right' interpretation. Understanding this prepares people to live in developing situations where participants 'construct and reconstruct meanings with reference to the performance of others and of themselves' (Mangham 1987: 10), learning how to step back from their own discourse 'to read it as they would the text of a play' (Mangham 1995: 510).

5   Finally, literature helps to break down rigid boundaries and could assist management to become a more genuinely cross-disciplinary study, gaining strength by drawing on different forms of knowledge and learning. In a time of disciplinary and cultural melt-down, when faith in universal truths is unravelling, space has opened for new styles of interdisciplinary learning, but as yet without any clear sense of what is relevant to management studies or why. Developing models of industry are already being defined through 'relational' images like clusters, chains and networks set in zones of uncertainty. By contrast, many management teachers prefer to define themselves narrowly as economists, sociologists, accountants, lawyers. A reconstructed form of academic management studies could more helpfully offer 'a pluralism of perspectives, a criss-crossing of intellectual boundaries and themes, an ability to explore alternative conceptual frameworks and improvise with different research questions' (Kallinikos 1996: 51). In such a 'pluralism', the study of literature can be helpful in thawing out frozen hierarchies, challenging dominant assumptions, inviting cooperation. Changing attitudes to subject boundaries can be actively realised in reading novels like Julian Barnes's *Flaubert's Parrot* (1984) or Kurt Vonnegut's *Slaughterhouse-5* (1970), which collapse conventional genre distinctions between naturalist fiction, fantasy, criticism, history and autobiography. More can surely be made of the potential relationship between mainstream management courses and the now well-established programmes in educational or arts management and policy. While these can be dismissed simply as derivative forms of the mainstream, those involved in teaching them are concerned to stress those personal and qualitative aspects that differentiate their fields, and to query the simple transferability of terms like 'product', 'demand', 'investment' and 'profit' (Bottery 1990; Pick 1986). When they do this, in effect they present a critique of what is currently lumped together under the heading of management education. It is strange that so few attempts have been made to plan and teach courses that link business and arts education, or that bring together groups of businessmen with senior teachers who are gaining advanced qualifications in management.

Conclusion

These five points have been advanced using literature as an exemplar, but their significance is not to be taken simply as a plea to introduce an additional bolt-on unit in management studies that would leave everything else unchanged. The case for undertaking a literary-critical approach of this kind is that it could result in reconsidering and reimagining all parts of the management curriculum. This would be a reversal of what was earlier called the 'colonising' tendency of management: turning everything else into itself. My argument, by contrast, is that – properly conducted – the study of literature could empower students and lecturers to question the nature of what is often called the 'mainstream' management curriculum, a pedagogy that sees the teacher as expert with 'answers', the downgrading of the personal and emotional, and the separation of theory from lived experience. It could prompt greater awareness of the way in which managers are made (or made up) and of the political and cultural dimension within which management knowledge is socially situated and constructed (Clegg and Palmer 1996). Instead of 'reconstructing' management education from the outside, it might be better to encourage teachers and learners to reinvent themselves and their subject continuously as situations change.

Questions for reflection and discussion

1   How successfully do you think the subject of management studies has established itself as a clearly defined specialist field with its own characteristic language?
2   What tensions (if any) do you see existing between the claims of management studies both to be an academic specialism and to provide a professional preparation for the world of work?
3   What steps do you think might be taken to make management studies a more effective agent of change in thinking and practice?
4   If you feel that there is a case for adding new courses to the mainstream management curriculum, how would you make room for them?
5   Choose any field of knowledge that you consider at present omitted or under-represented in management education and draw up a list of coherent reasons for including or extending it. How might you present your case to a curriculum committee?

Acknowledgement

I am indebted to John Pick for helpful criticisms and comments, which have contributed to this chapter.

References

Aktouf, O. (1996) 'Competence, symbolic activity and promotability'. In S. Linstead, G. Small and P. Jeffcutt (eds) *Understanding Management*, London: Sage.
Alvesson, M. and Willmott, H. (eds) (1992) *Critical Management Studies*, London: Sage.
Alvesson, M. and Willmott, H. (1996) *Making Sense of Management: A Critical Introduction*, London: Sage.
Andrews, R. (ed.) (1992) *Rebirth of Rhetoric*, London: Routledge.
Anthony, P.D. (1986) *The Foundation of Management*, London: Tavistock.
Anthony, P.D. (1994) *Managing Culture*, Buckingham: Open University Press.
Atkinson, P. (1990) *The Ethnographic Imagination*, London: Routledge.
Bakhtin, M. (1981) *The Dialogic Imagination*, Austin: University of Texas Press.
Ball, S.J. (1990) 'Management as moral technology'. In S.J. Ball (ed.) *Foucault and Education: Disciplines and Knowledge*, London: Routledge.
Barry, B. (1989) 'Management Education in Great Britain'. In W. Byrt (ed.) *Management Education: An International Survey*, London: Routledge.
Beck, J. and Cox, C. (1980) *Advances in Management Education*, Chichester: John Wiley & Sons.
Bottery, M. (1988) 'Educational management: an ethical critique', *Oxford Review of Education* 14 (3).

Bottery, M. (1990) *The Morality of the School*, London: Cassell.

Broekstra, G. (1998) 'An organization is a conversation'. In D. Grant *et al.* (eds) *Discourse+Organization*, London: Sage.

Burrell, G. (1992) 'The organization of pleasure'. In M. Alvesson and H. Willmott (eds) *Critical Management Studies*, London: Sage.

Business–Higher Education Forum (1985) *America's Business Schools: Priorities for Change*, Washington DC: Business–Higher Education Forum.

Byrt, W. (ed.) (1989) *Management Education: An International Survey*, London: Routledge.

Caulkin, S. (1998) 'The Management Column', *The Observer*, 5 July.

Clegg, S.R. and Palmer, G. (1996) *The Politics of Management Knowledge*, London: Sage.

Cohen, C. (1998a) 'How literature may be used to assist in the education of managers', *The Learning Organization* 5 (1): 6–14.

Cohen, C. (1998b) 'Using narrative fiction within management education', *Management Learning* 29 (29): 165–81.

Czarniawska-Joerges, B. and Guillet de Monthoux, P. (eds) (1994) *Good Novels, Better Management*, Chur: Harwood Academic Publishers.

de Fries, M.F.R.K. and Miller, D. (1987) 'Interpreting organizational texts', *Journal of Management Studies* 24 (3): 233–47.

Downing, S.J. (1997) 'Learning the plot', *Management Learning* 28 (1): 27–44.

Ehrensahl, K.N. (1995) 'Discourses of global competition', *Journal of Organizational Change Management*, 8 (5): 5–16.

French, R. and Grey, C. (1996) *Rethinking Management Education*, London: Sage.

Grey, C. (1998) 'Child's play: representations of organization in children's literature'. In J. Hassard and R. Holliday (eds) *Organization–Representation*, London: Sage.

Grey, C. and Mitev, N. (1995) 'Management education: a polemic', *Management Learning* 26 (1): 73–90.

Harré, R. (1990) 'Some narrative conventions of scientific discourse'. In C. Nash (ed.) *Narrative in Culture*, London: Routledge.

Hassard, J. (1993) 'Postmodernism and organizational analysis; an overview'. In J. Hassard and M. Parker (eds) *Postmodernism and Organisations*, London: Sage.

Hassard, J. and Parker, M. (1993) *Postmodernism and Organisations*, London: Sage.

Johnston Jr, J.S. and associates (1986) *Educating Managers*, San Francisco: Jossey-Bass.

Jones, T.B. (1986) 'Liberal learning and undergraduate business study'. In J.S. Johnston Jr and associates (eds) *Educating Managers*, San Francisco: Jossey-Bass.

Kallinikos, J. (1996) 'Mapping the Intellectual Terrain'. In R. French and C. Grey (eds) *Rethinking Management Education*, London: Sage.

Kanter, R.M. (1991) 'Change-master skills: what it takes to be creative'. In J. Henry and D. Walker (eds) *Managing Innovation*, London: Sage and Open University.

Leavitt, H.J. (1983) *Management and Management Education in the West: What's Right and What's Wrong*, London: London Business School.

McCloskey, D.N. (1990) 'Storytelling in economics'. In C. Nash (ed.) *Narrative in Culture*, London: Routledge.

MacLeod, D. (1996) 'Called to the breach', *The Guardian* , 24 December.

Mangham, I.L. (1978) *Interactions and Interventions in Organisations*, Chichester: John Wiley & Sons.

Mangham, I.L. (ed.) (1987) *Organization Analysis and Development*, Chichester: John Wiley & Sons.

Mangham, I.L. (1995) 'Scripts, talk and double talk', *Management Learning* , 26.4: 493–511.

Mutch, A. (1997) 'Rethinking undergraduate business education', *Management Learning*, 28.3: 301–12.

Nash, C. (ed.) (1990) *Narrative in Culture*, London: Routledge.

Pick, J. (1986) *Managing the Arts? The British Experience*, London: Rhinegold.

Protherough, R. (1983) *Developing Response to Fiction*, Milton Keynes: Open University Press.

Protherough, R. (1986) *Teaching Literature for Examinations*, Milton Keynes: Open University Press.

Protherough, R. (1999) 'Is culture an industry?' *Kenyon Review*, 21 (3/4): 135–46.

Pugh, D. (ed.) (1966) *The Academic Teaching of Management*, Oxford: Blackwell.

Raab, N. (1997) 'Becoming an expert in not knowing: reframing teacher as consultant', *Management Learning* 28 (2): 161–75.

Reed, M. and Anthony, P. (1992) 'Professionalizing management and managing professionalization: British management in the 1980s', *Journal of Management Studies* 29 (5): 591–613.

Scase, R. and Goffee, R. (1989) *Reluctant Managers*, London: Unwin.

Sinclair, A. (1997) 'The MBA through women's eyes: learning and pedagogy in management education', *Management Learning* 28 (3): 313–30.

Thomas, A.B. and Anthony, P.D. (1996) 'Can management education be educational?' In R. French and C. Grey (eds) *Rethinking Management Education*, London: Sage.

Thompson, J. and McGivern, J. (1996) 'Parody, process and practice – perspectives for management education?' *Management Learning* 27 (1): 21–35.

Thompson, R. (1987) *Perspectives on Management Training and Education*, London: British Institute of Management.

Useem, M. (1986) 'What the research shows'. In J.S. Johnston Jr and associates (eds) *Educating Managers*, San Francisco: Jossey-Bass.

Waldo, D. (1968) *The Novelist on Organization and Administration*, Berkeley, CA: Institute of Government Studies.

Williams, R. (1983) *Keywords* (second edition), London: Flamingo.

Further reading

The first four titles are crucially concerned with the question of what is to count as management knowledge and how it is to be acquired. The remaining three are short articles giving examples of the wider changes in learning and teaching that can be brought about through the study of literature.

Alvesson and Willmott (1996)
Anthony (1986)
Clegg and Palmer (1996)
French and Grey (1996)
Cohen (1998a and b)
Raab (1997)
Thompson and McGivern (1996)

6   Teaching management through reflective practice

Janet McGivern and Jane Thompson

Introduction

In this chapter we present our pedagogy, which draws on diverse perspectives in order to create frameworks that offer accessible and meaningful ways of exploring management for our students, who, coming from a variety of backgrounds and previous disciplines, bring with them a complex array of expectations and assumptions. We and our colleagues, some of whom have contributed to this text, have developed an approach to management education located in a 'critical' as opposed to 'orthodox' tradition. We encourage our students to develop skills that will enable them to be critical, reflective practitioners of management, capable not only of gaining insight into their behaviour but also of making sense of it in terms of their position and experiences in their social, psychological, political and physical world.

Critical approaches to management education

You may be aware that during the last decade there has been a lively debate in the field of management education. This has been informed by an increasing body of critical management research. In particular, critical approaches to 'making sense' of management have drawn on Marxist and labour process accounts, Weberian analyses, feminism, psychoanalysis, humanism, post-structuralism, cultural theory, discourse analysis and environmentalism (see Grey and French (1996) for a detailed overview). The 'paradigmatic wars' debate has encouraged an opening up of boundaries, a look beyond our immediate disciplines, borrowing ideas and ways of working from areas that were previously viewed as incommensurable. Such debate has generated a richness of perspectives and data and, more particularly, a focus on the development of 'critical approaches' to management education.

Working experientially

In our approach to teaching management, we begin with the premise that the nature of 'management' is complex, ambiguous, contradictory and uncertain; it is also recognised as a social and political activity (Anthony 1986). We state from the outset that we have no 'quick fixes' for 'managerial problems'. This departs from the way in which 'management' is traditionally conceptualised in many management education programmes, where functional approaches have dominated, competencies are key, and accreditation has proliferated at the expense of pedagogic style. A useful overview of management education is provided by Willmott, who notes a divide between practitioners and academics:

> Practitioners have voiced doubts about the relevance of the knowledge and skills imparted by academics; and, on the other side, academics have complained about the failure of practitioners to appreciate the importance of gaining an in-depth understanding of the disciplines and responsibilities that comprise the practice of management.
>
> (Wilmott 1994: 112)

We are sensitive to these issues and in our programmes have attempted to incorporate the needs of practitioners/employers and academics, and indeed those of our students.

Recent work in management studies demonstrates a body of knowledge at a level of critical analysis, for example Anthony (1986), Reed (1989) and Alvesson and Willmott (1992); we have put some of these ideas into practice. Thus in the following account we are able to illustrate an alternative approach to management education at the level of curricular development. We show how we have attempted to reflect the complexity of 'management' and the social and political dimensions of 'managerial practice' in the design and delivery of our curriculum. Issues around power are embraced and negotiated within the seminar group. Another dimension, that of our unconscious preoccupations, is also an area that we have attempted to explore in our 'managing with people' units. However, encouraging students to embrace such complexity is not always easy. Many students, as a result of their earlier educational experiences, expect 'answers'. They see tutors as 'experts' who have answers, in either their heads or their briefcases; the student's task is to get them to impart this 'knowledge'. How then do we encourage students to recognise the complexity that we describe and thus prepare them for the various aspects of managerial life that they may encounter?

Our thinking has been influenced by a number of writers, notably Pedler *et al.* (1990), Rogers (1967), Schon (1987), Morgan (1997), Hyman (1975), Whitaker (1989) and authors of novels. Writings emerging from organisation theory (Hassard and Parker 1993) employ notions of metaphor, ambiguity, contradiction and irrationality, and these we take as starting points to enable students to gain an understanding with a view to enabling them to become adept in the 'art of reading situations' (Morgan 1997). To encourage the reading of situations (an essential managerial skill, we suggest), we stress the importance of placing the latter in a wider philosophical framework. We therefore encourage students to draw from a range of disciplines: philosophy, psychology, sociology and the humanities. Attention is also drawn to labour process theory/industrial sociology, organisational symbolism, ethnomethodology, postmodern ethnography, literary criticism and post-structuralist feminist theory, while questioning paradigmatic boundaries.

Seminar work is central to our approach. We begin by suggesting that 'management' is often reified, presented to us in a mystical manner, as deeds carried out by remote and unapproachable individuals in the name of 'the organisation'. (See Chapter 9 for a more detailed exploration of this.) We offer students the possibility that they are already managers in the sense that they are required to manage various aspects of their social, domestic, emotional and working lives, and that these seminars could provide an opportunity for them to develop further in this direction through an investigation of 'self' and others. Our foundation-level handbook introduces the course with the following:

> Managing ME is the first step for the self-developer – unless I take charge of myself, how can I take charge of situations? Unless I can create order in myself, how can I

contribute to creating order with others? Managing ME first is the key of self-empowerment, and the empowerment of others.

(Pedler et al. 1990: 10)

In order to facilitate this notion of 'managing me', students are encouraged to perceive 'management' as something that they experience all around them 'here and now', rather than being abstract to them in organisations 'out there'. Drawing on ideas developed in action learning (Revans 1983), we therefore suggest that the seminar can be used as a 'live' learning resource – an organisation that mirrors the complexity of organisations 'out there'. Focusing on the dynamics of the group, we encourage members to recognise the social and political nature of their behaviour 'here and now'. Negotiating space to get points heard, giving constructive feedback, collaborating with others, creating trust, coping with uncertainty, confronting what is perceived to be oppressive behaviour and proposing an alternative view – all are 'managerial' activities. Issues such as non-attendance at seminars, apparent lack of reading/sharing of ideas, 'silence', posturing, etc. are not ignored but are raised as points for discussion. Such processes occur naturally in groups, and a recognition of these is encouraged, along with the opportunity to learn how to manage 'here and now' in what may be perceived as a relatively 'safe' environment. Thus our learning strategy is experiential and has a strong self-development focus. We attempt to encourage the acquisition of meta-qualities, described by Pedler *et al.* (1994) as creativity, mental agility, balanced learning habits and skills and *self-knowledge*. Burgoyne's research illustrates that an experiential approach is necessary to develop the higher-level meta-qualities required by managers (Burgoyne and Stuart 1976).

We draw on the humanistic writings of Carl Rogers (1967), viewing his concepts of significant learning – learning that leads to changes in behaviour – and that of self-discovery as central to the learning approach we identify. We encourage students to assume ownership of their learning, particularly the process by which (significant) learning occurs.

Using aspects of Schon's (1987) reflective practitioner model, we begin with students' experience, and opportunities are provided for students to recognise and reflect on their experience 'here and now' in the seminar, which, as we suggested earlier, can be perceived as an 'organisation'. The processes that occur in groups such as those described above can be seen to mirror processes in organisations 'out there'. Schon reminds us that we create 'theory' in our practice, and in order to challenge the mystique of theory, we need to recognise and give primacy to our own theories. Schon does not negate the role of theory, but he is critical of theoretical frameworks that are premised on a view of technical rationality. So with a focus, in the first instance, on students' experience and 'reflection in action', we complement aspects of humanistic philosophy with the reflective practitioner model (*ibid.*).

Indeed, there is often an initial reluctance to take responsibility for learning – students look to tutors to 'lead' and sort out issues for them – but as they begin to understand the nature of the course, many are able to make use of the seminar as an experiential learning resource and are thus able to prepare for what we consider to be the 'real theory' of managerial work. Such a learning approach does raise issues for tutors and students, but the evaluation of our approach is ongoing, and we are engaged in discussions with colleagues and students with regard to the content and delivery of our programmes.

Students are encouraged to describe and critically evaluate their own experience in their assignments: thus autobiographical, self-reflexive genres are encouraged. The following is an extract from a first-year undergraduate assignment.

> We were trying to talk about power, and really struggling. I hadn't done the reading which didn't help. There were lots of silences, often these give me time to think but today I felt uncomfortable. Caroline was talking about the definitions of power in Morgan (1997). Then someone commented on how difficult it was to talk about something as nebulous as power. The tutor stood up and drew a circle on the board: 'This dot in the centre represents the power in this group now. Come and put your initials where you think you are in the circle.' Most people were fairly good-humoured about it. I became even more uncomfortable. I didn't want to put up my initials. I felt I was quite influential in the group but suppose I put myself near the middle and the others disagreed. How would I feel then? When it got to me I said I didn't want to take part. One or two people were quite angry about it. Mathew said he hadn't wanted to be involved but felt he had to do it. The tutor suggested we looked at the reasons why some people had felt obliged to go along with something they didn't want to do and how that related to power. That really got us talking! The interesting thing was – when I looked at the reading I should have done, our discussion was all there. We'd actually talked about Stephen Lukes' (1974) third dimension of power without knowing anything about it.

What is your experience of how issues such as lack of preparation and silence are generally dealt with both in classrooms and at work. An experiential approach to learning makes use of everything that happens in a seminar. What other phenomena have you encountered that might lend themselves to this sort of approach?

Working with conscious and unconscious processes

A 'self-development' focus generated through experiential group work is a central feature of our management development courses. We draw on Revans' model of action learning (1983) and Kolb's concept of the learning cycle (1984) to illustrate to students the process of their development as 'reflective practitioners' (Schon 1987). However, the emphasis on conscious, individual action embodied in these models paradoxically goes only part of the way towards aiding our understanding of what underpins management action. A more 'reflexive' approach is required, enabling group members to locate their behaviour in the context of their political, social and psychological worlds and in so doing recognise the multifaceted aspects of self and others. We would agree with Vince (1996) that learning at an intellectual level is inadequate. Our experience suggests that for a more complete, experiential 'knowing' that leads to 'significant learning' (Rogers 1967), it is helpful for individuals to engage with and explore emotional experience, both in the 'here and now' and the 'there and then'. The insight gained seems to offer possibilities for understanding, tolerance and modification of previous behaviour.

To facilitate this process, we use some of the group analysis methods common to psychotherapy. When we refer to using therapeutic factors we mean using naturally occurring group dynamics to facilitate growth or change for individuals.

Drawing on psychoanalysis

In his obituary poem for Sigmund Freud, W.H. Auden wrote: 'Freud is no more a person now but a whole climate of opinion' (1952). This sentiment is reflected in the branch of psychology that Freud founded, psychoanalysis, where debate has generated many controversial developments to Freud's own theories. Psychoanalysis generally concerns itself with three areas of study: the long-term impact of our early experiences; the nature and role of the unconscious; and the theory and practice of psychoanalytic treatment. It is useful, when facilitating groups, to be familiar with some of the complex processes of the unconscious: the dynamics of learning and growth, defence mechanisms, and the unconscious interactions that occur in any relationship.

Early attempts to bring people together in groups for analysis took one of three forms. The first, analysis of individuals by the therapist in the presence of others, did not prove popular. The second, demonstrated initially in the postwar work of Bion (1959) in a military hospital, commonly referred to as 'Tavistock group therapy', was used by many group therapists during the 1960s and 1970s but recently not to the same extent. Bion, working originally with shell-shocked patients, studied not individuals but groups. This analysis of the whole group rather than individuals has been criticised strongly as 'not only ineffective but often countertherapeutic' (Yalom 1985: 193).

It is the third therapeutic approach that prevails and can be seen in many present-day 'support groups'. Rather than previous attempts at analysis *in* the group or analysis *of* the group, Foulkes (1948) developed a form of analysis *by* the group: noticing that the group formed a microcosm in which the relationship problems brought by individuals could not only be discussed but possibly observed as they were experienced in the 'here and now' by group members. The additional benefits of this dynamic maximised the potential for group members to bring data about their own behaviour from their unconscious into consciousness. In our own work, we use this phenomenon when the opportunity arises.

Application of group therapy to education

In 1946, Lewin, a social psychologist, was employed by the state of Connecticut to train groups of leaders, who would in turn help to change racist attitudes among the public. Lewin attached observers to his training groups (known as T-groups) for the purpose of research. After each session, the research team met to discuss observations on leader, members and group behaviour. Hearing about these meetings, some group members expressed a desire to attend. Reluctantly, the researchers agreed. The effect on group members of hearing an in-depth analysis of themselves was, according to observers, 'electric' (Benne 1964). Soon the format of these meetings changed to allow all parties to become involved in the analysis and interpretation of their interaction. Lewin realised that he had stumbled on to a powerful technique of human relations education – experiential learning. It is from Lewin's work that we have concepts such as 'feedback', 'unfreezing', 'observant participation' and 'cognitive aid'.

Carl Rogers, teacher, psychologist and originator of 'client-centred therapy' in the United States, first referred to these experiential groups as 'encounter groups' in the mid-1960s. Although this was a vague generic term encompassing a variety of forms of group, the common factor was that therapeutic groups were no longer seen as the preserve of the mentally ill but were also an environment in which personal development might take place. Rogers had brought therapeutic group work into the classroom.

Contextualising 'here and now' in a critical perspective

The psychotherapeutic approach outlined here is used alongside other methodologies. Intellectual rigour, according to Peter Anthony (1986), can only be introduced through a critique of management. 'Critique', as employed here, does not refer explicitly to a Marxist or neo-Marxist perspective, although it may include such approaches. Rather, 'critique in management is about analysing and problematizing the assumptions, discourses, practices and ideologies of management from a multiplicity of perspectives' (Grey 1996: 9). So our experiential study of individual and group behaviour associated with management action unfolds alongside a critical approach to analysing organisation and management.

Our units, both undergraduate and postgraduate, are structured in order to give students plenty of guidance in preparation for and following up seminars. This might include a week-by-week breakdown of themes, with recommended reading and discussion questions. Students are expected to bring two main ingredients to class – their experiences and their reading. In contrast to the preparation, the sessions are usually loosely structured; students are encouraged to manage the session, abrogating any 'rights' of the tutor to control the seminar, although this stance will frequently become a topic for discussion and a way of looking at concepts of power and managerial prerogative. Discussion may focus on the here and now, some aspect of previous experience or on reading. Part of the facilitator's role is then to encourage individuals to validate their own experience and encourage a critique of their reading with reference to their own experiences.

Students leave experiential groups with much more than the sum of their reading and experience, as is illustrated in the following passage, in which a student reflects on the process of her own learning.

> In preparation for the seminar I'd read Karen Legge's *Power, Innovation and Problem Solving in Personnel Management* [1978]. I'd enjoyed the book but it didn't really relate to my own experiences. In the discussion John described in detail some of the changes that had taken place in his own organisation. It was all the things Legge had been talking about. In the course of the seminar all the textbook issues became real for me. It gave meaning to what I'd read, I came away feeling I'd really understood and learned something!

You may wish to consider how you learn. Do you learn in different ways? Do you have preferred ways of learning? How do you respond when faced with something different to the teaching and learning methods with which you are familiar?

In an experiential, action learning environment students will inevitably experience different learning; they learn what is most pertinent and significant to them at the time. Perhaps more important is that students, through this method, begin to recognise and understand their own learning processes and so 'learn how to learn' (Pedler *et al.* 1994). We would concur with Alistair Mutch that there is a continuing tension, on business studies courses, 'between imparting a body of knowledge and using that body of knowledge to develop other qualities' (1997: 306). We tend to value the latter, although we acknowledge that many colleagues elsewhere operate in the predominant functionalist paradigm, which favours the teaching of information and techniques as 'knowledge'.

Our students are encouraged to keep diaries recording and reflecting on their own work and progress. We suggest an autobiographical approach to assignment work, encourage varied genres in assignment writing, including dialogue, second-voice device, plays, prose and pictorial representations. The predominant focus is on the student through an analysis of their own experiences in the light of their reading and seminar discussion. We suggest to groups that they are capable of producing their own theories, and they do indeed do this (Schon 1983). This is a phenomenon we have observed many times in groups, aptly illustrated above in the student's account of her seminar on power.

Marx, enjoying a comeback recently (see *The Guardian*, 20 October 1998), provides a compelling analysis of experience. Some might argue that he has never been away, only buried in a search for more acceptable or palatable ideologies of the right. We are exploring ways of linking critical Marxist theory explicitly to experience. So, in a foundation-level seminar on the theme of motivation, students may initially address questions about their own motivation. A few will remember references made in the lecture programme to the Hawthorn Studies (Roethlisberger and Dickson 1939), a study that appears to capture the interest of some. Others may refer to Maslow's hierarchy (1943), usually in terms of the model's inadequacies. There may be mention of the manager's job in terms of motivating the workforce; opinion is frequently split on the possibility that one person can motivate another. The tutor may then raise more searching questions: for whom are the theorists writing? Why is motivation an issue? In this way, the tutor can introduce the notion that people may be naturally 'motivated', as Rogers (1967) suggests, but the circumstances that they find themselves in militate against innate compunctions towards work and self-actualisation. An overview of Marx may be offered, illustrating the exploitative and alienating nature of the labour process. We find Paul Thompson's work (1989; 1995) and Gareth Morgan's *Images of Organisation* (1997) very useful here. Fiction, perhaps *The Ragged Trousered Philanthropist* (Tressell 1965), offers another approach. Reference to the writing of Marxist psychologist Ronald D. Laing (1967) may be used to suggest the part played by the family in our early socialisation into accepting this *status quo*. This is all offered to students as 'food for thought', to inform their discussion. In this way, we are able to help to generate a number of perspectives and demonstrate how they both complement and contradict each other.

In a postgraduate seminar, Marxist analysis might be used to suggest that managers occupy a contradictory position in the mode of production (Wright 1982). Initially unaware of this view, some students, through a reflexive process, may come to identify themselves as agents of capitalism (Willmott 1987), recognising themselves to be both exploiter and exploited. (This theme has been developed further by Joe Nason in Chapter 3.) In confronting individuals with the knowledge of the degree of their alienation, the process of education may cause them to question the process of career development for which they seek their 'qualification'. This may be a painful awakening – for some empowering, for others debilitating. The impact often goes beyond a re-evaluation of career to a crisis about the meaning of life, the place of relationships and the value of an individual's work. We frequently question our responsibilities in this.

All these things *might* happen in the group; part of the facilitators' skill includes making a judgement about when to intervene and by what process. This presupposes an awareness of what is going on in the group. It is to these complex issues that we now turn.

What to look for in groups

We value the writings of internationally acclaimed Dorothy Whitaker (1989), whose work with psychotherapeutic groups, along with that of Edgar Schein (1988) on organisational psychology, has helped us to clarify what it is we see happening in groups.

Authority

Issues of authority tend to emerge quite early on in a group's history, and an attentive facilitator can focus on this in a useful manner.

Ann had been writing continuously during the initial stages of the session. Students are encouraged to keep a diary, so occasional note taking is not unusual. In this case though, Ann was absorbed, she appeared to be oblivious to the group members around her. After several minutes, the facilitator caught Ann's attention, suggesting to her that she was not quite 'with us' today. Ann appeared embarrassed and put her papers down. Returning to this incident later, Ann recounted how she had felt punished by the facilitator. The facilitator explained that she was trying to make a helpful comment. Another group member responded by saying that she too had felt that the facilitator had been giving Ann a 'telling-off'. Other members of the group agreed that the facilitator had simply been helping Ann to reflect on her behaviour.

Why do you think there were such contrasting views on what took place on this occasion?

It is not unusual for an individual's attitudes towards authority, parental control, dependence, even God, to be seen as personified in the facilitator. Witness how, in the early stages, a tutor's entrance will reduce a group to silence. Her appearance seems to suggest that now the group must turn to its task; they are reminded of their responsibilities; they wait to be instructed by this person, who is in charge. Seating arrangements may reveal interesting feelings towards the tutor. It is not unusual for the tutor to find that large spaces have been left on each side of her chair as students draw away.

This sort of occurrence may be open to various interpretations. It is often the job of the facilitator to draw attention to 'that which can't be mentioned' (Dorothy Whitaker's expression). We would be reluctant to close down possible learning by introducing the psychotherapeutic concept of transference, preferring to focus members of the group on doing their own work on their own experiences and associated feelings.

Norms

Groups usually develop their own 'norms'. It may be appropriate for us to draw attention both to idiosyncrasies of the group and to wider cultural conditioning.

On one occasion, Graham was particularly challenging in the group. His neighbour, Helen, became visibly uncomfortable when Graham's questioning was then directed at the facilitator. Later over coffee, Graham approached Janet, embarrassed and apologetic. She suggested that his feelings might be useful material for discussion.

Resuming the session, Janet recounted their break-time conversation to the group. Graham explained that he only became aware that his challenging manner towards the tutor was inappropriate when he sensed Helen 'squirming'. Janet asked who had written the 'rules' about what was acceptable behaviour and enquired: 'What other norms are operating in here that govern the way we address each other, potentially inhibiting the possibility for communication?'

In this way, what might have been an uncomfortable exchange was used as a vehicle for learning, by focusing on group processes. What kind of 'rules' operate around you, at home, at work, in seminars? Are these implicit or explicit? What are the advantages and disadvantages of such rules?

Erving Goffman, in his seminal work *The Presentation of Self in Everyday Life* (1959), suggests that when an individual plays a role, he/she assumes that others will collude. Our communication with others depends on this assumption being maintained. Thus the relationship between student and tutor tends to embody traditional values about allowable behaviour on both sides. Even Janet's previous suggestion that part of the group's work might include challenging such norms did not prevent internalised rules from operating. Graham had also made an assumption that Janet would be made to feel uncomfortable by his behaviour. Perhaps the initial process of identifying our constraints is the most difficult part of understanding them. It is relatively easy for groups to acknowledge their social conditioning at a conscious level. Gaining insight, in an experiential way, is quite different. As tutors, we rely on the here-and-now opportunities that arise by chance to facilitate that process. Once recognised experientially, it was possible for the group to explore the potential impact that their communications had in either enhancing or inhibiting learning in the seminar situation.

In this sort of scenario, we are inviting students to experiment, in a relatively 'safe' environment, with behaviours that might be quite alien to their own. There is no attempt to criticise individual behaviour or any suggestion that individuals have to 'change', although we might point out to students that the very nature of learning suggests growth and therefore change. Rather, we aim to provide the opportunity for people to learn more about what drives their behaviour and so develop a greater understanding of themselves.

Following this particular session, one student said that she had learned that she was not obliged to please people by responding to their questions. This was significant learning that stayed with her and, she wrote later in an assignment, contributed to her self esteem.

Collusion

The notion of collusion in groups is poignantly illustrated in R.D. Roy's classic study *Banana Time* (1960), in which he documented the working practices of four male factory workers. His focus was on the way that their behaviour and conversation followed patterns, which observation revealed were structured and repetitive, each man having his part to play.

One regular conversation centred around the fact that George's daughter had married the son of a university professor, a fact that appeared to guarantee George a superior status in the group. As Roy recounts, one day Ike revealed to the group that he had seen the 'professor' teaching at a school for hairdressers. George responded with stony silence. For thirteen days the whole pattern of behaviour collapsed. Themes and conversations slowly re-emerged, but the professor theme never reappeared.

Janet had cause to recall *Banana Time* following an interesting occurrence in one group of postgraduate students. The group had been discussing the topic 'emotion at work'. The previous week, the tutor had returned marked assignments to the group. David had not been present so had not had his assignment returned.

The group was discussing the apparent contradiction between the aim of the unit, which was 'developmental', and the fact that their work was assessed, or 'judged'. Janet asked if any parallels could be drawn between this and an earlier discussion, which centred on their contradictory experience that 'workers' are expected to be completely committed to their organisation while accepting that they are disposable. The conversation became intense, and all group members appeared to be engaged in the discussion. However, the discussion seemed simply to remind David that he had not received his assignment back. He interrupted, loudly, silencing his colleagues:

D: Oh, Janet, have you marked our assignments yet?
J: (talking very quickly and quietly) Yes, I've given them back, I'll give you yours at the end of the session.
D: What mark did I get?
J: We'll discuss this later.
D: It wasn't very good was it?
J: I'll talk to you later about it.
D: I've failed, haven't I?
J: This isn't the best time or place to discuss this.
D: No, I don't care, tell me, what mark did I get. I've failed haven't I?
J: (now exasperated) Yes you got 38 per cent.

David sits back, apparently satisfied.

The group is able neither to continue its discussion nor to respond to David's interruption, and it remained quiet for some time.

Why did David's behaviour silence the group? This kind of incident provides excellent experiential material for studying group behaviour. Reflecting later, group members suggested that David had broken the implicit 'rule' of what was allowable as conversation in that situation. He also failed to act in a 'student' role.

Silence

Silence is frequently an issue for groups. There may be times when we, as tutors, have to exercise all our self-control to resist the temptation to play teacher and 'jump in' to fill the gap when there is a 'pregnant pause'. It is their (and our) previous experience of such silences that often makes them so difficult to handle. Some students (they tell us) will use the space to 'think' if the opportunity arises. For others, there is 'nothing happening'. Individuals will refer to the anxiety that they experience in the 'vacuum', a panic that paralyses them and is often expressed as anger: 'why isn't the teacher teaching us?' Invariably, there are individuals who, for a variety of reasons, can be 'relied upon' to speak, much to the relief of some others, who appear to be more concerned with 'keeping the whole thing going', whatever the value of the intervention. This is important material for discussion, revealing significant cultural norms and potential for individual learning.

On one occasion, a student was asked why she did so much talking in the group and was often the first to start a discussion. She appeared puzzled, replying that she did it in order to learn. Quizzed about what helped her to learn she became more perplexed, realising that talking contributed little to her learning; she felt responsible for 'keeping the group going' and felt she 'missed out' on the listening that she might like to have done. The group was able to see that they 'scapegoated' this student – while she worked hard for them they were able to avoid taking responsibility for what was or was not happening in the discussion. This is one of the many defence mechanisms that we see enacted in groups. These kinds of intervention provide opportunities for people to reflect on the reciprocal nature of their relationships, both inside and outside the group. Some time later, this student revealed to the others that she 'always talked' in the hope of being listened to. Since she had 'learned' that this had drawbacks, she described herself as 'much quieter', only to discover that people now paid more attention to what she said.

This is a useful example of 'experiential learning'. Based on this and what you have read so far, are you able to describe what is meant by 'experiential learning'? Can you think of an occasion when you learned through a similar process?

On other occasions, it may be more appropriate for the tutor to intervene during a period of silence: perhaps to comment on moods or themes that appear to have arisen; to underline events or feedback; perhaps to 'teach'. There are no rules here; we have found that we must develop our own styles based on experience.

Intervening in groups

Let us not suffer under any illusion – everything that tutors do or do not do in a group is an intervention, including silence. To further complicate matters, what some students regard as helpful, others will see as a threat.

In one group, a tutor may intervene at a level where they point out some of the assumptions that the current discussion appears to rest upon. Rather than 'confront' individuals, the tutor may try to challenge the generally accepted assumptions and values that appear to exist within the group. In a different group, we may openly challenge individuals.

> I once asked a male student if he had heard what the woman next to him had said to him. His response was vague, so I persisted: 'Did you hear her say that she felt intimidated by your comments?' Only when I finally said: 'One of your colleagues has just said that you are intimidating her; how do you feel about that?' did he seem to hear me and stop to reflect.
>
> This scenario is quite unusual, and we would never let this kind of open confrontation between a tutor and a group member go without some sort of review. Later in the same session, when the incident was referred to, Janet asked the group what they thought had been going on. Replies were interestingly quite mixed. One student suggested that she was defending the woman. Another suggested that Janet was trying to teach the male student to listen. Their different perceptions provided opportunities for various process issues to be discussed, including the appropriateness, or otherwise, of the tutor's comments and the power dynamics operating.
>
> Here again we have an example of differing perceptions on the same incident. What strategies might you implement in order to enhance communication and understanding in a group?

Dorothy Whitaker describes the purpose of therapeutic groups as 'to benefit the persons in a group through making as full a use as possible of the potentials of the group as a medium for help' (1989: 26).

Our experiential learning groups, we would suggest, work in a similar way, the multi-perspective focus on management dictating the employment of additional resources (e.g. reading) to enhance that potential. How then should the facilitator 'be' in the type of group we run? Psychoanalyst Patrick Casement (1994: 24) provides a cautionary note:

any strong adherence to a particular school or theory, or position on technique, can itself become intrusive. The analytic process can easily become tilted in a pre-determined direction, which means it ceases to be truly exploratory or psychoanalytic.

We observe that many tutors practising 'student-centred learning' use a style that combines care and challenge with a modelling of 'traditional' leadership – explaining, interpreting, providing solutions for the group. We have some difficulties with this as an image of effective group facilitation. It models some of the very values that we might at times seek to challenge, most notably the notion of 'leader' in terms of management of meaning and action. Sometimes, the best way of challenging students' preconceptions comes through the facilitator not behaving in their expected 'leadership role'.

In this case, Janet was working with a group of mature, part-time undergraduates. The group was working according to a content/structure that they had designed earlier in the semester. The topic on this occasion was leadership. There had been some reading. It was the beginning of the session: some students shuffled papers around; others were apparently lost in thought. The following are her recollections of the session, written after the seminar and subsequently confirmed by Stuart, the student involved.

Stuart: 'I know we were supposed to talk about leadership today, but I've brought in a newspaper cutting about Handy's book *The Empty Raincoat* (1994). He's talking about management taking responsibility for their actions. I think we ought to discuss this – it links in with Peter Anthony's idea of moral management. Here, I'll pass it round.'

This is received amid a mixture of mutterings from other students in the group: 'What are we talking about today?' … 'Leadership' … 'What's Stuart on about?' … 'Oh it's just Stuart, he wants to talk about something else' … 'Handy's book, is it about leadership then?' … 'I read a book by Handy' … 'You've read a book?' … (laughter).

Stuart: 'I think this is really important.'

A couple of the group members looked at the tutor. She did not respond. Stuart's neighbour was reading the newspaper extract. There was more banter. This continued for several minutes.

Janet wanted them to focus and reflect on what was happening: 'I think it might be helpful if we look at the way leadership has been exercised here, during the ten minutes we've been in the room.'

By using this sort of intervention, a somewhat abstract concept such as 'leadership' became pertinent, a 'real' problem for the group, 'here and now'. It was no longer just a topic, there were people involved, actions and real feelings at stake. This provided an opportunity for significant, experiential learning to take place: 'we permit the student, at any level to be in real contact with the relevant problems of his existence' (Rogers 1967: 280).

> What do you understand by the concept of 'leadership'? What assumptions does the 'traditional' view of leadership make about those who follow? What leadership qualities do you find most helpful in the classroom? At work? Why?

Rogerian 'leadership factors' of empathy, genuineness and unconditional positive regard fit more comfortably with our ways of working but do not embrace the flexibility of approach that is needed for working with groups that are usually very mixed in terms of ability, experience and motivation.

Some models of student-centred learning seem to be more suggestive of a participative teaching and learning strategy than an experiential one. Based on our teaching experience, we would make a clear distinction, in terms of teaching and learning, between *participative* learning and *experiential* learning. In practice, they lie along a continuum rather than being distinct, but different assumptions underpin each style. Participative learning suggests that students are engaged in the tutor's agenda and that there are some overall learning objectives. Experiential learning suggests that there are many diverse agendas and that learning is unique to the individual.

> With any group it may be appropriate to employ a balance of approaches, perhaps even a shift from participative to experiential, as the group matures. Our dilemma is often, do we 'drop students in at the deep end' or give security instead? For example, early in a course we might, using a participative approach, in the closing of a session, direct students to summarise what the learning has been. The advantage of this activity is that it ensures that every student has something to take away; she [*sic*] knows that she has 'learned' something. The disadvantage, which is quite worrying, is that we may inadvertently shut down further learning and exploration by forming a conclusion before students have reached their own.
>
> A real danger is ... when we bring a person up to a point of discovery and just as he [*sic*] is about to make the discovery, we tell him what it is.
>
> (Jenkins, in Blumberg and Golembiewski 1976: 30).

In an experiential session, the tutor avoids any suggestion that the session has come to a close, purposely leaves questions hanging, unanswered. The advantage is that students take ownership of what they have learned; learning becomes continuous, not just something that starts and ends in class. Students often find it necessary to carry on talking long after the seminar. One final-year student reported: 'We always spend hours in the refectory after a 2 hour session continuing the conversations'. This would seem to fulfil Rogers' (1967: 277) prediction that 'people would get together if they wished to learn.'

One of the disadvantages of an experiential approach is that some students come away feeling that they have not learned anything, although this may subsequently provide process material for the group to explore.

The role played by the tutor in individual student learning is not a dilemma that we have solved but rather fruit for our own learning – our own 'real-life' management problem. Even to suggest that we can package this in terms of advantages and disadvantages, as we have above, is misleading. The role is essentially one of facilitation – working alongside students who are pursuing their own learning. But as the examples here demonstrate, in the classroom we adopt whatever style seems appropriate for the group at that time. The tutor's role is complex and changing, thus we continually evaluate and rethink. Sometimes, it is important to share this process with our students. In this way, we model the reflective practice we seek to promote, sharing our own live management problems.

Emotional aspects of teaching and learning

Vince (1996) points out that emotional issues are often omitted in experiential approaches to management learning; that managers develop intellectual skills of reflecting on experience at the expense of connecting with their emotional experiences. Like Vince and Martin (1993), we see limitations in the action learning model. We find that we are able to address this issue by developing a pedagogy that includes humanistic values and psychotherapeutic techniques. The anxiety that students experience, for example when they realise that the tutor is not going to 'lead' or 'entertain' them, is often palpable. And it is not just the students who suffer!

It is often tempting to make students (and ourselves) feel better at the expense of possible learning. This is part of the wider dilemma that we have about allowing students to feel uncomfortable, even though there is evidence that some level of discomfort is almost a prerequisite for learning: 'If the security–disequilibrium condition is in tolerable balance … challenge may be experienced … the potential learner is pulled along by the challenge of self discovery' (Blumberg and Golembiewski 1976: 24).

A group will find a norm that is comfortable for its members. This level will allow trust to develop through which individuals will take greater risks. There is a snowball effect. Risks lead to greater learning, which in turn deepens trust; the norm shifts. Our part then will be different, as groups change.

We do agree with C. Von Nostrand (1993) about the importance of guiding the group into a position where members are able to challenge themselves and each other, and feel comfortable about it. If students are given too much 'guidance', they tend then to look for it – negating the value of the experiential approach. We struggle to find a balance between tutor as creating 'co-presence' (Laing 1987) and tutor as 'nurturing parent' (Berne 1968: 24). We remind ourselves of Morgan's work, borrowing from psychoanalytic theories, that we continually recreate and re-enact relationships we've learned within the family (Morgan 1997). In developing skills of reflection, we would draw the group's attention to how easy it is to allow students to become dependent on the tutor, just as later they may become dependent on a manager. The dependency relationship is known to all of us. Perhaps at some unconscious level both students and tutors are striving to return 'home' to those familiar roles that require no thought. As Mangham (1988: 32) suggests:

> Most of us, most of the time, in most circumstances, at home, work or play, perform without reflection. Even in circumstances where we are theoretically called upon to reflect – planned meetings, interviews, decision points in our life and the like most of us tend to enact our parts in well established scripts.

Conclusion

We are working with groups at undergraduate and postgraduate levels, and these demonstrate very mixed learning abilities. For some students, experiential learning may represent a significant step forward in their experience of learning, a culmination and extension of what has gone before. For others, it is alien and threatening; the removal of security. We try to remain sensitive to this, modelling the important skill of reflective practice in the classroom and in our research. In this chapter, we have attempted to describe our pedagogy, offering what we hope are illuminating examples of what 'experiential learning' in a critical, reflective context might look like in practice and the potential that it has to offer for organisational action.

References

Alvesson, M. and Willmott, H. (1992) *Critical Management Studies*, London: Tavistock.

Anthony, P. (1986) *The Foundation of Management*, London: Tavistock.

Auden, W.H. (1952) *Selected Poems*, London: Penguin.

Benne, K. (1964) 'History of the T-Group in the Laboratory Setting'. In L. Bradford, J. Gibb and K. Benne (eds) *T-Group Theory and Laboratory Method*, New York: John Wiley.

Berne, E. (1968) *Games People Play*, Harmondsworth: Penguin.

Bion, W. (1959) *Experiences in Groups*, London: Routledge.

Blumberg, A. and Golembiewski, R. (1976) *Learning and Change in Groups*, Harmondsworth: Penguin.

Burgoyne, J.G. and Stuart, R. (1976) 'The nature, use and acquisition of managerial skills and other attributes', *Personnel Review* 5 (4): 19 29.

Casement, P. (1994) *On Learning From the Patient*, London: Routledge.

Foulkes, S.H. (1948) *Introduction to Group-Analytic Psychotherapy*, London: Maresfield Reprints.

Goffman, E. (1959) *The Presentation of Self in Everyday Life*, Harmondsworth: Penguin.

Grey, C. (1996) 'Introduction', *Management Learning* 27 (1): 7–20.

Grey, C. and French, R. (1996) 'Rethinking management education'. In R. French and C. Grey (eds) *Rethinking Management Education*, London: Sage.

Handy, C. (1994) *The Empty Raincoat*, Oxford: Hutchinson.

Hassard, J. and Parker, M. (eds) (1993) *Postmodernism and Organisations*, London: Sage.

Hyman, R. (1975) *Industrial Relations: A Marxist Introduction*, London: Macmillan.

Kolb, D. (1984) *Experiential Learning*, Englewood Cliffs, New Jersey: Prentice Hall.

Laing, R.D. (1967) *Politics of Experience and the Bird of Paradise*, Harmondsworth: Penguin.

Laing, R.D. (1987) *Did you used to be R.D. Laing?* Recorded Interview, Channel 4.

Legge, K. (1978) *Power, Innovation and Problem Solving in Personal Management*, London: McGraw-Hill.

Lukes, S. (1974) *Power: A Radical View*, Basingstoke: Macmillan.

Mangham, I. (1988) *Effecting Organisational Change*, Oxford: Basil Blackwell.

Maslow, A.H. (1943) 'A theory of human motivation', *Psychological Review* 50 (4): 370–96.

Morgan, G. (1997) *Images of Organisation*, London: Sage.

Mutch, A. (1997) 'Rethinking undergraduate business education, a critical perspective', *Management Learning* 28 (3): 301–12.

Pedler, M., Burgoyne, J., Boydell, T.H. and Welshman, G. (eds) (1990) *Self-Development in Organisations*, London: McGraw-Hill.

Pedler, M., Burgoyne, J. and Boydell, T.H. (1994) *A Manager's Guide to Self-Development*, London: McGraw-Hill.

Reed, M. (1989) *The Sociology of Management*, Hemel Hempstead: Harvester Wheatsheaf.

Revans, R. (1983) *ABC of Action Learning*, Bromley: Charterwell-Bratt.

Roethlisberger, F.J. and Dickson, W.J. (1939) *Management and the Worker*, Cambridge, MA: Harvard University Press.

Rogers, C. (1967) *On Becoming a Person*, London: Constable.

Roy, R.D. (1960) 'Banana time: job satisfaction and informal interaction', *Human Organisation* 15: 158–68.

Schein, E. (1988) *Organisational Psychology* (third edition), London: Prentice Hall.

Schon, D. (1983) 'Reflection in Action'. In J. Walmsley, R. Woolfe, J. Reynolds and J. Shakespeare (eds) *Health, Welfare and Practice*, London: Sage.

Schon, D. (1987) *Educating the Reflective Practitioner*, San Francisco: Jossey-Bass.

Thompson, P. (1989) *The Nature of Work*, Basingstoke: Macmillan.

Thompson, P. and McHugh, D. (1995) *Work Organisations*, London: Macmillan.

Tressell, R. (1965) *The Ragged Trousered Philanthropists*, London: Panther.

Vince, R. (1996) 'Experiential management education'. In R. French and C. Grey (eds) *Rethinking Management Education*, London: Sage.

Vince, R. and Martin, L. (1993) 'Inside action learning: an exploration of the psychology and politics of the action learning model', *Management Education and Development* 24 (3): 205–18.

Von Nostrand, C. (1993) *Gender-Responsible Leadership*, London: Sage.

Whitaker, D. (1989) *Using Groups to Help People*, London: Tavistock/Routledge.

Willmott, H. (1987) 'Studying managerial work: critique and proposal', *Journal of Management Studies* May: 249–70.

Willmott, H. (1994) 'Management education: provocations to a debate', *Management Learning* 25 (1): 105–36.

Wright, O.W. (1982) 'The American class structure', *American Sociological Review* Vol. 47.

Yalom, I.D. (1985) *The Theory and Practice of Group Psychotherapy* (third edition), New York: Basic Books.

Further reading

We would recommend that you continue your explorations of management learning through a study of the following:

Rogers (1967) – an essential read that provides a thought-provoking perspective on understanding self and individual learning.

Blumberg and Golembiewski (1976) – offers a useful framework for understanding learning in groups.

French and Grey (eds) (1996) *Rethinking Management Education*, London: Sage – a 'critical' text that gives an excellent overview of current issues in management learning.

Pedler (ed.) (1991) *Action Learning in Practice*, Gower – focuses on practical aspects of action learning in groups within the workplace.

Pedler *et al.* (1994) – a helpful introduction to reflecting on your own management skills.

7 Circles of uncertainty in management learning

Judith Golding

Introduction

This chapter will examine in more detail the idea of a cyclical conception of learning and will investigate its appropriateness for management learning in the light of the kinds of uncertainty that pervade complex organisations. It will compare and contrast cyclical approaches to learning with the kind of more familiar linear approach (especially those that have emphasised a need for the prior identification of learning outcomes) that has been so popular in management studies.

The chapter will explore alternative ways of assessing when and where learning has occurred, focusing in particular upon the appropriateness of cyclical approaches in situations involving high degrees of uncertainty. In the course of this analysis, the chapter will present an argument for a more viable alternative than the tired old theme of 'back to basics', which is again in vogue. Indeed, the chapter will suggest that a theme of 'forward from basics' might be a rather more constructive way in which to proceed.

Beginning with an analysis of the problems posed by uncertainty, the chapter will examine the way in which as individuals we cling to our deeply held beliefs, resisting all attempts to invert those beliefs – a situation that leads to the taking up of organisationally fixed positions, correspondingly resisting all attempts to shift those positions. The chapter will seek to highlight the inadequacies of approaches that are based upon a belief in the attainability of certainty such as seems to pervade so many organisations. The analysis will contrast this situation with the apparently conflicting condition in which learning from experience is an accepted part of the activities with which we occupy our leisure time.

Through this comparative analysis, the chapter will present an alternative approach to management learning, involving the prospect of learning through uncertainty, and will develop the idea of a positive use of uncertain situations, such as those encountered in sport, through the documenting of a case study, designed to illustrate the possibilities for harnessing the opportunities presented by uncertainty.

Learning in circles

One of the themes of this book has been to emphasise that learning can be approached in a cyclical manner, in contrast to some of the more traditional concepts of learning, which assume that it occurs in a linear way. Indeed, in the history of ideas there have been periodic attempts to conceptualise knowledge acquisition in terms of circular programmes of understanding: circles or loops of learning, for example (Argyris and Schon 1978: 46); or 'verstehen' (Outhwaite 1975); or 'hermeneutic circles' (Bleicher 1980: 2); or indeed the idea of 'double hermeneutics' (Giddens 1976: 162).

In this chapter, I want to suggest that a view of 'circles of (mis)understanding', in which understanding is seen as 'tentative and supposed', with little chance of establishing permanent grounding and therefore without a particularly special status attached to it, might be equally apposite.

As an example of what I mean by this implied inversion, I was recently made aware of the way in which my 'knowledge', or 'supposed understanding' of one small element of my experience was undermined by an apparently innocent, although quite stimulating occurrence.

Consider the children's rhyme:

> As I was walking on the stair,
> I met a man who wasn't there.
> He wasn't there again today,
> I wish the man would go away.

Over the years, I have developed a view that might account for such experiences and situations as either fictitious, paranormal or in this case simply an example of a nonsense rhyme – until recently, when I was reading a newspaper article in which the rhyme appeared, but with a difference:

> As I was walking on the stair,
> I met a man who wasn't there.
> He wasn't there again today,
> He must be a hologram!

At this point, an explosive and wholly new (to me) area of 'explanation' was opened up, in which the final line presents a quite new possibility, in the form of what seems to be an entirely logical outcome, the kind of outcome that simply had not occurred to me before – one in which far from requiring an explanation such as that of a nonsense rhyme, I now had a perfectly feasible and logical explanation for a previously unexplained phenomenon.

While contemplating the implications of this, I was suddenly hit by another newspaper headline: 'Old MacDonald has a windmill farm'. Nothing surprising in that perhaps. Mildly amusing maybe. But in the context of my considerations I began to imagine the difference between the kind of impact such a headline might have now and the impact it would have had 25 years ago – assuming that it survived the subeditors of the newspaper where it was printed, for surely someone would have spotted it and identified it as a nonsense headline – wind farms being part of an unknown future.

It then began to occur to me that there was a distinct possibility that a great deal of what I define as 'nonsense' might turn out simply to consist of statements or situations lacking an appropriate framework for logical explanation. And since such situations clearly change over time, a more worrying question began to raise its head, namely, what if it should turn out that much of what I take to be logical/normal/acceptable forms of knowledge are based on nothing more than, well, nonsense, to put it bluntly?

Against this kind of fundamental challenge, I want to explore in this chapter the grounding of what we take to be 'understanding' and the implications that this might have for our conceptions of what constitutes learning – and especially management learning.

Belief in the attainability of certainty

One of the things that often strikes people as significant when thinking about managing in organisations is how lacking in certainty organisations are. Yet certainty is the thing that many people in organisations appear to need and in many cases profess to achieve if not strive to maximise. By implication, certainty is treated as an attainable end-point and handled with little awareness of the difficulties involved. Yet even writers such as Ackoff (1974) have shown how ignoring levels of uncertainty can so easily result in nonsense systems. He suggests that where it may be possible to create models that are apparently 'objective' and can be optimised, it is not possible to optimise 'reality' in the same way 'for reality does not consist of isolated and tractable problems, but complex, ever-changing interrelated messes' (Alvesson and Willmott 1996: 24).

In every decade, new panaceas appear that claim to make improvements to our understanding of how to organise more efficiently. Total quality management (TQM), for example, is based on the idea that it is possible to define and standardise the degree of quality necessary to satisfy customers, and having done that, to develop a system to monitor production to achieve that standard. TQM initially developed in industrial manufacturing organisations and has now spread virus-like into so many other organisations, including those involved in services, finance or even health and education. To develop such a TQM system clearly involves a presupposition that it is possible to have at least a reasonable sense of and agreement about what 'quality' means to the customer. Yet how can it be possible to define and regulate such a system without travelling into the realms of nonsense by excluding variables that some customers (less important, less valuable ones, no doubt) would include in their description of quality? Without such inclusions, quality becomes nothing more than a collection of pre-identified elements taken from a predetermined list, at any given moment. The fact that we all have the ability to change our views constantly as to what constitutes 'quality' in any given field clearly highlights the problems of any system based upon such assumptions. It is not too difficult to find examples of the fracturing foundations of such generalised systems – there are some particularly revealing ones in recent quality audits of UK transport systems.

The difficulties in deciding upon the factors that determine quality in any particular product are complicated by the fact that most people have what might be termed a series of bedrock assumptions about what constitutes quality. These assumptions may be largely unarticulated (indeed they may even be inaccessible to conscious thought) but nevertheless may frequently be called upon in situations requiring quick assessments of quality to be made.

Many of these underlying assumptions are likely to have derived from social and environmental factors in a person's particular background. One of the important factors in industrial societies, for instance, is the idea that quality is in some way counterposed to any concept of quantity (e.g. 'I prefer quality to quantity, if you don't mind please'). An extension of this principle can be seen in courses on management research, if not in the whole area of social research, where so-called qualitative methods are often presented in contradistinction to quantitative methods.

One unfortunate consequence of this kind of bedrock assumption is that it can quickly lead to a concentration on ensuring high standards of service and comfort to the detriment of quantity. In railway transport, for example, this has sometimes led to a concentration on the comfort of carriages and standards of refreshment service, which are desirable enough in their own right but are not the whole story – for if the train does not run to time, and a customer misses an important connection, it is unlikely that an excellent cup of coffee is going to be seen as compensation for the disruption caused. This is not to suggest that railway companies are not interested in running to time. However, the company that owns and operates the rolling stock may be a different company to the one that owns and operates the track.

This is certainly the case in the UK at the moment, and in the example above, the delay may have been caused by circumstances beyond the rolling stock company's ability to control. Accountability is thus seen to be fundamental to any concept of quality. Indeed, it may be that an inappropriate form of organisation is a more important criticism of the privatised scheme of railways currently operated in the UK than is any political argument about privatisation or nationalisation.

While on the subject of trains, it was reported on the radio in the UK recently that a rail company was having a 'hundred per cent day' – a day in which every train was to run on time. Such was the determination to meet this perfect performance figure that on several occasions it appeared that trains did not stop at stations to pick up passengers, since the delay caused by this operation would impede the chances of meeting the target. Needless to say, a spokesperson for the company denied any link between these sudden failures to stop and the 'quality' initiative.

Can you think of any examples from your own experience of occasions when you have found it difficult to ascertain where precise responsibility for poor quality lay? And can you think of any examples where deteriorating quality would seem to have arisen from an inappropriate form of organisation, such as that caused by the separation of responsibility between crucially interdependent components of quality, or where apparently good intentions had somehow become subverted?

A frequent problem faced by those who attempt to encompass the variety of problems that can occur in any complex organisation and represent them with a system based upon predetermined ends is underlined in, for example, the area of safety and risk audits. It might seem appropriate in healthcare and other social sector organisations to attempt to identify the limits of safety and risk, but at what point does a system designed to assist the smooth and effective operation of an organisational unit itself become a source of problems? A potent example of this can be seen in a current research project that I am engaged in concerning a UK children's home, where the constant emphasis on safety and risk audits has become itself a source of merriment and lack of respect for the management by the staff. Staff at all levels in this children's home consider that their main role is to encourage, develop and sustain young lives rather than criminalise them. However, the impact of audits has become so predominant, with monitoring having to be carried out so frequently, that staff consider they are impinging too much on time to carry out their caring and development work with the children. The result has been that staff have begun a process of over-reporting, where any minor detail is reported in an attempt to highlight the nonsense of the audit. To give just one example, it was recently reported that an air freshener had been found in the toilet. The grounds for concern? 'Well, clearly dangerous for children who potentially could develop into glue sniffers!'

Learning through uncertainty

It would appear that people employed in organisations often attempt to attain certainty in one form or another. Nowhere is this more evident than in the realm of what we have come to call 'management'. Perhaps this is not surprising, given that the history of ideas is littered with successive attempts to conceptualise this constant striving to (in some way) contain the complexity around us (Berlin 1978). The constant pursuit of meaning (or search for understanding), which is sometimes referred to as making sense, might almost have been designed to produce over-simplification by prescribing ways of avoiding the chaos that comprises organisational environments.

Perhaps it is also not surprising in management to hear so often a new variation on the old music hall joke – the one thing that I am certain about is that there is no such thing as certainty – especially in organisations (in this discussion, I shall confine my analysis to a consideration of organisations in which people do the work, which is worth emphasising in this context, since we may well be on the verge of having organisations where robots, or viruses, do the work!).

One starting point for such an analysis might be to question why so much energy is expended on attempting to abolish the supposed evils of chaos and complexity, which are manifest in everyday concerns such as cash flow, profit volatility, rapid uncontrolled change, etc. Might it not be that with a little appreciation there could be more fruitful alternatives?

Suppose for a moment that we were discussing leisure activities rather than thinking about management – for example, visits to the theatre or an art gallery, or the annual holiday. I suggest that we might find a rather different, if not contrary, approach towards the lack of certainty. The excitement of a holiday taking us to places of which we have little prior knowledge and no experience – in other words little understanding, and clearly no certainty, of what to expect – is likely to produce a quite different response. Indeed, the depth of uncertainty may even be more desirable – for example, expensive holidays are more highly valued than ones that take us to the 'same old place'. Similarly, an art exhibition that presents extraordinary aspects of the human condition in a new way may be valued in relation to an inverse uncertainty ratio, just as with a new theatre production that shows us a new story, or an old story in a new light. In such situations, we are not certain of what to expect, and we are obviously not certain how it will affect us. Yet this uncertainty frequently appears to trigger the enjoyment felt at artistic events. The same can be said of adventure holidays, where confrontation with nature (for example, defying gravity by climbing mountains, canoeing down rapids or bungy jumping) has a lack of certainty as one of its main attractions.

Learning from experiences

Perhaps one source of our willingness to invest money in holidays or entertainments that are based upon a lack of certainty lies in the observation that we appear to derive some kind of emotional satisfaction from facing, or perhaps from overcoming, them. This can sometimes result in personal development that can lead to individuals seeing and understanding things in a way that they had not before. 'I learned something that I didn't know about myself' is a typical reaction of those asked to explain why they put themselves through such dangers.

This kind of learning from experience is also important in work organisations, although the part played by emotion in this is rarely acknowledged in the management literature (see Fineman (1993) for a notable exception). The traditional apprenticeship system (sometimes referred to as 'sitting beside Nellie' – gendering being a predominant feature of organisational history too) is based on our ability to watch and learn, rather than read textbooks on how to sew a seam, spin a thread, oil a tractor. Such work-based learning is founded on a clear assumption that the one thing we do not have on our first day at work is a clear idea of exactly how to do anything. In these traditional apprentice-based approaches, we are presumably meant to be guided through the uncertainty by sometimes kind, sometimes unkind, fellow workers ('unkind' in the sense that it is often believed by the proponents of such schemes that we learn only by feeling pain, discomfort or even humiliation). Thus new workers are meant to be cured of their lack of knowledge through the medium of others showing them how to do things, in the course of which being cured of any emerging overconfidence or arrogance by being humiliated (a more subtle 'use' of uncertainty than is sometimes acknowledged!).

Modern work organisations are often ideologically cast in a context that emphasises a necessity to learn and develop. It is said to be no longer possible for people employed in management in any organisation to continue to work in the same way as their predecessors, or even in the way that they did themselves a mere decade before. Constant learning and self-development is said to be not a luxury but an essential quality. I shall not, however, concern myself here with the kinds of reification required to embrace some of the more questionable concepts of 'organisational learning' that are currently in vogue (see Furze and Gale 1996: 271).

One of the declared aims of this book has been to explore some of the contradictions inherent in management situations, and one of these would seem to lie in the realms of current calls for more 'learning organisations' in the wider context of what has been termed 'lifelong learning'. There are obvious attractions in such ideas, but rarely do their proponents stop to consider any opposing forces that might need to be addressed to achieve that kind of change. Rarely, for example, do such calls deal with contextual factors, which might militate against such movements – for example, the opposing forces residing in the fact that such calls often take place in a context of increasing control.

As an example of the kinds of effect that such unexamined contradictions can have, consider a recent occurrence in an organisation in the north of England, where a manager who had only recently been extolling the virtues of a learning organisation, and arguing for more investment in facilities that would promote lifelong learning, was asked to name the three most important things in management. His reply:

Loyalty, loyalty and loyalty.

There were a number of different levels of response to this. Some took it as a humorous play on the estate agent's story concerning the three most important things about a property (i.e. position, position and position) but that such a pronouncement could not have any serious relevance beyond being a good joke. Some accepted, albeit with a smile, that it was a serious contribution to the running of the organisation but then quickly transformed it into an opportunity to call for more co-operation between different levels of management – beginning with the suggestion that such a statement served only to confirm that management was a team effort. Some regarded the pronouncement as a transparent confirmation that managers were only really interested in control. Some suggested that it should be treated as a useful parody, in which something about the difficulties involved in management were being illustrated. Some reacted with horror, on the assumption that the manager concerned really believed what he had said – and the fact that he thought he might be able to sustain and even engender such a belief in others was an example of the extent to which management control sometimes (often?) extends into attempting to control others' perceptions of what they do.

Whatever your own reaction to such a situation, can you think of any occasions when humour has been used to say something important but that has instead served to disclose something about submerged intentions and/or deeply held beliefs? And can you think of any occasion when you have tried to use humour yourself to avoid or defuse a situation in which fundamental tensions were about to be exposed?

There is a sense in which pronouncements concerning the need for continual development do indeed reflect the essentially dynamic nature of complex organisations. Any idea that may have been grasped, or understanding that may have been learned from previous situations, can be suddenly irrelevant, and out of date, because of a change that takes place in another part of the same organisation, or indeed outside that organisation. This is compounded by the emphasis placed in the educational approaches that management graduates are likely to have encountered in the development of their careers. Unfortunately, management education has too often been channelling students' attention towards particular functional areas of management – often as though they were dynamically independent and sometimes even unrelated (Reed 1989: 16). Whatever the reality and particular clusters of life's experiences that managers bring to their work, it is clear that the ability to continue learning is an important element in the achievement of the most common success criteria that are applied to organisations (Anthony 1994: 17).

As has already been suggested, many of the approaches to learning in management education have been based on the same kinds of assumption as traditional school teaching, where, beyond the primary level, teaching continues to be dominated by subject-based, didactically conveyed knowledge. The extent to which such approaches are based on education theories deriving from behaviourist psychology (often based on animal testing) is sometimes forgotten. Thus we are left with a largely unexamined intellectual tradition in which information is conveyed, with repetition being considered the best way to reinforce the receipt and retention of that information in others (for a critique of the 'one-way' conception of the role of a teacher in this context, see Musgrave 1965: 218). Moreover, this situation has been maintained despite periodic attempts to challenge these assumptions and introduce more innovative approaches – such challenges generally being followed by equal attempts to discredit innovations by describing them as 'trendy', with accompanying calls for a return to so-called 'basics'. That management education has followed this path is easily demonstrated by a cursory examination of syllabuses, where it will be found that courses are invariably made up of subjects taught in the same manner, based on the same beliefs about how we learn (for a critique of some of the implications of this, see Alvesson and Willmott 1996: 203).

But what would an alternative approach to management education look like? Well, French and Grey (1996) have set a context for rethinking management education, but I want to stay for a moment with a particular strand that this might take. Suppose that someone were to suggest that it could more appropriately be carried out using the learning methods used in sport. For example, perhaps management could be 'taught' in the same way as football. It might be said that footballers have to make quick decisions based on a combination of prior knowledge, previous experience, drawing upon images of great footballers, knowledge gained through training in ball skills and strategies, and not least, criticism from fans and the media – and all this in a context of extreme win/lose uncertainty. Could it not be said that managers face situations in which the application of similar approaches might be beneficial?

It is said that one of the favourite axioms of the highly successful former soccer manager Brian Clough was to the effect that 'football is ninety per cent good habits'. What I believe he meant by that was that in facing situations of great uncertainty (bearing in mind that he was particularly concerned with the role of defending players when he said that) then an approach to the game that engendered 'good habits' would mean that the necessary reactions would be more likely to occur when required if they had become habitual.

The correlation between habit and appropriate action is logical enough, and the implications for training follow quite naturally from that. Thus it seems fairly straightforward to accept, for example, that if defending players were to concentrate in their training on always staying on the goal side of attacking players, then they would be less likely to be caught out of position in real games. On the other hand, in order to do that, defending players would need to watch closely the bobbing and weaving of any attacking player trying to deceive them as to the direction that they were going to move in.

This kind of training would require a suspension of the oft-quoted dictum that every child engaged in sport from an early age is told, namely, 'keep your eye on the ball'. In the circumstances of Brian Clough's axiom, perhaps that latter dictum needs to be amended to 'do not keep your eye on the ball until the moment before you are about to play the ball yourself'. Prior to that moment, if you are caught 'ball watching' you are vulnerable to the attacking player slipping in behind you while you are frozen to the spot keeping your eye on the ball.

Do you think that the engendering of ideas like the 'good habits' example above, could have any part to play in improving the relationship between action and thinking about management? Could this be achieved by the kind of innovation that might encourage more constructive reflective practice?

Could it be that attention might be more fruitfully turned towards an appreciation of the immense learning value of individual experiences in coping with uncertainty, and away from the constant search for certainty. Indeed, one of the main problems of certainty-led management learning is that it leads to a search for the right answer (reflections of the answer that teacher wanted at school, in the later management education assignment, which merely repeat all the theories correctly). Whereas organisations are living entities, complex associations of people, each with brains and emotions capable of producing unlimited numbers of ideas and decisions (not forgetting diversions and circumlocutions!) that can lead to vast numbers of choices and alternatives.

Alternative approaches to learning in management education

I have suggested that an alternative to the pursuit of certainty in management might be to attempt to harness learning through uncertainty. I have also suggested that the words 'learning' and 'self-development' are frequently used when referring to leisure activities. I referred in particular to leisure activities in which individuals see themselves as being challenged and appear to enjoy and seek out such challenges. Perhaps one reason why we find it difficult to accept that there may be some correlation between leisure and work learning is our inherited Victorian work ethic (sometimes referred to in the UK as a 'Protestant ethic'), which from an early age engenders a feeling that because something is enjoyable it cannot be work!

However, there is another paradox here, because clearly enjoyment does sometimes occur in the workplace. This often arises from adversity (see the resistance and control literature, e.g. Salaman 1979; Edwards 1979; Esland and Salaman 1980), but it can also be as a result of people spending time together in a project, or indeed in socialising at work, weekends or in attending educational courses.

It was fun working with the others, not like being at work at all.

I learned some interesting ways of handling people from the kinds of things that happened, I can tell you.

It was so much easier talking about work when we met in the pub after the course each day.

These examples taken from some previous field notes are the sorts of phrases we are all familiar with. Yet from this kind of experience, involving interaction that is seen as casual, relaxed and 'enjoyable', it is difficult to define the extent of learning that has taken place – and especially in any precise way that will allow tabulation of how many staff understand and now know how to use the new software, or have grasped the operating principle of the new financial plan. The kind of learning that results from experiential approaches is extremely difficult to assess, calculate or cost. It therefore tends to become ignored in the staff development plans of most organisations.

A case study in learning through uncertainty

At this point, it might be useful to consider an example of learning through uncertainty in a little more detail through the medium of a case study. A case study that is particularly appropriate for this was occasioned by a recent attempt by the UK government to influence the way in which lecturers in higher education taught their students.

The background to this case derives from the way in which the Conservative UK government of the 1980s had made changes in the manner in which post-16 education was managed. Chiefly, the changes involved the way the sector was funded, by moving away from externally directed financing to making each institution more responsible for its own financial affairs. As part of this, an attempt was made to steer institutions towards designing their work in more cost-effective ways. Clearly, this was intended to involve a consideration of the cost of lecturing staff compared with the number of students who graduated, and central to this was the style of teaching that was taking place.

To achieve these aims, the government initiated the Enterprise in Higher Education scheme, in which, for those institutions successful in their bids, £1 million over five years would be allocated, provided that the institution was able to match this with the same amount of money raised elsewhere. They were clearly expected to attract these additional sums of money from industry. This was to be used as a specific budget exclusively to develop the institutions in particular areas that the government felt would assist its general aim of overall cost reduction.

My own involvement in this initiative, and hence in this case study, was as the staff development manager of the enterprise initiative at a university in the north of England. In this role, I was part of a team whose job it was to define, design and carry out a programme of work that would fulfil the remit we had submitted to the appropriate section of the Department of Employment (which placing provides some clarification of the government's intentions). The areas that our particular enterprise team specified (deriving from our perceptions of what might be seen to satisfy the government's needs) were to be information technology, European membership, student-centred learning, staff development and the development of industrial links.

For most student-related staff (lecturers, administrators, librarians, computer technicians, etc.) at the university, the government's initiative was initially seen as extremely threatening, and the majority tended to have a very negative attitude towards it. In fact, they were exhibiting some classic signs of worrying about their future, stemming from the kinds of uncertainty that the enterprise project created.

It was recognised by the enterprise team that merely to launch a programme of work with reassuring noises to the effect that the initiative was not designed to make them redundant, or change ways of working without consent, etc., would have no useful consequences. Many would clearly not have believed us. Such a reaction would not have been at all surprising, since we knew that the introduction of the initiative nationally had been unable to escape the suspicion that it was a scheme dreamed up by a government whose main (if not only) intention was to save money on higher education because it was seen as a very expensive system. These suspicions were confirmed as a result of information received from the enterprise initiative's national headquarters, which tended to highlight issues such as the many 'experts' that we could employ to provide training to our staff in teaching large student groups, using computers to teach more students, student-led supervision, and so forth – frequently, it seemed, aimed at reducing the amount of time a student would spend with a lecturer.

Despite these misgivings, we did feel that we were being presented with an opportunity and that we just might be able to encourage staff at the university to benefit from new ideas that were relevant to modern higher education institutions, but without coupling those ideas to financial consequences. Thus we decided, for example, that the increasing use of computers by all staff (many lecturing staff at that time had never touched a computer, let alone used one regularly) was worth supporting, whereas the development of systems that removed students' entitlement to appropriate staff contact time was not.

After long deliberation, we decided in essence to attempt to harness the uncertainty not by resolving it but by offering it for consideration within the confines of what we had undertaken to do. We decided to adopt a 'guiding philosophy' along which our own actions could be steered. That philosophy was basically one in which the role of a higher education institution was considered to be one of enabling students to learn as effectively as possible. We did not therefore take it as our responsibility to either attempt to reduce costs or to support existing jobs. Our aim in those areas was to remain as passive as we could, our main job being seen as enabling learning to take place.

Having clarified our guiding philosophy, we decided to design an initial programme that all staff who worked with students (academic, library/learning resources, administrative) would be invited to attend. It did not seem very sensible to repeat the kinds of workshop that staff had attended previously. Lecturers, for example, had been on courses on using new pieces of teaching machinery and equipment or designing marking schemes; administrative staff were often invited to courses on updating their computing skills, etc. For this programme, we felt that we had to present some opportunities that, at least initially, were different and preferably challenging.

Since the 1960s, there have been three main types of university in the UK: the traditional ones, including 'Oxbridge' and the so-called 'redbrick' universities; the 'greenfield' universities established in the 1960s; and the ex-polytechnics that became the 'new' universities in the 1990s. The original division between the 'academic' research-based work of the traditional universities and the more 'applied' work of the polytechnic sector has increasingly blurred into a situation in which the bulk of institutions attempt to carry out the full range of work. Research that takes place in all these universities is funded mainly by government, in various guises, but also by a number of other bodies such as charities and occasionally by industry. The expectation is that lecturing staff who teach in these institutions will normally relate their research to their teaching work. One result of this expectation has been to produce a homogenisation of teaching approaches, whether that be through the traditional lecture and seminar programme, the laboratory demonstration and practice or the use of life drawing to study art.

Unfortunately, some of these approaches present problems in an era in which more and more students want to enter higher education, and moreover an era in which greater recognition is being given to the need to offer continuing education for people throughout their lives. Against this kind of background, the enterprise team felt a need to develop a programme that could face these issues without losing the benefits achieved through centuries of higher education – how to make possible developmental changes without 'throwing the baby out with the bath water'.

A decision was made that it was not the team's job to define a new system that could do all these things. Rather, we should attempt to provide a structure that would enable staff to think about this dual need for themselves, with each of them working out something that would relate to their own area of work. We considered that it was our role to encourage others to realise that learning was concerned with the individual developing, not a way of instilling certain predefined end-points in teaching and learning. Thus while we felt a need to try to encourage staff to think more individually, and to be aware of the fact that they were moving into a more and more uncertain future, we also knew that it would be counterproductive to attempt to do this in a conventional way.

We therefore designed our first programme of introductory workshops based on the idea that it would be more successful if we could get staff to identify with learning through uncertainty. Our first step was to hold two-day workshops, away from the workplace, with the participants in each workshop coming from different departments. Therefore we had, for example, lecturers from engineering, art, sociology, food studies, languages and business, a librarian, administrators and computer support staff, all on one workshop.

The programme was designed in such a way that a number of activities took place requiring participants to work in small groups – planning and then producing ideas and plans that were acceptable to all the members. Engineers and sociologists, for example, found themselves going back to the basics of their understanding about their own subjects in order to explain to their colleagues why a certain way of teaching could or should work. They questioned each other and offered shared solutions, which finally became shared designs developed by larger groups. Many of these ideas were imaginative, many were quite crazy, but they were reconsidering what their role was as part of a system that attempted to help students to learn.

We were making the workshops as uncertain as possible by mixing staff from different areas, which initially they found quite threatening. We did not keep to a specific timetable (other than meals), because we were trying to give them the space to think about their work in a way that they never normally had time for. On the other hand, we were also conscious of the questions as to how many of us would reconsider why we do the basics of our job, even if we did have the time. Faced with such questions, we therefore tried to use uncertainty to get staff to develop and learn with each other and through such uncertainty steer them into reconsidering how to enable students to learn more effectively. The results and ensuing feedback showed that there were some notable successes – people are still talking about, and drawing upon, their experiences of the workshops eight years later!

Concluding note – embracing uncertainty

This chapter has suggested that a great deal of action in organisations is oriented towards the pursuit of certainty (e.g. the treatment of financial information as though figures such as those presented on balance sheets had a surety beyond the accounting conventions that have led to their collection in that particular form). The chapter has highlighted problems in the pursuit of certainty and has suggested that rather than trying to erect fixed parameters as an automatic response to uncertain situations, it might be more fruitful to consider alternative responses. Indeed, the chapter has suggested that a more appropriate approach to managing the kinds of uncertainty that pervade complex organisations might be to attempt to harness such situations and convert them into opportunities for learning.

This chapter has highlighted the essential (and perhaps curious) differences between the ways in which we approach work and the ways in which we approach leisure. It has suggested that a realisation of the incongruities in this difference might present some possibilities for the development of alternative approaches to dealing with uncertainty in organisations.

References

Ackoff, R. (1974) 'The social responsibility of operational research', *Operational Research Quarterly* 25: 361–71.

Alvesson, M. and Willmott, H. (1996) *Making Sense of Management*, London, Sage.

Anthony, P. (1994) *Managing Culture*, Buckingham: Open University Press.

Argyris, C. and Schon, D.A. (1978) *Organizational Learning: A Theory of Action Perspective*, Reading, MA: Addison-Wesley.

Berlin, I. (1978) 'An introduction to philosophy'. In B. Magee (ed.) *Men of Ideas*, London: BBC Publications.

Bleicher, J. (1980) *Contemporary Hermeneutics*, London: Routledge & Kegan Paul.

Edwards, R. (1979) *Contested Terrain, The Transformation of the Workplace in the Twentieth Century*, London: Heinemann.

Esland, G. and Salaman, G. (1980) *The Politics of Work and Occupations*, Milton Keynes: Open University Press.

Fineman, S. (1993) *Emotion in Organizations*, London: Sage.

French, R. and Grey, C. (eds) (1996) *Rethinking Management Education*, London: Sage.

Furze, D. and Gale, C. (1996) *Interpreting Management – Exploring Change and Complexity*, London: International Thomson Business Press.

Giddens, A. (1976) *New Rules of Sociological Method*, London: Hutchinson.

Musgrave, W. (1965) *The Sociology of Education*, London: Methuen.

Outhwaite, W. (1975) *Understanding Social Life, The Method called Verstehen*, London: Allen & Unwin.

Reed, M. (1989) *The Sociology of Management*, New York: Harvester Wheatsheaf.

Salaman, G. (1979) *Work Organisations, Resistance & Control*, London: Longman.

Further reading

Russell, B. (1967) *The Problems of Philosophy*, London: Oxford University Press. Beginning with the first sentence of the book: 'Is there any knowledge in the world which is so certain that no reasonable (person) could doubt it?', this classic work on the nature of intellectual enquiry is an excellent introduction to the question of what is to count as valid knowledge.

Vattimo, G. (1988) *The End of Modernity*, Cambridge: Polity Press. An illuminating essay on the idea of 'claims to truth' being treated as nothing more than 'persuasive accounts'.

Burrell, G. (1998) *Pandemonium*, London: Sage.

Morgan, G. (1993) *Imaginization*, Newbury Park, CA: Sage. Some more imaginative approaches to conceiving and dealing with the uncertainties of organisations.

Ditton, J. (1977) *Part-time Crime*, London: Macmillan. An excellent study of what happens when the pursuit of organisational certainty becomes too widespread for its own good.

8 Promises, promotion and pristine porcelain

Rhetorics and essences in management action

Fred Dobson

Introduction

This chapter explores the author's struggle to come to terms with the 'nature' of management. Starting with personal experiences of managing organisations and subsequent experiences, first as a student and then as a member of staff, in a business school, the author explores his own and students' ideological preconceptions of control in management action. Following the author's perception of serious incongruity between some of the models used in management training and his experiences of management, a dialectical position is used to suggest that much of the underpinning of pedagogic processes is based on 'virtual reality' – an idealised position unrealisable in practice.

On pristine porcelain

The export sales director of the manufacturing company in Germany from which I was attempting to obtain the exclusive distributorship for Britain was arriving later that morning, together with his sales manager. Their product range was exciting and profitable, and it complemented our existing product profile perfectly. Unfortunately, at the time we needed them more than they needed us, so I felt that we needed to impress them with our efficiency. I had already been to visit their factory near Cologne, and, to me at least, they appeared to exhibit all the hallmarks of what I can only describe as anal compulsiveness. These were frighteningly efficient people running a factory and distribution network as if it were a well-oiled Swiss clock. So, in recognition of this efficiency, our own offices were made especially tidy for the visit. Freshly ground coffee was gurgling in the percolator, and the warehouse floor was made unusually clear of packing waste and other detritus. Even the two delivery vans had received their first ever coat of polish. These vehicles were then positioned artistically at the front of the building, displaying the company logo to its full advantage. Impression management was the order of the day.

I was in a state of excitement imagining the profitable increase in turnover that their comprehensive range of electronic timers, counters and liquid-level sensors would offer us. The Germans produced sophisticated process-control products with a very high profit margin for the distributor. We had all the necessary expertise in this area of electronic control, but we were only a small company in their terms. Would they want us or not? The uncertainty of the situation transferred itself to my bladder. I went for a pee. Once in the 'gents' toilets I decided that I had better check the cubicles for cleanliness. With a gasp of disgust I saw that in one of the stalls some dirty bugger had pebble-dashed one of the toilet bowls – obviously, I reasoned, the result of a heavy night on the beer. Despite the cleaning materials and toilet brush to hand, he, whoever he might have been, had left the disgusting mess for somebody else to deal with. I hurriedly left the toilets to find the warehouse operator, Sid. I found him behind one of the racks dabbing with his broom at a small pile of dust displaying all of his usual phlegmatic lethargy.

'Sid, one of the toilets is blathered in shit, would you clean it please before the Germans arrive.'

A look of incredulity came over Sid's normally impassive face. He removed the saliva-stained dog-end of the ever-present untipped cigarette from his mouth before speaking. I felt a twinge of unease, I had seen this telling piece of body language a number of times before, and coupled with his toxic body odour, it made any confrontation doubly unnerving.

'If you want that toilet cleaning Fred, you can clean the fucking thing yourself.'

'Sid, you know how important this visit is to us all. And, after all, I am the managing director, and I do have other more important things to do before they arrive.'

'I don't give a toss if you are the prime minister Fred. I am not cleaning up somebody else's shit.'

I felt anger at his unreasonableness. Should I give the bugger his P45 at the end of the week, or sack him now? However, I had to weigh this against the fact that he had been with me for five years, and I had no other cause for complaint outside his malaise. Sod it! Angrily, I went back into the toilets, got a toilet brush and bleach, and scrubbed vigorously at the bowl until the porcelain was pristine. Ugh! Dirty, inconsiderate bastard, whoever he was, and bollocks to that ungrateful bastard Sid after I had given him a job – he had spent two years on the dole before had I employed him. Mind you, some niggling little voice deep inside me did keep on suggesting that he had a valid point, why should he clean it, apart from the fact that I did not want to be the one who had to do it. Employees are nothing but a pain in the arse, I told myself. They never appreciate anything that you might do for them. But the truth was, I remained uncomfortable with the trappings of control, I disliked giving orders or exercising any form of authority. I knew that I had experienced too much of it in my youth, and I still felt uncomfortable when confronted by authority figures myself.

How should I have dealt with this, I asked myself. Is this how you are supposed to 'manage' in these situations. How are you supposed to manage when you do not like exercising overt authority over others? I had spent an hour the previous day listening to the complaints of one of the sales representatives. The other two sales people in the company had sun-roofs in their vehicles, he whinged, and he did not have one fitted in his new company car. He was the representative that had been with me the longest, so it was not fair. Did I not value his efforts? He was, he told me, a hard-working and conscientious employee, and it was a question of prestige and 'face' to him as far as the other two sales representatives were concerned. Holy shit, I thought, was that all he had to worry about? Tiring of the monologue, and not really knowing how to say no, I told him to take the bloody thing back to the distributor that afternoon and have a sun-roof retro-fitted. Should I have been harder? On the other hand, could I have been harder given my acknowledged problem with control? Why was I not assertive enough to say 'no' when I felt that I should? Could I have 'managed' this predicament better? What would John Harvey-Jones or Richard Branson have done in this situation, or in the thousand and one similar situations that arose in the day-to-day running of a small business. Or did I really care? More to the point, at this time, resonances of an earlier undergraduate period came to mind. I had started the business shortly after I had graduated; at the time, I really did not know what else to do. I remembered fondly the political philosophy seminars that I had attended: it was there that I had been at my happiest. I wondered what a philosopher such as Wittgenstein would have made of these particular 'language games' in which I seemed to be permanently involved. What would a critical theorist such as Habermas have made of the assumptions implicit in the 'systematically distorted communication' when I communicated with employees? At the time, I remember putting these lofty thoughts on one side, for it was clear that what I needed was a better understanding of 'control'. What I really required was some professional instruction on how to 'manage' people better in an organisation!

Becoming a manager?

On the other hand, though, perhaps I did know what I was doing, because shortly thereafter we were awarded the German distributorship for the UK. Turnover increased rapidly. Unfortunately, so did cash flow problems. These were a consequence of company turnover reaching the £1 million mark for the first time. The company was under-capitalised, so growth of this dimension was definitely problematic. The time had come, I felt, to stop being an entrepreneur and become a 'manager'; it was time to switch the firm's main focus temporarily from growth to consolidation. It now seems strange that I chose to make such a distinction between the two activities; but I did wonder if I did have the ability to be a 'real' manager.

At about this time, I saw an advert in the local press offering a part-time MBA course in a local institution. Finance and people – that was my problem, I reasoned, and the MBA obviously represented the answer to a personal prayer in these crucial areas of commerce. I had been told that MBAs were the 'Flash Harrys' of the business world; they had all of the answers. I attended the business school for an interview. I was interviewed by a gentleman approaching middle age who looked like a refugee from the 1960s – complete with a carefully cultivated 'Zapata' moustache and a haircut that looked like Sid's floor mop, the only difference being that Sid did not dye his mop to disguise its advanced age – all that was missing to complete the picture was an Afghan coat and a Bob Dylan album playing in the background. What the hell, this was academia, the people here were obviously different to the hairy-arsed electrical engineers that I had to deal with in my usual working environment – what had I to lose but my managerial ineptitude and the tax-deductible dollop of cash that represented the fees. I enrolled.

As it turned out, there did seem to be several people teaching on the MBA who seemed prepared to tell me how to 'manage'. Unfortunately, those who did seemed singularly unconvincing. It appeared obvious to me that these people had never had to deal with the really important issues that arise in industrial organisations – issues such as getting shit scraped off a toilet by a subordinate. Management was treated by members of this group as unproblematic. It seemed that orders had merely to be given to be obeyed by an enthusiastically compliant colleague. Many of my fellow students absorbed this learning as if it were holy writ – they obviously believed it! I rationalised interminably: the problem evidently rested in me; it was obvious that I was weak; and my personality would preclude me from ever joining the ranks of 'good', effective managers. Effectively, I felt that in the long term, I was doomed, I was a managerial 'wimp'. A cloak of self-doubt hung around me like the skin on a cold school rice pudding. But one effect of this new environment was that I had acquired the 'taste' for education again, so should I go back and enrol for that postgraduate degree in political philosophy that I had half-heartedly started when I first graduated all those years ago? Fortunately, at this time I encountered a small group of management lecturers who presented a subject that questioned the whole basis of the validity of the managerial prerogative, who offered a different perspective on organisational behaviour. The majority of my fellow students appeared to hate these people in so far as they claimed that there were no simple answers, merely 'uncertainty', which one had to learn to live with. I think that I knew this already but to this point had assumed that it must be myself that was wrong. There had to be an answer. Given this new data, where now was the holy writ? What had happened to the tablets of stone, the 'official' theory (Anthony 1986) offered by other members of the teaching staff? Questions that I had tried to ignore previously came to the fore. What was the nature and basis of managerial control? Why did some managers appear to get a 'kick' from power and the domination of others while others, such as myself, did not?

These questions took me back to my undergraduate days, to a time when I was reading for a law and politics degree and had illusions about becoming a barrister. In my second year in law school, I joined one of the Inns of Court in London and started the obligatory 'dining-in' to fulfil the criteria of membership. My perception at the time was that never in my life had I encountered so many pretentious people to the square metre as I did at 'the Inn'. It appeared to be full of people desperately pretending to be something that they were not. Something in the back of my mind made me very uncomfortable with this type of behaviour, and I consequently decided that a career at the bar was not for me after all. This feeling of dissonance was echoed to a large extent on the MBA, where I also experienced students' behaviour as disconcertingly familiar. A strange and, at the time, unplaceable feeling of *déjà vu* occurred frequently in their presence. With my fellow students, I felt myself to be an 'outsider', part of but not in the group. Many of these MBA students, to my mind at least, appeared to think of themselves as almost 'precious', part of an elite. 'Anointed', 'special', even 'arrogant', were adjectives that immediately sprang to mind at that time when describing what appeared to be their attitude to themselves. But during this period I was ignoring the knowledge of the influence that my own 'masks' had on my behaviour, to use what I later came to recognise as a Goffmanesque dramaturgical metaphor (Goffman 1967).

First reflections

These feelings of discomfort came to a head during an MBA 'residential' in a hotel in a nearby city. It was during this 'residential' that I looked long and hard at myself and realised, painfully, that I did not like what I saw – I realised that in my own way I was just as phoney as everybody else. I looked at my colleagues and realised that the feelings of *déjà vu* that I had experienced were grounded in my childhood memories of school, and particularly of the similar attitudes of the theological students who constituted half of the Irish Catholic college in which I spent my teenage years. It was at this time that I began to wonder whether the MBA was merely a vehicle that allowed access into yet another belief system, one that was as grounded in ritual and theological certainty as was the Catholic priesthood (the metaphor of the 'newly ordained' MBA 'laying hands' on the sick company in order to bring it back to health, springs to mind here). Resonances of the half-formed questions that I had asked myself during my youth came again to my mind. The truth is that they had never really gone away. Who the hell was I? What was it that made us behave in the way that we did, I asked myself? Why was I surprised by Sid's refusal to clean the toilet when requested? Why did the formative experiences of my youth still influence my perceptions so strongly? I realised that many of these questions had been at the back of my mind for a long time. An understanding of why I was attracted to philosophy as a subject became clearer. I needed answers, I needed certainties, and I, like most other people, had blinded myself to the 'reality' of everlasting uncertainty. Here lay the magnetic seductiveness of philosophy, as I am sure it must have done for many other people who also needed 'answers' in their lives. It was at this point that I felt I knew that Descartes' 'method of doubting' transcended mere scepticism (Descartes 1988). Can we really ever know anything for certain except that we are sentient and thinking beings? I had been well and truly 'decentred' by the experience of the weekend.

Dialectical reasoning

But where did this leave me as far as my management career was concerned? On the one hand, of what practical use were many of the traditional models taught by some members of the business school? On the other hand, like those people who claim that musically the Beatles said all that there was to be said in the 1960s, I was rapidly arriving at the belief that the German philosopher Hegel (1977) had identified much of what was important in the realm of management all those years ago.

> The work of Georg Wilhelm Hegel (1770–1831) influenced many subsequent philosophers, including Karl Marx. His writings have therefore strongly influenced the course of nineteenth- and twentieth-century world history. One of Hegel's more important philosophical concepts was that of the 'dialectic'. Hegel thought that all logic and world history followed a dialectical path whereby all internal contradictions were transcended, but these gave rise to new contradictions, which themselves required resolution (Singer 1983).

Why did Hegel influence my view of management? Well, my perception by this time was that much management education was grounded in the idea that human beings are essentially rational creatures, that human behaviour is somehow predictable and rational. Answers in management, exemplified by the proponents of 'official' theory, were to be found in an inverted image of ourselves, an idealised image whereby we and others were capable of overcoming our raw 'animal' irrational selves. Put simply, the new inhabitant of the business school is, in effect, a flawed and imperfect being seeking perfection for him or herself through the acquisition of arcane knowledge and, more to the point, learning how to create it in others. The language of psychoanalysis might help to explain this concept more clearly.

> Freud divided the mind into three 'provinces', the *id*, the *ego* and the *superego*. These 'provinces' have no actual existence as such but are hypothetical constructs used by Freud to explain his theories. The id is the seat of the *pleasure principle*, and its sole aim is to seek satisfaction of pleasurable drives. The ego is governed by the *reality principle*, which it tries to substitute for the pleasure principle of the id. The superego is guided by the *idealistic principle*, but as it has no contact with reality it is unrealistic in its demands for perfection. The superego has two subsystems, the *conscience* and the *ego-ideal*; the former is thought to develop as a result of punishment, while the latter is thought to develop as a result of rewarding 'proper behaviour'. The ego-ideal is therefore grounded in the notion of what ought to be (Freud 1933/1990).

The ego-ideal, to use one of these psychoanalytical concepts, is rather like what we know as 'virtual reality' in the present day; however, the paradox of the ego-ideal is that like virtual reality, you can *see* that perfection exists, but it does not exist in the 'real' world. It definitely exists, so to speak, but only in a parallel universe.

To emphasise this point, I am reminded of a question asked by a postgraduate management student in a seminar. 'Why do people not just do as they are told?,' I was asked by this student. My answer to this question was simple – if people did what they were told, why would we need managers in the first place? However, it is the implications of the question that are important. First, there is an assumption in the question that people are, or should be, susceptible to rational control systems; but, second, the question is underpinned by what appears to be an inverted caricature of reality. If we use the language of psychoanalysis again to explain this phenomenon, the student's question appears to assume that the ego-ideal is unaffected by a demanding id and is somehow sustained by a severe superego imperative, an idea that we can somehow control the irrational aspirations of the superego (the superego, like the id, being those parts of our mental life that are totally irrational in their demands on us). So the student's question reflects what we might describe as a mirror image of reality – a reality that appears to be commonly held by some teachers in business schools, who espouse a more functionalist approach to management education, and by some practising managers.

Hegel recognised 'inversions' of this type in his description of an 'upside-down' world in his *The Phenomenology of Spirit* (1977: 97):

> According, then, to this law of this inverted world, what is *like* in the first world is *unlike* to itself, and what is *unlike* in the first world is equally *unlike* to itself, or it becomes *like* itself.

If we use a religious metaphor to explain this phenomenon, this dialectic suggests that 'here', where sin and injustice reign, can ideally be 'inverted', through due process, to 'there'. 'There' is where we can find, through repentance and prayer and subsequent salvation, the purity and justice that cannot be achieved 'here'. My perception is that for the average person who is new to the study of management, the 'modern' organisation, characterised by uncertainty, ambiguity and imperfection, can be 'inverted', through acquired arcane knowledge, to clarity, certainty and perfection – an organisational *nirvana* characterised by the unquestioning compliance of its staff. Like the old Desmond Dekker song from the 1970s, 'You Can Get It If You Really Want', you only have to reach out and grab it! But the problem remains that this perfect world, as it remains 'virtual', and thereby never 'real', must always be merely symbolic – it eludes the grasp, a symbolic world that is always and everywhere absent but also paradoxically always 'virtually' omnipresent.

It might be argued that much management education, like its religious counterpart, must remain hooked into this symbolic and 'inverted' world in order to survive, for it is through this contradictory dialectic that it produces its *raison d'être*. If this were not the case, what would be the rationale for the business school and management training in the first place? Outside of teaching the 'mechanics' of IT or the 'composition' of a balance sheet, of what use would it be to the modern organisation? But an additional problem raised by this Hegelian theme is that this 'inverted' world is itself already inverted:

> We have to think pure change, or *think antithesis within the antithesis itself*, or *contradiction*. For in the difference there is an inner difference, the opposite is not merely *one* of *two* – if it were, it would simply *be*, without being an opposite – but it is the opposite of an opposite, or the other is itself immediately present in it.
>
> (*ibid.*: 99)

Perhaps this 'double inversion' of our pre-existing world hinges on our own pretensions and stupidities. Could it not be argued that it is this double inversion that the management 'guru' identifies, in fact depends on, and ultimately 'hooks' into in order to offer what pass for 'answers' for the credulous? If we look at our existing world from its 'inverted' perspective, that is from that virtual reality position of the ego-ideal, it must appear a ridiculous spectacle. My own experience of organisations suggests that some everyday examples of this second inversion might include 'posturing', 'brown nosing', back stabbing or 'empire building', or any number of other such 'cluster behaviours' encountered in the modern organisation (see for example, Hodson 1991).

Can you think of examples of these 'cluster behaviours' that you might have observed in operation in your own organisation? Using a dialectical approach, think of your own workplace from the position of the 'ego-ideal' and see what you come up with.

It is within this virtual reality position that I believe the 'guru' thrives by identifying the 'ideal' from a parallel universe. He or she views the organisation and discovers opportunities by looking back through a second inversion. 'Answers' are then offered that will 'resolve' those problems that are identified by the guru – 'answers' that invariably involve control, no matter how well disguised they might be. Indeed, the Swedish organisational theorist Czarniawska-Joerges (1993: 17) identifies such 'answers' as linguistic 'control devices' and suggests that those who supply these 'answers', such as consultancy firms and university departments, are actually suppliers of production tools for the 'manufacturers of control' in organisations. It might be asked to what use these production tools are put. A sceptic could argue that they lead to nothing but a continuous hysterical tinkering with the fabric of organisations – change for change's sake – a situation that results in either a continuous and inexorable tightening of control or, in many situations, to unmitigated chaos within the organisation.

In this context, I think that it might also be said that many of the highly abstruse metaphysical doctrines of management, such as those of 'quality management', could be interpreted as part of a greater cosmology that has its foundations in control – a cosmology serving as a direct corollary to its religious counterpart. Tuckman (1993: 54), for example, argues that the very emergence of TQM is an attempt to create new forms of managerial and political control, a control that arises not by coercion but through the consent of those involved. Following the TQM analogy, there is, I believe, a sense in which both 'quality' management and religion are underpinned by the illusion of an attainable 'perfection' that can be achieved through practice and adherence to the rhetoric of 'right first time'. Are both systems not intended to create an unbroken continuum between the theoretical and the behavioural? This puts me in mind of the seminary where if I do the 'right' thing, 'salvation' is there for the asking, the 'right thing' (whatever that might be) ensuring that the chances of 'rejection' by a 'higher' authority are minimised. Yet another way of looking at this might be to suggest that in the case of both quality management and religion, the control is depoliticised. Those doing the control, the priests and those who are in charge of quality initiatives, are merely neutral conduits for the 'word' as laid down in the 'gospels'. Those exercising control are, in its performance, merely performing a fundamental religious activity in distinguishing between the 'sacred' and the 'profane', so it cannot really be defined as the exercise of power and control in a traditional context. Might I therefore suggest that it is not by accident that those individuals who developed the doctrines of quality management, such as Deming and Oakland, are termed 'gurus' by their acolytes, the usual synonym for a spiritual leader. My experience in seminars with students working for a masters or postgraduate diploma in quality management is that they will inevitably refer to these 'gurus' in the same hushed and reverential tones that a 'devout' Catholic will use when referring to Mother Teresa of Calcutta or to the Papacy.

Can you think of any 'systems' that are in place in your own organisation that are intended to ensure compliance without the direct intervention of a superior?

To recapitulate, the perspectives held by those new to the study of management frequently serve to emphasise the nature of this 'already inverted' world postulated by Hegel, a parallel universe where 'perfection' is possible. I have to be honest and admit that as far as this chapter is concerned, these perspectives were 'everyday' and 'taken for granted' by myself; in fact, I had ceased to think of them as unusual until I underwent the process of writing this chapter. Such is the nature of reflexivity. This is a state of affairs acknowledged by Garfinkel (1984: 35) when he informs us:

> Familiar scenes of everyday activity, treated by members as the 'natural facts of life', are massive facts of the members' daily existence both as a real world and as a product of activities in a real world.

To put this into some sort of context, one of the first seminars that is held for first-year undergraduates at the institution where I teach addresses the question 'what is management?' I ask the students during these sessions to discuss the 'nature' of management, and why they as individuals want to be part of it. The following are fairly representative of the multiplicity of responses that have been given:

- I want to control people.
- I want to tell people what to do.
- Managers have real power.
- Managers can get things done.
- Managers set the agenda in an organisation.
- Managers can motivate people in the workplace.

As one 'wannabe' Gordon Gecko said to the group during one of these first-year seminars:

> Yeah – I want some of that too, I like the idea of being in a position to control people.

When I asked the same person how he saw the bulk of his time being used as a manager, his ingenuous response was:

> I expect to be making decisions, and other people will carry them out. I'll have the authority to make them do as I tell them.

Talk about an imaginary 'inverted' world of compliant subordinates! Of course, this last statement is a perfectly 'meaningful' one in the same sense that 'This is a warp drive engine, Captain Kirk' or 'Beam me up, Scottie' are also meaningful. But it is hardly a senseful 'perceptual' statement from an undergraduate in so far as my own experiences of getting toilets cleaned has taught me that the speaker had as much chance of 'making people do exactly what I tell them' as he or she has of making a career with Starfleet Command fighting Klingons. The naïveté of responses such as these, as well as initially driving the tutor (me) momentarily speechless, can take a considerable length of time to 'unpack' in seminars (I have subsequently learned how to maintain an ironic distance during these 'happenings'). This is not a reflection on the intellectual capacity of the students; it is just that their notions of what 'doing' management means are grounded in ideological preconceptions – put another way, it seems that they are like seismologists tracking the spirit of the age. Not that this state of affairs is unique to students – some writers on management echo this frightening preoccupation with control and domination in their work – texts such as that offered by Kakabadse (1985) can demonstrate a quite breathtaking arrogance when it comes to issues around dealing with subordinates. There appear to be some specific preconceptions of the nature of management, and many students appear to recognise 'ideologically' what the function of management is – and I suppose that we could argue in this context that this recognition excludes reflective cognition in that it is based on assumptions of intersubjectivity (Crossley 1996). 'Everybody *knows* this without having to articulate it, don't they?' appears to be the subtext of statements of this nature, a sense of something that is *said* to be so and therefore *is* so. It appears to be very much 'taken-for-granted' knowledge, to use the language of the sociologist. To counterbalance this apparently one-perspective position, many other responses from the seminars that I referred to above focus on 'communication' or 'earning potential' in the management arena; however, in my experience, it is the perception that one can 'control' or 'motivate' subordinate 'others' that is the primary rationale for many of those contemplating management as a career. However, it must be said that explanations based on 'wealth accretion' or sumptuous lifestyles are frequently articulated, seemingly grounded in the notion that 'conspicuous consumption' is synonymous with 'happiness'.

How do you define the 'nature' of management? Perhaps more to the point, how would *you* define a good manager? Is such a definition possible?

But should these perceptions surprise us? Perhaps Rorty puts his finger neatly on the point when he says:

> there is nothing deep inside each of us, no common human nature, no built-in human solidarity, to use as a moral reference point. *There is nothing to people except what has been socialised into them* – their ability to use language, and thereby to exchange beliefs and desires with other people.
>
> (1980: 177; my italics)

'There is nothing to people except what has been socialised into them', as Rorty puts it; so perhaps one ought not to be judgemental of misconceptions about 'doing' management. Are these students not merely echoing an inevitable *Weltanschauung*, that is to say that they are echoing a specific world view that affects their beliefs and conduct (and what has morality to do with management anyway)? These graduate or postgraduate students are members, or aspiring members, of a community that has created a common social reality around control. At least one writer (Ritzer 1996: 106) claims that those whom the teacher encounters in the seminar room are those who have submitted to control mechanisms themselves in order to end up in university.

However, these possible explanations notwithstanding, many of the assumptions held by those new to the study of management can still afford some fascinating primary data for the organisational sociologist. The management of human resources appears to be perceived by many management students as an unproblematic activity, and my experience suggests that it is thought by them to be one that they can, and will, be taught. 'What is a good manager?' or 'What is the best way to motivate people?' are just two examples of the type of question I am asked regularly in seminars. As in the seminary attended by the religious postulant, it appears that many business students are locked into the fantasy dimension of the ego-ideal. For the religious, it is the somewhat misanthropic notion that the self is imperfect in that it is stained by 'original sin', but this can be overcome and controlled – in other words, 'redemption' is an ever-present possibility. In a similar manner, it appears that the same misanthropic rationale applies to the business school student. Others are imperfect, whether due to 'original sin' or not, but *they*, the subordinates, can also be readily controlled and motivated by use of the arcane expertise that comes with acquisition of a specific qualification. In both cases, the perception appears to be that appropriate skills can be gained through being given received 'truths' as if piped through a conduit. (With me positioned in this metaphysical dreamland as one of the 'suppliers'!) From the position of the conceptual ego-ideal, the absurdity of this position is obvious. As Hegel (*ibid.*) might have put it, our existing world is already 'inverted' between reality and its idealised counterpart, with our 'normal' world, viewed from this hypothetical 'perfect' position, appearing as a ridiculous spectacle in that it is already 'inverted' in itself. The nearest appropriate analogy might be the anthropomorphism of a Tom and Jerry cartoon, which in effect caricatures the absurdity of the human condition in that it caricatures 'normal' human behaviour. Might one suppose that the subtext of this genre is to ridicule the absurdities of everyday behaviour from an 'inverted' position? Perhaps justifiably in this context, we could afford to be slightly more cynical of much management education. Given the ideological foundations of students' understanding, perhaps one could be tempted to paraphrase Oscar Wilde and claim that many of the new inhabitants of the business school might be defined as 'the unspeakable in pursuit of the unreachable', but then the perceptions articulated are not of their own creation.

My argument has been that management has come to be defined by many as part of a set of 'self-evident truths', with 'management is synonymous with control' being the central premise of its unfolding development. In an effort to make sense of this ideological position, I intend to return to the dialectical philosophy of Hegel. However, to contextualise this, at this point I would like to consider briefly the position on knowledge adopted by another German philosopher and predecessor to Hegel, Immanuel Kant – more specifically to focus on Kant's distinction between the concepts of *a priori* and *a posteriori* knowledge. For the distinction between the *a priori* and the *a posteriori* is, I believe, one issue that is central to ideologically created perceptions of 'doing' management.

The *a priori* is knowledge that is free of empirical contingencies, in other words, it is knowledge that is true simply by definition, in so far as it does not depend for its authority on the evidence of experience (Moser 1987). So, if I were to make a statement such as 'Harry's father is a male', 'Joe's aunt is a woman', these would be examples of *a priori* or 'analytic' knowledge, because in theory neither statement could be proved false through experience. In other words, I do not have to meet Harry's father to know that he must by definition be male. Simple analytic truths do not give us any additional understanding of the world, so if I were to say 'It is either raining or it is not', the statement is true by the meanings of the words.

On the other hand, if I were to say that 'Harry's father is a transvestite', 'Joe's aunt sucks lollipops while trimming her beard' or 'peaceful resistance is effective', these would represent *a posteriori* or 'synthetic' statements, because they are contingent truths, and experience could prove them to be false. For example, I may discover on meeting Joe's aunt that she dislikes all sweet confections intensely and is not at all hirsute! The essence of all synthetic statements is that they contain new information in their predicates that may or may not prove to be 'true'. However, let us consider other statements, such as 'all bodies have mass' or 'peaceful resistance shuns violence'. In neither of these statements is the concept of the predicate contained in the subject, so while these statements are not analytic, they are nonetheless true. These statements are examples of what Kant defines as 'synthetic *a priori*' knowledge.

Now, what I am suggesting is that it can be argued that it is to the latter group of synthetic *a priori* statements that many students and practitioners ascribe the essence of management – 'management is synonymous with control' – a taken-for-granted truism that appears to be as analytically 'true' to many management students as much as is the truth of 'rain is wet'. How this particular 'truism' arises in the first place would be the subject of another chapter, so I will have to settle here for an attempted refutation of this ideological position on philosophical grounds.

First, it would be too simple to refute this perception simply by claiming that the boundaries between the analytic and the synthetic are so blurred as to render them almost meaningless. Recent philosophers such as Quine and Putnam have dismantled these concepts beyond rehabilitation. We all 'know' that the Earth was once flat, and that the notion of the 'epicycle' was considered *analytic* prior to the Copernican revolution. Was not phlogiston an *analytic* 'truth' prior to the discovery of oxygen? – and let us not even consider 'Harry's father' in the era of the sex-change operation! As Quine (in Honderich 1995: 739) tells us, the analytic–synthetic distinction has to be abandoned, because 'any statement can be held true come what may, if we make drastic enough adjustments elsewhere in the system.'

The intention of my assertions regarding newcomers to the study of management and the nature of analytic truths was not to set up a 'straw man' in order to easily beat the stuffing out of it, but to demonstrate the scepticism of modern philosophy towards the 'truth value' of analytic statements. Indeed, even more recent work, such as that of the philosopher Richard Rorty (1980), has laid to rest any notion that a secure foundation can exist that would act as a touchstone for knowledge; and as he tells us of Kant's philosophy:

> Kant put philosophy 'on the secure path of science' by putting outer space inside inner space (the space of the constituting activity of the transcendental ego) and then claiming Cartesian certainty about the inner for the laws of what had previously been thought the outer. He thus reconciled the Cartesian claim that we can only have certainty with the fact that we already had certainty – *a priori* knowledge – about what seemed not to be ideas.
>
> (Rorty 1980: 137)

This point enables me to return to the dialectical philosophy of Hegel, a philosopher who balked at the notion of any fixed *a priori*, self-evident 'truths', and who saw reason as always relative to reality. Knowledge develops, according to Hegel, not like a mathematical deduction but like a tree blossoming. This wonderful metaphor is to be found in the first few pages of *The Phenomenology of Spirit* and is one that appears to dominate his dialectical thinking:

> The bud disappears in the bursting forth of the blossom, and one might say that the former is refuted by the latter; similarly, when the fruit appears, the blossom is shown up in its turn as a false manifestation of the plant, and the fruit now emerges as the truth of it instead. These forms are not just distinguished from one another, they also supplant each other as mutually incompatible. Yet at the same time their fluid nature

makes them moments of an organic unity in which they not only do not conflict, but in which each is as necessary as the other; and this mutual necessity alone constitutes the life of the whole.

(Hegel 1977: 2)

In contrast to Kant's insistence on a world filled with pure, rational knowledge, Hegel offers us a world filled with uncertainty and contradiction; our knowledge, according to Hegel, is always fragmentary and incomplete. A bud cannot be a blossom or a fruit at the same time, but all are part of a flow – like knowledge, it is a question of *becoming*. We cannot say at what point a river is its 'truest', in the same way that no idea can lay claim to the possibility of its eternal 'truth'. Similarly in management, there are no absolutes, for as a discipline it is also constantly in the process of *becoming*. As one 'absolute' arises laying claim to veracity, another contradictory claim will emerge to challenge it; and out of this dialectical process emerges the synthesis, the *negation of the negation*. And thus it always was, and presumably always will be. But then I think I have already demonstrated that I cannot be certain about anything, so who knows! The question that should perhaps be asked is: 'is this not the pathway to "understanding" down which those who aspire to management as a career should be heading?

Conclusion

Perhaps most management training attempts to reinforce the idea that we can exorcise or, at the very least, minimise contradiction and uncertainty, while the reality is that we cannot. In order to address what appear to be the high levels of certainty experienced by many management practitioners and business students, would not the study of subjects not normally found on the business school curriculum help people to live with the complexity and high levels of ambiguity found in the modern organisation? Perhaps it is within an interdisciplinary approach to management understanding that a significant contribution to the intellectual growth of practitioners can be achieved.

As for me, I think that I have just about got it now, so come back Sid, all is forgiven. Honestly!

References

Anthony, P. (1986) *The Foundation of Management*, London: Tavistock.

Crossley, N. (1996) *Intersubjectivity – The Fabric of Social Becoming*, London: Sage.

Czarniawska-Joerges, B. (1993) *The Three Dimensional Organisation – A Constructionist View*, Lund: Chartwell Bratt.

Descartes, R. (1988) 'Meditation One'. In G. Bowie, M. Michaels and R. Solomon (eds) *Twenty Questions: An Introduction to Philosophy*, San Diego: Harcourt Brace Janovitch.

Freud, S. (1933/1990) *New Introductory Lectures on Psychoanalysis*, The Penguin Freud Library Vol. 2, Harmondsworth: Penguin.

Garfinkel, H. (1984) *Studies in Ethnomethodology*, Cambridge: Polity Press.

Goffman, E. (1967) *Presentation of Self in Everyday Life*, Harmondsworth: Penguin.

Hegel, G.F. (1977) *The Phenomenology of Spirit* (trans. A.V. Miller), Oxford: Clarendon Press.

Hodson, R. (1991) 'The Active Worker: Compliance and Autonomy at the Workplace', *Journal of Contemporary Ethnography* 20 (1): 47–78.

Honderich, T. (1995) *The Oxford Companion to Philosophy*, Oxford University Press.

Kakabadse, A. (1985) *The Politics of Management*, Aldershot: Gower.

Moser, P.K. (1987) *A Priori Knowledge*, Oxford University Press.

Ritzer, G. (1996) *The McDonaldisation of Society*, Thousand Oaks, CA: Pine Forge Press.

Rorty, R. (1980) *Philosophy and the Mirror of Nature*, Oxford: Basil Blackwell.

Rorty, R. (1991) *Contingency, Irony and Solidarity*, Cambridge University Press.

Singer, P. (1983) *Hegel*, Oxford University Press.

Tuckman, A. (1993) 'Ideology, Quality and TQM'. In A. Wilkinson and H. Willmott (eds) *Making Quality Critical: New Perspectives on Organisational Change*, London: Routledge.

9 Nothing starts from nowhere

David Currie

Introduction

In this chapter, we will be exploring the important contribution made by the concept of the social construction of reality in our explorations in and critical thinking about management. The chapter draws on the work of two sociologists, Peter Berger and Thomas Luckmann, introduced briefly in Chapter 2, whose text, *The Social Construction of Reality*, has provided a seminal contribution to the development of our thinking in sociology.

However, for the next few thousand words, I am going to adopt a less conventional style than you have so far encountered in this book in order to widen the scope of our explorations. I shall be attempting to produce a reflexive text where my intention is to try to 'find some way of exemplifying … rather than just offering a disengaged description' (Cooper and Woolgar 1993) of the concepts under consideration. Readers of a more nervous disposition may wish to proceed directly to a second introduction, which can be found later in the piece (imaginatively headed 'Introduction too') and through to the end of the chapter before coming back to read what now follows.

Nothing starts from nowhere (again)

'Right then, for next week I want you all to read the short story I'm about to hand out. It's called "Glenmore Breakpoint", and it will help us to prepare for next week's session on the social construction of reality.'

Glenmore Breakpoint (a short story by Jimmy McNietzsche)

It didn't need to be like this. Well, that's what he told himself anyway. There must be a thousand different ways he could do it. Sadly, the other nine hundred and ninety-nine eluded him. He was unhappy. He had started out with such good intentions. Things were going to be different this time. But no! He had done things just exactly as he had always done. And so he found himself feeling trapped by his own behaviour and threatened by the inevitable consequences of his repeated actions. Bollocks!

Bollocks? What the hell is that about. He wasn't in the habit of saying 'bollocks'. He was usually much more effusive in his choice of expletive. He was holding back. Self-censoring. He knew that others would read and judge him. But he also knew that his editor, the publishers even, would not have objected to one of his more usual utterances. But what are editors' and publishers' and readers' judgements compared with his mother's. He wasn't sent to Sunday school for all those years on all those cold, grey Maryhill Sunday mornings to come out with obscenities. Even more evidence of being trapped. Bastard! **BASTARD!**

Bastard? He can write 'bastard' as often and as boldly as he likes but no one will be fooled by it. It's a hollow act of bravado. Perhaps when he grows up, we might be more persuaded by such things, but meantime we recognise it for what it is; no, picking your nose in the pub and breaking wind – breaking wind? more censorship – farting on the bus are definitely not evidence of breaking the chains. And what do I mean, 'when he grows up'? *If* he grows up is much more to the point.

Well at least he managed to end that paragraph without one of his pathetic little outbursts. Does this indicate progress? No, I don't think we can claim that. Anyway, lest we digress – and I think he would rather enjoy a digression at this juncture – like it or not, he still has to face up to his predicament. Or I should say his current, most pressing, predicament. Because I can assure you that predicaments are not in short supply. You've probably already gathered that from what's gone on so far. And I think it's timely for us to spot this. Because his other favourite ploy is to write about not getting on with the task in hand in such a way that he tries to create the appearance of activity. He calls this 'self-reflexivity' and claims that it's at the leading edge of management research. Pretentious prat!

Quite!

In fact, his entire repertoire consists of this one theme, which he regurgitates over and over, ever more tediously. Although in fairness, he appears to have some appreciation of the tedium. That said, it doesn't stop him from doing it. Can you imagine what a Cliff Richard concert would be like if he sang one song twenty times over? What, you say he does? Okay, bad choice. What about Mike Oldfield then? Now *Tubular Bells*, that was surely a seminal offering. A defining moment for an entire generation? What? He's just released *Tubular Bells 3 – A Dance Remix*? Bloody hell!

This expletive business is catching. Okay, so perhaps he isn't unique in terms of returning to this recurring theme. Perhaps we might even recognise a Nitzschean flavour to this. And who is being a pretentious prat, now? That's catching as well. While we're on the subject: did you know that Cliff Richard stayed up the road from him in Maryhill (although upwardly mobile locals consider themselves to be in Kelvinside!) for a week back in the late fifties while performing a series of evangelical pop concerts in Glasgow? He claims it as one of his earliest memories: being taken in his pram to see the great Cliff. His best man, Davie, retold the tale at his wedding and made a joke about him and Cliff having shared the same interest in celibacy in the 30 years since. That's friends for you!

What does it mean when we say things like that? No, it must mean something: 'there you go'; 'that's life'; 'enough said'. Funny business. Words, I mean. But hold on! We're letting him off the hook here. These little diversions. The jolly banter. It's a smokescreen. The game's up. 'The game's up' – that's another one. What game? Up where? What does it mean? The game's still up no matter how much he might try to tell us the contrary. We're well into the piece and all there's been so far is a half-hearted reference to Nietzsche. And to the best of my knowledge that wasn't quite his brief. Time to get tough. Kick some ass. Throw the book at the bastard. Throw which book, exactly? Not this one surely? It doesn't exist yet. Oh! the rule book! Is that what that means? What rules? Let's throw the book and kick some ass anyway.

He was suddenly distracted. Although in fairness, it didn't ever take much to distract him. He had never quite seen her in this light before – and no!, don't ask what light, it's just a saying, okay? Slowly, she started to edge towards him. That looked like a new dress. At least he had never noticed it before. Perhaps it was an old dress, then. Let's just agree that it was 'new' to him. But let's not worry too much about the details regarding the dress, because even as I was telling you about it, she had started to remove it. First the left shoulder strap. Then the right. Soon not a shred of evidence of the dress having ever adorned her could be found on her body. Meanwhile he hadn't been slow to size up the situation and had followed her lead and just as slowly divested himself of his dress. He was now walking towards her …

'Right, that's it! You really have gone too far now. You're way beyond the edge. Not even you can justify this little episode. You're out of the game, pal. Finished. Washed up.'

'Whatdoyoumean,washedup?,I   …   bastardandI'mnotmakingthisup,thespacebaron-mykeyboardhasstoppedworking.Honest.It'sthetruth!!'

'Pathetic! Absolutely bloody pathetic! Don't you agree? That's it, I want nothing more to do with you. How about that? Have you ever seen anything remotely as bad as he's just written?'

'Well … '

'Oh, come off it. It's just rubbish. And as for that last little trick with the spacebar on his keyboard. Is that really the best he can come up with?'

'Maybe it did actually malfunction.'

'Don't be daft, of course it didn't. It was just a stupid stunt.'

'How can you be so sure about the keyboard. It might actually …'

'No! I'm not buying that. The whole piece is a load of unmitigated crap. He's out! So, are you in?'

'Well, I … '

'For God's sake, man, what is there to think about. It's the big chance you've been waiting for. Your chance to get published. What do you need to think about?'

'Sure, I want to get published, but you asked him to do the chapter and somehow it just doesn't seem ethical for me to take his place like this.'

'Ethical my arse. He had his chance and he's blown it big time. I mean, Cliff Richard, sex scenes – and there's an unlikely combination if ever there was one. Just tell me what the hell any of that thousand words of crap has to do with Berger and Luckmann? Eh? Can you? No, of course you can't. So, will you take over the writing of this chapter?'

'As I was trying to say, it just doesn't feel right.'

'What have feelings got to do with it? It's just a job, for God's sake.'

'Well actually, I think feelings are very important.'

'Rubbish. Business – and publishing's a business in case you're forgetting – is about the bottom line, making profits. Feelings, yours, mine, or anyone else's for that matter, simply don't come into the equation. All I'm looking for is someone i.e. YOU, to take over the writing of this chapter.'

'But he might actually have been working to the brief. You did stop him after only a thousand words. He was really only getting started.'

'Rubbish! If he couldn't spell out in his first five hundred words never mind a thousand just exactly what he was going to be doing in his chapter, well as far as I'm concerned that's all the evidence I need to convince me that he wasn't up to it.'

'That's a bit simplistic. Why should an author "spell out exactly" what's going on. Isn't it up to readers to think for themselves, sometimes at least, just occasionally?'

'In a work of fiction, perhaps. Yes, I can agree with that. But this is an academic text we're talking about. And that's different.'

'Why?'

'Why? I'll tell you why. Because academic texts are just different. Everyone knows they have to be written in a particular way – everyone except this idiot, that is.'

'But who says that academic texts have to be written in a particular style. Is the situation really so certain, so unambiguous. I mean, my life is full of ambiguity and uncertainty, and while I don't deny that it would be nice to get rid of some of it I've never really found a lasting solution.'

'It doesn't really matter whether your life, or mine for that matter, is full or empty of ambiguity and uncertainty. Just take my word for it – I know what a book about management should look like. Now, will you take over the chapter.'

'But have you discussed this with him. You know, given him some feedback about your reservations?'

'Reservations? They're hardly reservations. The piece is crap. He's beyond the pale. So, no! I haven't given him feedback. He's history as far as I'm concerned.'

'That's hardly fair, is it. I mean not even giving him feedback.'

'He'll get feedback enough when the book's published and he's not in it. Yes, I'm sure he'll find that more than enough feedback. And in any case, where did you get the idea that life was fair.'

'You're a hard woman.'

'You've got to be in this business. First sign of weakness and they're out to get you. And I mean really get you – no holds barred.'

'Who?'

'The management, and sometimes even other editors in the company.'

'I'm sure it's not as bad as that. I mean, surely people are professionals. And when it comes down to it, you're all on the same team at the end of the day.'

'Professionals? In name maybe. But this is a cut-throat business nowadays. And, yes they all talk about being on the same team, but nobody really means it. At the end of the day, at the end of my day anyway, it's "shit on or be shit upon". I mean, all these recent mergers and takeovers in the industry, they've really destabilised everyone. No one can afford to have a book flop. All that downsizing. It's really bad.'

'It's interesting that you should use the term "downsizing" in the present context. You mean redundancies, job losses, people being sacked, don't you?'

'Yes, I suppose I do. We all just use the jargon. And I guess it somehow doesn't sound quite so bad.'

'It might make it sound better from management's point of view, but how do the poor sods who have lost their jobs feel, eh? And for those who stay on, it must be so counter-productive. All that back-stabbing and back-watching must take up so much energy. Energy that could surely be put to better use. Not to mention having to work twice as hard as before.'

'Well, you might say that, and you might be right. But it's just the way things are. No point fighting it, no point at all. You know, when I came here at first, I took everyone at face value. Believed the rhetoric that we were all part of the same team, one big happy family. So the first few times another editor tried to drop me in it I didn't see it for what it really was. I just assumed that I had misunderstood his intentions. But I soon discovered that it was how everyone was. Now I know these things for what they actually are. But it's not like I actually blame the managers or the other editors. I mean, at the end of the day, they're just doing their jobs, aren't they? And what choice do they have? What choice do any of us have, really? None, if you ask me. At least not if we all want to keep our jobs. We've all got mortgages to pay at the end of the month.'

'That sounds quite depressing. I mean do you really have no choice. God, it sounds awful.'

'Not really. As I said, you do get used to it.'

'And it must rub off on how you treat your authors, surely?'

'Oh no! I don't think so. Definitely not. Well, some – yes – I guess I do lose my patience with some. Especially writers like this one. He deserves whatever I do to him.'

'It must have really changed you, then; made you hard, untrusting – and perhaps untrustworthy?'

'Not at all. It's just a job. Ask any of my friends. They'll tell you. It hasn't changed me one little bit. When I leave the office at the end of the day I go back to being myself. But look, I don't want to talk about me. What I want to know is whether you'll take on the chapter? Come on, a simple yes or no!'

'Hmmm! I really would like some time to think it over.'

'Unfortunately, time is the one thing we don't have. If you can't give me an answer now, just forget it. I can't spend any longer trying to persuade you. I'll find someone else. You know, you've missed a golden opportunity here. There'll be plenty of others ready to bite my hand off. This is going to be a gem of a book. Never mind, see you again sometime.'

'Cheers, yeah, see you.'

'I wonder if I've done the right thing? It's not as if I've actually got lots of offers at the moment. I wish I could feel more positive about the decisions I make. But I am sure about one thing, I'm glad I don't work in publishing. It sounded really horrible. All that political in-fighting and the redundancies. Thank goodness it's not like that in academia!'

Suddenly, the scene changes. (This takes us by surprise, as up to this point the author has chosen to omit detail about scenes. Perhaps he's too lazy to bother, or perhaps he thought it unnecessary. Or perhaps he thought you'd provide your own scenes – a study first, then an office, then perhaps a public house, one with real ale, of course, or maybe that last scene was played out in a car, or a toilet, or – and what a convenient device that is for an (alleged) author to let his reader do all the work. But now he tells us the scene is changing. What is going on?)

The scene changes from offstage right, where the narrator has been eating a cheese and pickle sandwich (in wholemeal bread, of course) washed down with a slightly warm but still refreshing bottle of French lager (and so providing an international dimension to the narrative), to offstage left. Two rather aloof men are engrossed in a deep and meaningful analysis of preceding events. Let's see what they have to say.

'What do you think? Any good? Do we need to scrap the lot? Can any of it be salvaged? You must admit, it's quite a good idea, isn't it? Tell me, tell me.'

'Mmm! It's taken nearly three thousand words to get to this point. Three thousand words!'

'Okay, but so what?'

'So what? The editor was voicing concern after only one thousand words and what's happened since? Another two thousand words, that's what.'

'Well, what's wrong with that? We've still got several thousand more to go.'

'But … '

'But?'

'But what's it all about. Where is it going? You're about a third of the way through the chapter and you've made only a few obscure remarks about Berger and Luckmann. I've no problem with the 'new literary form' aspect of the brief. That's okay. Well "okay" if you like that sort of thing – and on the evidence so far I can see why some people don't particularly like it. But the new literary form is only the medium. Instead it seems to have taken over. So Berger and Luckmann's ideas have been kept well in the background.'

'But what do you think about the casting, the characterisations, the costumes.'

'That's just my point. You've let the medium get in the way of the message. And this is surely why the postmodern concept of "serious fun" is such a shallow one. It allows people – including academics like you – to hide behind what appear to be clever, content-full narratives, which when stripped to the bones are actually very thin accounts. I take it you were trying to have "serious fun"?'

'You always make me feel really guilty.'

But before he could reply, another abrupt change occurs. Yet again we find ourselves in the company of two men. Collective brows are clearly furrowed – they must be thinking about management.

'Well, that's as far as I've got so far. What do you think. Am I on track, following my brief?'

'Mmm, yes, but … '

'Oh, I know your "yes, buts" – "yes, but" I've got to make it more rigorous, tighten the narrative up, ground it more in the literature. That sort of "yes but".'

'Yes, actually, that's what I meant. But I have every faith in you. There's just one more thing. I think this would be an opportune place to put your second introduction.'

'I was wondering about that. If you think so, then I guess that's good enough for me.'

Introduction too

As promised, here is the second introduction. I wonder how you got here? Did you come straight here from the earlier introduction, or have you worked your way through 'Glenmore Breakpoint'? Either way is fine by me. I haven't yet reverted to a more conventional academic register (style), but you won't have to wait much longer now as the process of transition has already commenced.

There is another change of scene. A lecturer is about to address a group of management students.

'You will recall that last week I asked you to read "Glenmore Breakpoint" as a prelude to this week's discussion on the social construction of reality. Yes? Good. Well I would still like us to look at Berger and Luckmann; however, since last week I have received indirect feedback that some of you are still struggling with the approach I'm taking here. Now, I've no problem with that, but to be honest I'm a little disappointed that you didn't try to sort it out with me first rather than talk to a third party. I thought I was approachable, open to feedback. But look, let's not dwell on this. What I propose we do is for me to highlight some of the key aspects of Berger and Luckmann's work in the light of our reading of "Glenmore Breakpoint". Then I suggest that I spend a little more time going over with you why I am taking the approach I am and why I think it's valid. Is that okay? Good.'

Perhaps an initial example might help to get to the core of Berger and Luckmann's treatise.

A few years ago, I was teaching some final-level undergraduates. They were doing a group activity, and one sub-group had completed ahead of the other. Two of the students in the finished group started to talk about the unit being studied and in particular the reading. I sidled over so that I could eavesdrop. The conversation went along the following lines:

'Have you bought any of the books yet?'

'No, but my grant has finally come through, so I'm going to go to the book-shop this afternoon. What about you, have you bought any?'

'Yes, I got Rogers – *On Becoming a Person* – and Berne – *Games People Play*. I enjoyed those, especially Berne. But I also got the Berger and Luckmann book. But it was rubbish, just rubbish. I couldn't make any sense of it, a complete waste of money.'

'Thanks for the warning.'

By this time I had moved right up to the students.

'I just heard what you were saying about Berger and Luckmann. I take it you didn't enjoy it then?'

'Er, no actually I thought it was just crap. Sorry, but that's what I think.'

'Didn't you get anything from it at all then?'

'No. Not really, just confused.'

'Okay, let's see if we can make something of it in terms of the conversation you've just had with each other about the merits of the text. Could we develop objective criteria that would definitively determine what constitutes a good, as opposed to a crap, text? Number of sales; number of pages; lack of typographic errors; level of interest that it raises in readers; critical acclaim; etc. Perhaps we could. But are they really objective? Could we not find deficiencies in each of these criteria? Just because a book sells well doesn't necessarily make it good; just because one reader gets nothing from a text doesn't mean that someone else won't experience it as the greatest read ever; and so on. No, I would argue that it would be difficult to agree on objective criteria that were free from subjec-tive interpretation.

'But, just think back to your conversation about the books on the reading list. This afternoon when you are browsing along the shelves in the bookshop you'll no doubt remember the details. 'Ah, yes, Rogers, Joanne said that was a good one and here's Berne, that was good too. Oh no, there's that horrible book by Berger and Luckmann, what was it she said, don't waste your money on that – it's crap.'

'Now, is it really crap? While we can't say objectively that it is crap we can at least determine that in your shared reality it is crap. Joanne tells you it's crap and subsequently your actions, influenced by what she has told you, maintain that social construction. And no doubt, given time, you'd be able to persuade many more of the seminar group that it is indeed crap. And this, very crudely put, is the core of Berger and Luckmann's text. That rather than us pursuing an objective reality already out there, waiting to be discovered through the applica-tion of appropriate research methods, reality is instead created by us through our social interactions with each other.'

'Why couldn't they just say that, then?'

Now that example, although real, is quite simplistic and reductionist in terms of Berger and Luckmann's text, but I think it does capture its essence. This concept is referred to as 'reification'.

> Reification is the apprehension of human phenomena as if they were things, that is, in non-human or possibly supra-human terms. Another way of saying this is that reification is the apprehension of the products of human activity as if they were something other than products – such as facts of nature, results of cosmic laws or manifestations of divine will. Reification implies that man is capable of forgetting his own authorship of the human world … The reified world is, by definition, a dehumanized world.
>
> (Berger and Luckmann 1966: 106)

Other important concepts in the social construction of reality include:

- objectivation
- institutionalisation
- internalisation
- legitimation

Let me say something briefly about each of these concepts before showing how they contribute to the process of reification.

Objectivation

'The process by which the externalized products of human activity attain the character of objectivity is objectivation' (*ibid*.: 78). Also,

> The reality of everyday life is not only filled with objectivations; it is only possible because of them. I am constantly surrounded by objects that 'proclaim' the subjective intentions of my fellowmen, although I may sometimes have difficulty being quite sure just what a particular object is 'proclaiming'.
>
> (*ibid*.: 50)

Most readers of this chapter have never met or even heard of me before. You know of my existence only through your reading of my work. This piece of work is an objectivation of the subjective process that I have gone through to create the chapter. The chapter is not me, but it is only through the chapter that you know of me. Berger and Luckmann are particularly interested in the role that language plays in objectivating our subjective realities. 'Everyday life is, above all, life with and by means of the language I share with my fellowmen' (*ibid*.: 52).

I once worked for a manager who held fairly regular staff meetings. Whenever he was criticised about decisions he had made, or about lack of resources, or whatever, he invariably pointed to the fact that he 'had a mortgage to pay off'. In other words, his actions were objectivated in terms of his need to meet his financial commitments. He also invariably made reference to our mortgages as well.

Thus, an understanding of objectivation highlights the role of language and our everyday social interactions in creating and maintaining our various realities. This is centrally relevant to seeing at a macro level the ways in which management theories have come into existence and at a micro level how we ourselves are involved in such reality creation.

Institutionalisation

> the developing human being not only interrelates with a particular natural environment, but with a specific cultural and social order, which is mediated to him by the significant others who have charge of him.
>
> *(ibid.*: 66)

> Social order is not biologically given … Social order exists only as a product of human activity.
>
> *(ibid.*: 70)

Berger and Luckmann go on to argue how institutions come into being. In the first instance, this involves the repetition of actions – habitualisation. Habitualisation frees us from the constant problem of having to make numerous decisions. For example, the wearing of a neck-tie by male employees was the habitual (customary) practice in the first two organisations I worked for. This meant that when dressing for work in the morning I did not have to spend time wondering whether or not to wear a tie. I still had to decide which tie to wear, so I was not entirely absolved from decision-making activity. You may consider this a trivial example. But just think of all the similar trivial events that occur in your daily routine. Indeed, these are probably so habitualised that you might not think of many at first, but once you start to recall them, you will soon realise that if you actually had to expend effort on them you would not have had much time or energy to get on with the really important tasks.

> Habitualisation provides the direction and the specialisation of activity that is lacking in man's biological equipment, thus relieving the accumulation of tensions that result from undirected drives.
>
> *(ibid.*: 71)

Institutionalisation arises out of our habitualisations:

> wherever there is a reciprocal typification of habitualised actions by types of actors … The typifications of habitualised actions that constitute actions are always shared ones.
>
> *(ibid.*: 72)

In other words, at the point at which one person can anticipate the action of another on the basis of past, often repeated actions, our habitualisations become typifications – what we always do – and if that understanding is reciprocated, then we have institutionalisation: we start to act in predetermined ways within understood parameters. We come to know 'how things are done around here'. Institutions can, therefore, be as few as two people or can be many times more. Management in an organisation can become institutionalised – as evidenced, for example, in 'Glenmore Breakpoint'. Similarly, the discipline of management can be seen to be institutionalised – as evidenced by the proliferation of MBAs, business studies degrees, management textbooks and so on. It is worth noting that this institutionalisation leads to further limiting of options in everyday decision-making situations. Berger and Luckmann also remind us that these institutions are entirely created by people, although we experience them as objective entities.

Internalisation

The next 'stage' is internalisation, by which process 'the objectivated social world is retrojected into consciousness in the course of socialization' (*ibid.*: 78–9).

While much of our socialisation takes place in the early years of our lives, we can also note the ongoing process of secondary socialisation that occurs throughout our lives. When we are inducted into a new organisation, we are going through a process of secondary socialisation. At first, we might still prefer to do the things that we did elsewhere, but at some stage (unless of course we leave) we internalise the new institutional order into our consciousness and start to act in accordance with the rules of engagement.

> Golding (1986: 196) gives the following interesting account of his first encounter with the managing director of a company he had just started to work in:
>
> > The meeting was, in fact, being held in the 'Round-Table Room' (that well-known symbol of hierarchies of control) and there were four other directors and three other managers present. Being engrossed in my files, I did not actually detect the precise moment of the Managing Director's entry, but I became aware that something was amiss, and on looking up saw that everyone in the room had stood up because the Managing Director had arrived. I made an embarrassed gesture of standing up, by which time everyone else had sat down. The Managing Director gave me a vague wave of his arms, perhaps even as embarrassed as myself – or perhaps annoyed that no-one had initiated me.
>
> We can see in this example, without making any value judgement about the nature of the institutional order in question, that Golding's lack of understanding of the way things were done caused a breakdown, how ever temporary, in the action. This appears to have been experienced by all concerned as an embarrassing episode. Can you think of a situation where you have experienced such a breakdown? What were the consequences for you or the other actors involved?

Legitimation

In the foregoing example, we can deduce that the institutional order was taken as legitimate by the actors involved in the light of their compliance with the rule. Golding actually points out that one or two of the actors had developed their own responses to the rule, which allowed them to appear to comply without actually complying. But they were the exception. Berger and Luckmann tell us that we can determine whether an institution is seen to be legitimate by the extent to which it can survive through time by the successful socialisation of the next generation into the social order. As they put it:

> The same story, so to speak, must be told to all the children … These legitimations are learned by the new generation by the same process that socialises them into the institutional order.
>
> (Berger and Luckmann 1966: 79)

Reification

It is but a short step to complete the process of our originally subjective creations coming to be experienced as objective entities not of our making. Berger and Luckmann refer to this as a paradox: 'man is capable of producing a world he then experiences as something other than a human product' (*ibid.*: 78).

Or to put it slightly differently:

- woman creates reality;
- woman internalises this subjective reality;
- woman comes to experience this subjective reality as an objective entity.

This recognition of the human agency at the core of our everyday reality is important, because it leads us to see that management theory is likewise not an objective entity out there waiting to be discovered. Rather, it is actively created by us – even us, right here, right now.

You might want to revisit 'Glenmore Breakpoint' to see if you can identify instances of reification, objectivation, institutionalisation and so on before proceeding further.

Implications for thinking about management

So, what if any are the implications of Berger and Luckmann's treatise for us? I will describe some in the following subsections, which develop the theme of 'connections'. An initial example might help to further set the scene.

I was working with an MBA group a few years ago. Most of the group members appeared to be struggling to see the relevance of some of the theories being encountered in the unit of study. They were complaining about being too busy to do any reading before seminars. One of them put it like this:

'Look, I'm far too busy trying to manage the core and periphery workers in my company to bother about all these theories.'

'But,' I replied, 'the idea of core and periphery was once just such a theory. It was 'invented' by Charles Handy and others in the 1980s when they were speculating on the future nature of work.'

So, it transpires that less than 20 years on Handy's theory has become conventional wisdom and has become incorporated into the social stock of knowledge concerning management. It had then come to be experienced by the manager as a reified, objective entity – and as such had far more legitimacy that any theory about the social construction of reality or other such 'woolly' sociological theories.

My connections

I will now expand on the various connections between my attempt to combine an examination of key concepts in the social construction of reality and wider aspects relevant to exploring the nature of management. This may also help to clarify why I have chosen to proceed as I have in this chapter. I see the main connections as:

- the management of meaning;
- the implications for undertaking critical enquiry;
- Friedrich Nietzsche: lived philosophy and issues of method; and
- issues of representation and styles of narrative.

It is clearly beyond the scope of this chapter to go into a detailed description of each of these. Hopefully, this will lead to you extending your own explorations into these issues. These are also 'my' connections. They do not purport to be exhaustive in terms of the relevance of social constructionism to the study of management, but in exploring them they may provide an insight into why I have written the chapter like this rather than in some other way. This should also serve to demonstrate that far from being an old idea 'past its sell-by date', the social construction of reality serves as an important foundation for the sort of critical enquiry we have been encouraging you to engage with in this book.

Connections to the management of meaning

This concept was introduced in Chapter 1, where reference was made to the seminal work of Gowler and Legge (1984). The notion that reality may be of our own creation comes to be seen as significant in terms of what managers actually do in the day-to-day management of organisations. While our review of Berger and Luckmann's work points to the inevitability of institutionalisation occurring, consideration of the concept of the management of meaning shows how managers may be able to shape the nature of the institutional order. The following two examples may help to exemplify this issue.

I was in Malaysia recently, teaching on a masters programme. One evening, my colleague Vince and I were watching a live football match on satellite television. (The qualifying rounds for the 1998 World Cup were reaching their conclusion.) At half-time, some advertisements were run. At one point, the screen went blank and a message to the effect that 'inappropriate material has been removed' was displayed. I remember thinking at the time that I objected to such censorship.

The next day, I asked one of my students what sort of material would have been censored in this way. He suggested that the adverts could have been for tobacco products or alcohol, or have contained unsuitable images of women. He also told me that the 'live' football match was in fact shown on a delayed transmission, so that there was time to edit the adverts. As with the night before, I must admit to feeling just a little annoyed that I had experienced this censorship.

However, upon further reflection I remembered that tobacco advertising is completely banned on British television, and alcohol advertising is strictly regulated. Significantly, I had forgotten this. Because the adverts are simply banned, apart from occasional debates in the media or parliament about the scope and effectiveness of such bans, it is not a topic that I routinely consider during my normal television viewing. In my day-to-day reality, the regulation of such adverts is essentially covert. The censorship is assimilated into my daily reality as a matter of taken-for-granted fact, to the extent that I routinely forget about it. Now at least in Malaysia, because of the pan-national nature of satellite television, the censorship has to be overt. It is harder to forget about it in the face of constant reminders on the screen, although I suppose that there comes a point when even the overt signs become such a normal part of the satellite televisual landscape as to eventually become 'forgotten' about by locals, until prompted by inquisitive visitors, that is.

My final reflection at the time led me to think that I was actually 'happier' with the surface-level nature of the censorship encountered in Malaysia than the 'underground' censorship experienced in my normal reality in Britain. I am left thinking: what else is being kept from me, without even knowing that things are being kept from me? (For an interesting debate on the different perspectives on power in relation to these issues, see Lukes 1974).

Management's ability to control agendas by defining what is and what is not legitimate discourse is a powerful tool in terms of managing meaning and thereby shaping the institutional order. Can you think of any situation where you have been aware of such 'shaping'?

Recently, I heard an item on national radio in Britain. The presenter announced that two young male lions were causing problems within their pride at a private zoo. As a result, unless suitable alternative accommodation could be found, the two young lions were to be exterminated. She then went on to introduce a manager from the zoo to give more details. At the outset, the manager said that he wanted to put the presenter right on an important issue, namely that the lions were not to be exterminated but rather were to be euthanised (*sic*). 'Euthanisation', he went on to explain, was a management tool; extermination was far too emotive a term.

> I cannot ever recall a manager being so blatant about the use of language to manage meaning. (Actually, for me, his self-disclosure quite undermined his attempts to so manage meaning.)
>
> What does the use of the term 'management tool' by the zoo spokesman imply to you about the nature of management? Can you think of any circumstances where you have either employed particular terms or phrases or witnessed others doing so in order to manage meaning? Have you ever subsequently been challenged yourself or challenged another person over such attempts to manage meaning in this way?

We appear to live in an age of conspiracy theories – from the death of US President John F. Kennedy and Princess Diana through to the popular US television series *The X Files*. But I am not trying to imply here that managers are universally engaged in some grand conspiracy of manipulation and control but rather I am pointing to the rather mundane ways in which reality can be managed. (You may choose to interpret the management of meaning as manipulation and control, or you may be persuaded by Nason's account of hegemonic conditioning in Chapter 3.) If we simply internalise acts of censorship or management speak without criticism, we have seen how it is not long before such things become institutionalised and assume an unassailable status – this is just the way things are. This relates directly to the implications for undertaking critical enquiry.

The implications for undertaking critical enquiry

In referring to the work of Berger and Luckmann and other constructivist social scientists, Ravn states that

> For these social scientists, the point that social institutions are the constructions of a community of human agents implies that the same human beings possess the power to radically change those institutions.
>
> (in Steier 1991: 96)

If we want a critique to lead to new insights opening up the possibilities for change, then we need to be able to recognise whatever it is we are critiquing – in our case, the nature of management – as something that we have the ability to change. If management is experienced as something already out there, fixed, objective, then how can we ever hope to overcome it? This is not something that can be done easily. As someone who is an active member of the very institution(s) that I am seeking to critique, I am constantly open to charges of biting the hand that feeds me. We now recognise such citations as legitimatory devices. But it is one thing to recognise something for what it is or might be; it is quite another to actually do something about it.

Indeed, you may rightly protest that you do not want to change things! You may feel that the institutional order in your sphere of operation serves you well. Or you may choose to acknowledge that there is perhaps the possibility of change, but you prefer not to do so yourself. The manager who made constant comments about the need to pay his mortgage was making a pertinent point – there are many pressures simply to conform, to buy into the institution. But at least we have opened up the possibility, pointed to the human agency at the core of our institutions – at the core of management. And this leads me to Friedrich Nietzsche.

Nietzsche: lived philosophy and issues of method

Friedrich Nietzsche was born in Saxony in 1844 and died in a mental asylum in 1890. In his introduction to Nietzsche, Bryan Magee states:

> Nietzsche was the first philosopher fully to face up to Western man's loss of faith in religion, or in the existence of any world other than this one. If there are no God and transcendental realm, then morals, values, truth, rationality, standards of every kind, are not given to man from outside himself but are created by man to meet his own needs. We choose our values – or at the very least we collectively create our values. It's a highly challenging and deeply disruptive view, and Nietzsche realised that to the full.
>
> (Magee 1987: 234)

I think that this clearly shows a central connection to Nietzsche in our present exploration. However, I am also interested in Nietzsche's concern with developing a philosophy that could be lived. In rejecting the current dogma of the day, he did not simply want to substitute his own dogma but rather to find ways of actually enacting a meaningful philosophy – a philosophy that would enhance his existence through his actions in the world. In this sense, he was very much a philosophical experimenter – he tried things out. As Kaufmann (1974: 89) puts it:

> Questions permitting of experiment are, to Nietzsche's mind, those questions to which he can reply 'Versuchen wir's!' Let us try it! Experimenting involves testing an answer by trying to live according to it. To many of Hegel's questions, Nietzsche would thus say that they were of no interest to him because they were too abstract to be relevant to his way of living … Only problems that present themselves so forcefully that they threaten the thinker's present mode of life lead to philosophic inquiries.

Nietzsche became so disillusioned with the lack of vitality among his colleagues that he gave up his lecturing job. He referred to this in his most famous publication, *Thus Spoke Zarathustra*:

> For this is the truth, I have left the house of the scholars and slammed the door behind me … They [other scholars] are excellent clocks: only be careful to wind them up properly! Then they tell the hour without error and make a modest noise in doing so. They work like mills and rammers: just throw seed-corn into them! – they know how to grind corn small and make white dust of it.
>
> (Nietzsche 1961: 147–8)

You may deduce that Nietzsche was less than enamoured with his fellow academics. We can also see that he had the resolve to walk away from the institution that fed him. He wanted his search for knowledge to be a challenge. He wanted learning to be dangerous – in the sense that it might change us, and what could be more 'dangerous' than that? He developed a critique of the predominant approach to knowledge based around the Greek gods Apollo and Dionysus. He saw most of the antecedent approaches to knowledge being based on, as Kaufmann puts it, 'the classical Greek genius'. The Apollonian is rational, measured, controlled. The early Nietzsche did not actually distinguish greatly between Apollo and Dionysus. However, in his later works he sees the spirit of Dionysus as much more vital. Kaufmann (1974: 129) tells us:

> It has been overlooked that the Dionysus whom Nietzsche celebrated as his own god in his later writings is no longer the deity of formless frenzy ... but later the Dionysian represents passion *controlled*.

Nietzsche also recognised that this passionate engagement, as opposed to dispassionate rationality, marked him out as being somewhat dangerous, as the following passage from his autobiography, *Ecce Homo*, illustrates:

> One day there will be attached to my name the memory of something tremendous – a crisis without equal on earth, the most profound collision of conscience, a decision that was conjured up against everything that previously had been believed, demanded, hallowed. I am no man, I am dynamite.

(in White 1990: 4–5)

Nietzsche's desire for experimentation and his dissatisfaction with abstract theories points him out as a pragmatist, a philosopher of action. And as the quotation above illustrates, he was prepared to criticise the establishment, the institutional order of his day, if you like, with little regard for the personal consequences. He rejected idealism, so rather than dreaming of an unattainable (for him at least) world of ideals, he sought to focus on the world 'as it is'. I find this a helpful focus when exploring the nature of management. Much of what has been written about management is highly prescriptive and points to what should be rather than critiquing what is. However, it is worth noting that Astley tells us that such idealised prescriptions can still serve management in a 'practical' manner:

> Management theory is not predominantly oriented toward achieving higher levels of organisational performance ... Management theorists are engaged in the provision of a cosmology within which managers can locate their missions and actions as meaningful. In this regard management theorists affect managers not so much at a practical level ... but at an ideational level, in terms of managers' attribution of meaning and significance to these practical actions.

(in Anthony 1986: 178)

I think that it would be absurd for me to suggest that all these prescriptive or functional accounts of management ought to be completely disregarded. An understanding of the functions of management is essential if we are to develop a rich picture. But since my first encounter with the works of Nietzsche I have been challenged by his assertion that believing one thing and doing another means we lead inauthentic lives: 'ours is a dead way of living', he proclaimed. Is it possible to act in ways that are consistent with one's beliefs? Is it possible to be a manager and act in ways that are consistent with one's beliefs? When I first qualified as a trading standards officer, I used to work for a manager who regularly asserted 'Don't do as I do, do as I say!' In the many years that have passed since then, I have come to recognise ever more clearly how much easier it is to say rather than do!

The whole concept of authenticity has itself become problematic as a result of post-modern accounts of epistemology, which point to the impossibility of establishing the clarity and certainty necessary to be able to claim that thoughts and actions are indeed congruous (see, for example, Vattimo (1988)). The postmodern position suggests that since everything is open to interpretation we can never actually know anything in any absolute sense. French writer Albert Camus pursued this issue. He argued that on the one hand humans have a deeply embedded nostalgia for certainty, but on the other this postmodern critique of knowledge renders the establishing of such certainty impossible. Interestingly, Camus tells us that what we should be concerned with is the tension of living out our existence between this need for certainty and the knowledge of its impossible attainment. Camus, like Nietzsche, is interested in action, and while he acknowledges the place of theory in our lives he rather pointedly asserts that 'The preceding merely defines a way of thinking. But the point is to live' (Camus 1975: 63).

I find it a little ironic that the person who introduced me to the concept of authenticity, Nietzsche, is cited by many postmodern philosophers (for example, Vattimo (1988)) as the person responsible for beginning the end of modernism. This leads me into a potentially contradictory position. Indeed, this experiencing of contradiction – Camus actually refers to it at as 'absurdity' – has been a central focus of my recent research. And this leads me to the next connection.

Issues of representation and styles of narrative

I have found it easier to develop my exploration of the tension between my nostalgia for certainty (modernism) and my understanding of the impossibility of achieving such clarity (postmodernism) through less conventional (in the context of academic conventions in organisational analysis) styles of narrative. Initially, I used a second-voice technique – new literary form (NLF). Indeed, my PhD proposal was written in this style as a short drama. More recently, in my thesis I have been writing semi-fictional accounts based loosely around autobiographical events. Barbara Carniawska explores some of the issues relating to the use of fiction in two articles in the journal *Organization* (1995; 1997). Central to the use of fiction is the argument that the boundaries between scientific discourse (knowledge) and our everyday discourse is becoming increasingly blurred the more we come to recognise the human agency underlying scientific knowledge (another important development arising from the seminal work of Berger and Luckmann). It is argued that so-called fictional accounts of organisational events might actually be more 'factual' than apparently non-fictional accounts (see Protherough in Chapter 5). What attracted me to the approach was the degree of freedom that the use of fiction (or apparent fiction) allows. I can always disclaim events as 'not actually having occurred' if readers take exception to what is written. For example, I am at the time of writing the chairman of my university's branch of NATFHE, one of the lecturing trade unions. I am also a member of the board of governors at the university. (And if you think you can detect potential for some tensions between those two roles, you would not be wrong.) I have been privy to a vast array of events and insights, which for a variety of reasons – not the least of which is my desire to keep my job – I would have extreme difficulty in writing about overtly. However, by weaving such incidents into a work of fiction I can use the inherent ambiguity afforded by the genre to protect the innocent – and try to keep my job. The events portrayed then become examples of events rather than straightforward, factual accounts. I have also found it easier to write about what I might euphemistically refer to as 'embarrassing episodes' from my past in a fictional manner. As I said, the blurring of what is and what is not reality gives me the freedom to introduce issues that I would otherwise be reticent about mentioning. I am sure that my Calvinist upbringing in a working-class Scottish family has much to do with the origins of this reticence. It is also just as important to me that the use of the genre gives my reader(s) room to manoeuvre as well. I may be saying here that Jimmy McNietzsche is better placed to write more insightful accounts of organisational reality than David Currie. It occurs to me as I reflect on this section that I am much less reticent in classroom situations. This can possibly be put down to the rather less concrete nature of what is said than what is written.

Because I have resorted to such unconventional accounts, my work (what little there is of it!) is often labelled 'postmodern'. However, as I indicated earlier, I feel that it is more to do with the tension between modernism and postmodernism. It seems to me that critics are too quick to attach the label of 'postmodernism' to anything that is deemed unconventional in a particular context. NLF has been quite well critiqued, and it could be argued that it has failed to transform our accounts of organisational life in the way in which some hoped it might. More often than not, such work is treated as game playing, in some way not taking the reader seriously. However, in the spirit of Nietzsche, I think that it is still worth a try. I suppose I could develop case studies, change names, etc., but I just feel that much more scope is offered in a less conventional genre. I have not engaged in this discourse to play some sort of smart-arse trick on you (Woolgar 1988). Rather, I see this as a genuine attempt to bridge a gap – that between our theoretical conceptions or abstractions about the nature of management and our lived experience of management. I also suspect that the gap is unbridgeable, but like a moth around a naked flame, I still find myself returning to this problem over and over again, stumbling to find ways of capturing the experience authentically. As Barnes (1984: 161) put it:

> Sometimes you talk, sometimes you do not. The words are not the right ones; or rather the right ones do not exist. 'Language is like a cracked kettle on which we beat out our tunes for bears to dance to, while all the time we long to move the stars to pity'.

Problems of language apart, I might also suggest that part of what that gap involves is the overly rational – Apollonian – accounts that prevail. This chapter has been a small attempt on my part to produce a more Dionysian account. I want to acknowledge my engagement, my passion, not in an apologetic manner as something that is getting in the way of objectivity but rather as an essential element of any account of my experiences. As Carl Rogers (1967) suggests, we are feeling beings as well as thinking beings.

It may also be worth emphasising that fictional accounts are more obviously ambiguous than non-fictional accounts. I am much more predisposed to interpret a work of fiction actively. There is therefore something appealing about the use of fiction in so far as it militates against closure. Nietzsche often wrote in aphorisms, which were highly susceptible to interpretation. He did not do this by chance. He wanted his readers to have to work hard to apprehend his meaning. As a result of the proliferation of differing interpretations of his work on offer, to this day there is probably no more argued about philosopher than Nietzsche. He would not be too unhappy about this, as he subtitled *Thus Spoke Zarathustra* 'A book for everyone and no-one' and went to lengths to say 'my way may not be your way'. He did not want people to accept his writings in a dogmatic way but rather sought active readers who would strive to glean his meanings. As Protherough (see Chapter 5) suggests, there is value to be gained from reading literature in a non-mechanistic way: 'Literature has to be read as literature, not as something else'. In writing a piece like 'Glenmore Breakpoint', I know that I want to represent certain concepts, in the main to do with my, sorry Jimmy McNietzsche's, frame of reference and manifestations of the social construction of reality as enacted in the various discourses within the piece. But in drawing explicit attention to my position as author, hopefully I make you more aware of the sort of device that authors use to draw you into their world and persuade you of their authority to write about something in the first place. Is this really a central issue in thinking about management? I would argue that it is, that it should be of central concern. Whenever I or anyone else writes about management – or for that matter gives a lecture or leads a seminar – we are not passively reporting on events. Rather, following directly from our analysis of Berger and Luckmann, we play an active role in shaping the very practices we would seek to describe. As indicated earlier, I am writing about institutionalisation, for example, as one who is well and truly institutionalised. The process of bringing this chapter into print also means my having to engage with the institution of publishing. And I happen to think that you as a reader should be reminded of that. Just as the incident in Malaysia provided me with a helpful reminder of the extent to which my reality is managed by others through acts such as censorship and institutional rules, so we need to actively remember that when authors write about management it is always done from some position or another. We might try most of the time to disguise this fact – by claiming to be 'scientific' or 'objective' or 'unbiased' – but this is not so. As Willmott (1996) says:

> to understand the nature of management we also need to take into account how theories about management come into existence and in particular to recognise the power of managers and their role in the generation of management knowledge.

Conclusion

In this chapter, I have attempted to combine an exploration of the importance of social constructionism to our examination of the nature of management with the adoption of a different genre of representation. In seeking to uncover the human agency at the heart of what we claim to know about management, I have hopefully also shown that acts of representation are themselves affected by the practices we would seek to critique.

References

Anthony, P. (1986) *The Foundation of Management*, London: Tavistock.

Barnes, J. (1984) *Flaubert's Parrot*, London: Pan Books.

Berger, P. and Luckmann, T. (1966) *The Social Construction of Reality: A Treatise on the Sociology of Knowledge*, Harmondsworth: Penguin Books.

Camus, A. (1975) *The Myth of Sisyphus*, Harmondsworth: Penguin Books.

Czarniawska, B. (1997) 'A four times told tale: combining narrative and scientific knowledge in organisation studies', *Organization* 4 (1).

Czarniawska-Joerges, B. (1995) 'Narration or science? Collapsing the division in organization studies', *Organization* 2 (1).

Cooper, G. and Woolgar, S. (1993) 'The research process and organizational change: the importance of audience in research practice', paper to British Sociological Conference, Colchester, April.

Golding, D. (1986) 'On becoming a manager', *Organization Studies* 7 (2).

Gowler, D. and Legge, K. (1984) 'The meaning of management and the management of meaning: a view from social anthropology'. In M.J. Earle (ed.) *Perspectives on Management*, Oxford: Oxford University Press.

Kaufmann, W. (1974) *Nietzsche: Philosopher, Psychologist, Antichrist* (fourth edition), Princeton and London: Princeton University Press.

Lukes, S. (1974) *Power: A Radical View*, London: Macmillan.

Magee, B. (1987) *The Great Philosophers*, London: BBC Books.

Nietzsche, F. (1961) *Thus Spoke Zarathustra*, London: Penguin Books.

Rogers, C. (1967) *On Becoming A Person*, Trowbridge: Redwood Burn.

Steier, F. (ed.) (1991) *Research and Reflexivity*, London: Sage.

White, A. (1990) *Within Nietzsche's Labyrinth*, London and New York: Routledge.

Willmott, H. (1996) 'A metatheory of management: omniscience or obfuscation? a comment', *British Journal of Management* 7 (4).

Vattimo, G. (1988) *The End of Modernity*, Cambridge: Polity Press.

Woolgar, S. (1988) *Knowledge and Reflexivity*, London: Sage.

Further reading

If I have hooked you on Nietzsche, read his *Thus Spoke Zarathustra*. For a text that deals with ambiguity in a masterful way, read *If on a Winter's Night a Traveller* by Italo Calvino (1968).

Reflective

You may have deduced by now that this book is clearly not an encyclopaedia of management theory. From its very inception at proposal stage, this was always intended to be a text that grew out of the experiences of the contributors. All sorts of relevant theories are therefore 'missing' from the piece. It is also fairly clear to us that had the contributors drawn on different theoretical frameworks they would have gleaned different insights from their analysis of experiences. The point here is that the authors have used what they found helpful at the time. At another time, upon further reflection, no doubt different frameworks will be used and new insights gained.

Reflective practice, as exemplified in the pages of this text, does not lead to concrete endings – although the act of translating the analysis into written form may appear to give solidity, finality, to the issues under consideration. Rather, we are concerned to open up reflective practice as something that is ongoing, unending. It is therefore implicit that the sort of analysis performed by the authors is intrinsically ambiguous. What is today's helpful insight is tomorrow's problem. In fact, all the contributors have told us about the extreme difficulty that they had in reaching some sort of closure in their text; reflecting on what they had written previously often led them off in new directions. This is part of the difficulty of writing about experiences, as the act of writing invariably changes our understanding – endings lead to beginnings, and so on, and so on. But they had to stop somewhere! It might be more helpful, then, to think about them as commas – brief pauses – rather than full stops – dead ends. And the process does not end with the authors but starts afresh with each new reader, who will make sense of this or that in their own way. Interpretation upon interpretation. (Mis)understanding upon (mis)understanding. What a rich tapestry we find ourselves weaving, unpicking, redoing.

So, what of you? Where are you going? What will you do? Has our text affected you, made you think? We might speculate that if you have stuck with it right to this point, then you probably have been hooked and are now mulling over your own understanding of the nature of management. If that is so, then we will certainly have achieved one of our objectives in writing a book like this. But does your thinking, bringing with it new insights, have any relevance for future management action? In short, has your reading of this text the potential to change the way you act in the world, the way you manage?

It might be argued that action is easier when freed from the constraints of thought. Sportswear manufacturer Nike's admonition to 'Just do it' has certain attractions. You might now perceive some aspects of management action to be problematic, especially given the focus on moral issues in several of the contributions to the book. Can reflective practice, drawing on a critical literature, be a positive force for action, or are we simply reinforcing our helplessness within a system that must be obeyed?

We referred to juggling in the preface and suggested that in thinking about management we had to move beyond self-fulfilling solutions or 'how-to-do' questions and try to ask more searching questions about the nature of management. It is worth having a final reflection on the juggling metaphor. We might speculate that thinking about more searching questions may be dysfunctional for a juggler. Gary Player, the highly successful South African golfer, refers to this as paralysis through analysis; practice, practice and yet more practice – but do not think too much about what you are doing. Might it not be the same for managing? Perhaps yes, perhaps no. And whether it is a 'yes' or a 'no' for you is out of our hands. You must consider your own position, develop your own insights and solutions through, among other things, your own reflective practice.

For our part, we continue both to juggle and think – a messy business for sure, but great 'fun', nonetheless. And as Camus, so succinctly, put it:

> But it is hard to stop, hard to be satisfied with a single way of seeing, to go without contradiction, perhaps the most subtle of all spiritual forces. The preceding merely defines a way of thinking. But the point is to live.
>
> (Camus 1975: 63)

And who could argue with that?

Reference

Camus, A. (1975) *The Myth of Sisyphus*, Harmondsworth: Penguin.

David Golding
David Currie
Kingston-upon-Hull
May 1999

Name index

Ackoff, R. 100
Aktouf, O. 77
Alvesson, M., and Willmott, H. 34, 50, 68, 100, 105
Andrews, R. 77
Anthony, P.D. 28, 50, 69, 71, 76, 81, 86, 104, 140; and Reed, M. 68, 69, 70
Apple, M. 44
Argyris, C., and Schon, I. 35
Armstrong, P. 45
Atkinson, P. 73
Auden, W.H. 85

Babbage, C. 61
Bach, J.S. 59
Bakhtin, M. 73
Ball, S.J. 71
Barnes, J. 142
Barry, B. 65
Barthes, R. 20
Beardwell, I., and Holden, L. 23
Beck, J., and Cox, C. 69
Benne, K. 85
Berger, P.L., and Luckmann, T. 25, 26, 46, 125, 130–2, 133, 134, 135
Berlin, I. 102
Berne, E. 95
Bion, W. 85
Blumberg, A., and Golembiewski, R. 94, 95
Bocock, R. 43
Bottery, M. 71, 77
Boydell, T.H. (Pedler *et al.*) 82–3; and Pedler, M. and Burgoyne, J. 83, 87
Braverman, H. 61
Buchanan, D., and Huczynski, A. 18
Burgoyne, J. and Boydell, T.H. and Pedler, M. 83, 87; (Pedler *et al.*) 82–3; and Stuart, R. 83
Burns, T., and Stalker, G.M. 21
Burrell, G. 22, 68; and Morgan, G. 19, 34
Byrt, W. 66

Camus, A. 141, 146

Casement, P. 92–3
Caulkin, S. 65
Child, J. 43
Clegg, S.R., and Palmer, G. 69, 77
Clough, B. 105–6
Coe, J. 75
Cohen, C. 74, 75
Cooke, S., and Slack, N. 19
Cooper, D.E. 24
Cox, C., and Beck, J. 69
Cronkite, W. 4
Czarniawska-Joerges, B. 117, 141; and Guillet de Monthoux, P. 72

de Vries, M.F.R.K., and Miller, D. 76
Deal, T.E., and Kennedy, A.A. 30
Descartes, R. 115
Donne, J. 59
Downing, S.J. 76
Drucker, P. 18
Dunford, R. 29, 31

Eagleton, T. 41, 44, 50
Edwards, R. 55
Ehrensahl, K.N. 68

Fayol, H. 18, 19, 46
Fincham, R., and Rhodes, P. 29
Fineman, S. 28
Foot, P. 58
Foulkes, S.H. 85
Fox, A. 28, 29
French, R., and Grey, C. 69, 105
Freud, S. 85, 116
Friere, P. 34
Frost, P.J. *et al.* 31

Garfinkel, H. 118
Garson, B. 55
Gibson, J. 58
Gill, J., and Johnson, P. 48
Goffee, R., and Scase, R. 68

Goffman, E. 46, 57, 63, 89
Golding, D. 6, 134–5
Golembiewski, R., and Blumberg, A. 94, 95
Gowler, D. 10; and Legge, K. 136
Gramsci, A. 43
Grey, C. 76, 86; and French, R. 69, 105; and
    Mitev, N. 65, 68, 71
Guillet de Monthoux, P., and Czarniawska-
    Joerges, B. 72

Handy, C. 93, 135–6
Harré, R. 74
Hassard, J., and Parker, M. 77, 82
Hayek, F. 47
Hearn, J., and Parkin, W. 28
Hegel, G.H. 115–16, 117, 121, 122–3
Heller, J. 59
Hilton, I. 58
Hodson, R. 117
Holden, L., and Beardwell, I. 23
Honderich, T. 122
Huczynski, A., and Buchanan, D. 18

James, Baroness P.D. 59
Jay, A. 20
Johnson, P., and Gill, J. 48
Johnston, Jr J.S. 65
Jones, T.B. 70

Kallinikos, J. 69, 77
Kant, I. 121–2, 123
Kanter, R.M. 55, 69
Kaufmann, W. 139, 140
Kennedy, A.A., and Deal, T.E. 30
Kolb, D. 84

Laing, R.D. 87, 95
Larrain, J. 41, 44, 45
Leavitt, H.J. 70
Legge, K. 10, 23, 86; and Gowler, D. 136
Lewin 85
Luckmann, T., and Berger, P.L. 25, 26, 46, 125,
    130–2, 133, 134, 135
Lukes, S. 50, 84

McCloskey, D.N. 73
McGivern, J., and Thompson, J. 74
Magee, B. 24, 139
Mangham, I.L. 73, 77, 95
Mannheim, K. 40
Mant, A. 48
Martin, L., and Vince, R. 95
Marx, K. 87
Maslow, A.H. 25, 87
Miller, D., and de Vries, M.F.R.K. 76
Mintzberg, H. 18, 21, 47; and Quinn, J. 21

Mitev, N., and Grey, C. 65, 71
Morgan, G. 22, 25, 30, 40, 82, 87, 95; and
    Burrell, G. 19
Moser, P.K. 121
Mullins, L.J. 18
Musgrave, W. 105
Mutch, A. 69, 87

Newby, H. 57, 63
Newton, I. 20
Nichols, T. 45
Nietzsche, F. 139–41, 142
Nostrand, C.V. 95

Palmer, G., and Clegg, S.R. 69, 77
Parker, M., and Hassard, J. 77, 82
Parkin, W., and Hearn, J. 28
Pedler, M.; and Burgoyne, J. and Boydell, T.H.
    83, 87; (Pedler *et al.*) 82–3
Peters, T.J., and Waterman, R.H. 30, 52
Pick, J. 77
Player, G. 146
Protherough, R. 73, 74, 142
Pugh, D. 66

Quinn, J., and Mintzberg, H. 21

Raab, N. 74
Reed, M. 104; and Anthony, P. 68, 69, 70
Revans, R. 83, 84
Rhodes, P., and Finchan, R. 29
Ritzer, G. 120
Rogers, C. 83, 84, 85–6, 87, 93, 94, 142
Rorty, R. 120, 122
Rowe, C. 55
Roy, D. 58

Scase, R., and Goffee, R. 68
Schein, E. 88
Schon, D. 83, 84, 87
Schon, I., and Argyris, C. 35
Shakespeare, W. 72, 74–5
Sinclair, A. 76
Soames, N. 11
Sparks, K. *et al.* 52
Stalin, J. 31
Stalker, G.M., and Burns, T. 21
Steier, F. 138
Storey, J. 20, 50
Strobes, E. 11

Taylor, F.W. 18
Thompson, J., and McGivern, J. 74
Thompson, P. 87
Thompson, R. 68

Tressell, R. 87
Tuckman, A. 118

Useem, M. 69

Vattimo, G. 141
Vidal, G. 10, 11
Vince, R. 84, 95; and Martin, L. 95

Waldo, D. 72
Waterman, R.H., and Peters, T.J. 30, 52
Watson, A. 35
Weber, M. 21

Welshman, G. (Pedler *et al.*) 82–3
Whitaker, D. 88, 92
White, A. 140
Williams, R. 66
Willmott, H. 81–2, 87, 143; and Alvesson, M. 34, 50, 68, 100, 105
Wilsher, P. 48
Wintour, P. 11
Wittgenstein, L. 24, 25
Woolgar, S. 142
Wright Mills, C. 14
Wright, O.W. 87

Yalom, I.D. 85

Subject index

adventure holidays 102
advertising 136–7
air traffic controllers 5
alienation 87–8
ambiguity perspective 31
apprenticeship system 103
Association of Teachers in Management 66, 67
authority 88

breakfast meeting 42
BSE (mad cow disease) 11
bureaucracy 21
Business Higher Education Forum 69
business schools 35, 70; growth 22; postgraduate 65

call centres 30
censorship 136–7
certainty, attainability of 100–2
class conflict 22, 28
computers, use in HE 108
conspiracy theories 138
critical enquiry 138–9
critical management 18, 25–8
cross-cultural studies 66
cultural industry 71
cultural manipulation 18, 30

deference, concept 55–7
deferential hierarchical relationships 57–61
differentiation perspective 31

education; and group therapy 85–6;
    management 71; *see also* higher education
emotional issues 95
empowerment 20
enjoyment 106–7
Enterprise in Higher Education scheme 107–8
euthanisation 137
experiential learning 83–4, 85–8, 91, 94, 103–6
exploitation 42; structure 22

female managers 26

feminisation, of management 76
fiction 72, 73–7, 141–3
film industry (USA) 52
fire-fighting 31
Flaubert's Parrot (Barnes) 77
football 105–6, 136–7
functionalism 19, 55

group therapy, and education 85–6, 92–5
Guardian 58, 87
Gulf War syndrome 9

habitualisation 133
Hard Times (Dickens) 75
Hawthorn Studies (1939) 87
hegemony 43–6
Henry V (Shakespeare) 72
higher education 69; lecturers 107–9
historical context, management 17, 20–1
House of Sleep, The (Coe) 75
human resource management (HRM) 23, 53
humanities, in management education 73–7

ideology 40–2, 44; beliefs 34
Images of Organisation (Morgan) 22
impression management 111
industrial relations seminar 8
industrialisation, history of 52
information technology 54
Inns of Court (London) 114
Institute of Personnel Development (IPD) 23
institutionalisation 133–4
integration perspective 31
intellectual craftsperson 14
internalisation 134

knowledge, *a priori* or *a posteriori* concept (Kant)
    121–2

leadership 93–4
learning; in circles 98–9; experiential 83–4, 85–8,
    91, 94, 103–6; life-long 103–4; participative

94; student-centred 93–4; through
    uncertainty 102, 107–10; work-based 103
lecturers, higher education 107–9
legitimation 134–5
leisure 102, 106; industry 71
literature 72–3, 73–7

management; 'colonising' tendency 78; defined
    1–5; feminisation of 76; middle 36; scientific
    18, 24; senior 37–8; technical-rational pursuit
    18, 21–3
Management Charter Initiative (MCI) 23
management education 56, 66, 68–71;
    humanities in 73–7
management speak 25
management studies, growth 65–6
Master in Business Administration (MBA) 3, 23,
    65, 113–14; spirituality 20
master/slave relationship 58
meaning, management of 10–13
meta-qualities 83
middle management 36
modernism 142
motor sport, sponsorship 61
myth, role 20–1

narrative 72, 73–7, 141–3
National Coal Board (NCB) 54
needs hierarchy (Maslow) 25, 87
networking 20
new literary form (NLF) 141, 142
Nice Work (Lodge) 75
norms 89–90
North and South (Gaskell) 75
novels 72

objectivation 132–3
Observer 11
office politics 48
organisations; conflict 29; hierarchy 51–5; rituals
    of deference 61–2
outplacement 24

Pandemonium (Burrell) 22
patriarchal organisations 26
patronage 59, 60
personal assistant 58
personnel department 2
personnel management 53
Phenomenology of Spirit, The (Hegel) 116, 122–3
pluralism 29, 77
political parties (UK), ideology 44
postgraduate business schools 65
postmodernism 28, 31, 141, 142
power 84

practical activity 13
Prison Notebooks (Gramsci) 43
Private Eye 11
production manager 42
psychoanalysis 85, 115–16
psychotherapy 85–6

railway transport 101
reality, social construction of 132
redundancy 53
reflective practice 5, 6, 13–15, 46, 145–6;
    DMS/MBA 6–7; teaching through 81–97
reification 132, 135
ring-fenced 36
rituals 62
Romeo and Juliet (Shakespeare) 74–5

sales representatives 27
scientific management 18, 24
seminars 82–3, 86, 87, 119–21; industrial
    relations 8; MBA 3
senior management 37–8
sexuality 28
silence 91–2
Slaughterhouse-5 (Vonnegut) 77
social interaction 27
social research, qualitative/quantitative methods
    100
socialisation 34, 41
spin doctors 11
sport, learning methods 105–6
stress 36, 42
structure 25–6; exploitation 22
support groups 85
symbolism 27, 38

Tavistock group therapy 85
teaching; homogenisation of approaches 108–9;
    through reflective practice 81–97
teamwork 20
technical-rational pursuit, management 18, 21–3
television news 4
Thus Spoke Zarathustra (Nietzsche) 139, 142
total quality management (TQM) 100–1, 118

uncertainty 98–110
undergraduate assignment 83–4
universities, UK 108

Wolf (Cross) 76
work ethic, Victorian/Protestant 106
workshops 109
World Tonight 58

ZTC Ryland 35